About Island Press

Since 1984, the nonprofit organization Island Press has been stimulating, shaping, and communicating ideas that are essential for solving environmental problems worldwide. With more than 1,000 titles in print and some 30 new releases each year, we are the nation's leading publisher on environmental issues. We identify innovative thinkers and emerging trends in the environmental field. We work with world-renowned experts and authors to develop cross-disciplinary solutions to environmental challenges.

Island Press designs and executes educational campaigns in conjunction with our authors to communicate their critical messages in print, in person, and online using the latest technologies, innovative programs, and the media. Our goal is to reach targeted audiences—scientists, policymakers, environmental advocates, urban planners, the media, and concerned citizens—with information that can be used to create the framework for long-term ecological health and human well-being.

Island Press gratefully acknowledges major support of our work by The Agua Fund, The Andrew W. Mellon Foundation, The Bobolink Foundation, The Curtis and Edith Munson Foundation, Forrest C. and Frances H. Lattner Foundation, The JPB Foundation, The Kresge Foundation, The Oram Foundation, Inc., The Overbrook Foundation, The S.D. Bechtel, Jr. Foundation, The Summit Charitable Foundation, Inc., and many other generous supporters.

The opinions expressed in this book are those of the author(s) and do not necessarily reflect the views of our supporters.

Artful Rainwater Design

Artful Rainwater Design

Creative Ways to Manage Stormwater

By Stuart Echols and Eliza Pennypacker

ISLANDPRESS

Washington | Covelo | London

Keywords: biofiltration, bioretention, Clean Water Act, detention basin, flood control, flow splitter, gray infrastructure, green infrastructure, landscape architecture, porous paving, rain, rain garden, rainwater harvesting, rainwater trail, site design, stormwater management, watershed

Library of Congress Control Number: 2014951544

Printed on recycled, acid-free paper

Manufactured in the United States of America
10 9 8 7 6 5 4 3 2 1

Contents

Acknowledgments

Many thanks are in order, as many people helped us transform some intriguing ideas about stormwater and landscape design into this book. First we'd like to thank J. William Thompson, who as editor of *Landscape Architecture* magazine in 2005 encouraged our foray into Artful Rainwater Design (ARD), provided great information on projects, and published some of our early articles; and Elen Deming, then editor of *Landscape Journal*, who saw worthy scholarship and professional information in an article she helped us publish in *LJ* in 2008. Thanks also to our then–graduate student and fellow ARD fanatic, Seth Wilberding, for undertaking a thesis that provided us lots of good stuff. Special thanks also go to Tom Liptan, Portland pioneer and champion of green infrastructure whose "why not" attitude has led to the creation of many seminal ARDs.

We could not have filled this book with thought-provoking projects and ideas without the contribution of many talented designers nationwide. Steve Benz of OLIN; Warren Byrd of Nelson Byrd Woltz; Steve Koch of Koch Landscape Architecture; environmental artist Stacy Levy; Tom Liptan, retired environmental specialist for Portland, Oregon's Bureau of Environmental Services; Carol Mayer Reed of Mayer/Reed; Kevin Perry of Urban Rain | Design; Michael Vergason of Michael Vergason Landscape Architects, Ltd.; and Sue Weiler of OLIN deserve special thanks for sharing their ideas in a 2013 ARD symposium at Penn State. To all the designers who provided us case study information, we feel enormous gratitude: José Alminaña and Tom Amoroso of Andropogon Associates, Ltd.; Leo Alvarez of Perkins + Will; Mara Lee Baird of ML Baird & Co.; Kevin Burke of Atlanta BeltLine Inc.; Maxine Coleman of Perkins + Will; Bruce Dees of Bruce Dees and Associates; Herbert Dreiseitl of Atelier Dreiseitl; David Elliott of the Pennsylvania Horticultural Society; Mike Faha of Greenworks; Peggy Gaynor of Gaynor, Inc.; Ian Holzworth of Walker Macy; environmental artist Lorna Jordan; Jonathan Martin of RDG Planning & Design; Jeffrey Miller of Miller Company Landscape Architects;

Joan Nassauer of the University of Michigan; Alex Perove of Greenworks; Nancy Rottle of the University of Washington; Lee Skabelund of Kansas State University; environmental artist Buster Simpson; Peg Staeheli of SvR Design Company; Christie Ten Eyck of Ten Eyck Landscape Architects Inc.; Mark Tilbe of Murase Associates; Nick Wilson of Atlas Landscape Architecture; Sara Wilson of Siteworks; and David Yocca of Design Conservation Forum. Of all of the above, a special shout-out goes to Warren Byrd, longtime friend and ARD advocate, who always encourages us to spread the word further.

For support in the form of time and funding, we thank Ron Henderson, head of Penn State's Department of Landscape Architecture; Nat Belcher, director of the Stuckeman School of Architecture and Landscape Architecture; and Barbara Korner, dean of Penn State's College of Arts and Architecture.

This book wouldn't look nearly as good as it does without the artistic assistance of Chris Maurer, creator of our diagrams, and Lacey Goldberg, designer of our icons.

Finally, we owe deep thanks to Courtney Lix, our editor with Island Press, whose helpful collaboration made producing this book a pleasure.

Introduction

On a rainy day in Portland, Oregon, a man stops at New Seasons Market at Arbor Lodge to pick up a few items for dinner. As he hurries inside, he looks up above the entrance canopy and notices that rain is spewing from a spout near the roof and onto a metal sculpture of salmon that appear to be swimming upstream against the current of the falling rain. For just a moment he's reminded that runoff from rain flows from rooftop to river; it had better be clean and plentiful!

Across the country, in Gainesville, Florida, a student at the University of Florida indulges in an evening workout at the Southwest Recreation Center. The position of her treadmill gives her a view through the glass facade to the entry landscape, where she can see that a water runnel leads from the building, across the sidewalk, into a lushly planted landscape; at the sidewalk edge, a filigree sculpture contains a column of blue light. She's intrigued but puzzled—can't quite figure out the message. As she leaves the building after her workout, she stops at the sculpture and reads a small plaque at its base; there she learns that the sculpture represents the palmetto's cellular structure, and the blue light suggests the plant's slurping of water that comes from the building roof. Like the man in Portland, she realizes that roof runoff is feeding the plants and that rain is a resource, not a waste product.

These brief examples highlight features of Artful Rainwater Design (ARD), an approach to sustainable stormwater management in which the management system is designed as a landscape amenity. ARD not only controls the quantity of runoff and improves its quality but adds experiential value to the landscape. The visible aspect of the design educates, entertains, or enlightens—it celebrates rainwater's resource value and tells the story of how it's being managed. The term was coined by Stuart Echols in 2005, as we began to research the topic. *Artful* is meant to suggest that the design is beautiful and engaging; *Rainwater* is used instead of *stormwater* because "stormwater management" has histor-

Figure I.1. *(left)* The rain scupper at the New Seasons Market at Arbor Lodge in Portland, Oregon lets people realize rain's important impact on rivers (design: Lango Hansen Landscape Architects PC; Ivan McLean; photograph: Stuart Echols).

Figure I.2. *(right)* Students exercising in the rec center at the University of Florida are given the opportunity to come to a realization about rain (design: RDG Planning and Design; photograph: Kevin Thompson).

ically treated rainwater as a waste product to be removed. By using the term *Artful Rainwater Design* we want to emphasize that rain is a precious resource worthy of experience and celebration.

Onsite management of rain is required in more and more municipalities, as sewage- and stormwater-carrying pipes exceed capacity in cities and towns around the country. The days of combined sewer systems, which regularly sent untreated sewage into waterways during major storms, are waning. In fact, increasingly forward-looking regulations across the United States require that the first flush of large rain events (i.e., the initial—and dirtiest—rainfall up to 1½ inches) be managed on site, and more and more states expect site design to manage a ½- to 1½-inch storm. Rather than a burdensome regulation, we see this as an opportunity to create a more vibrant site design by using green infrastructure (soil and plants) rather than pipes to manage rain on a site. As Tom Liptan, retired environmental specialist of the Bureau of Environmental Services of Portland, Oregon, has said, "Use the landscape!"[1] This approach is both logical and beneficial: Let the water nourish plants while the plants absorb pollutants, and let the water then function within the natural hydrologic system through infiltration and evapotranspiration.

Urban sites often lack the space necessary for traditional large stormwater detention ponds; expensive urban land demands clever thinking about rain capture. Runoff management can be achieved in this context through multiple small, dispersed systems, from green roofs to flow-through planters, from water harvesting systems to rain gardens. The end-of-pipe, back-of-lot, out-of-sight and out-of-mind stormwater management approach is losing viability. And making those small, dispersed runoff management systems visible and "legible" is a design opportunity. By creating sustainable stormwater management systems that visibly communicate their management strategies, we can make people aware of rain as a resource, and we can make them realize that we must both control the quantity and ensure the quality of rain for it to truly serve as the resource needed for natural systems to thrive.

This strategy gives designers an opportunity to advance the agenda of environmentally responsible design by making the systems not only visible and legible but beautiful. As Elizabeth Meyer stated in her manifesto published in *Landscape Architecture*, "A concern for beauty and aesthetics is necessary for sustainable design if it is to have a significant cultural impact."[2] ARD gives designers a further opportunity to advance the agenda of environmentally responsible design by making the systems beautiful. If we create a landscape that people enjoy and value, it will be maintained and sustained, and its environmental benefits will endure.

Therefore, this book is grounded in a set of principles we consider imperative for the future of rainwater management design:

- Rainwater is a vital resource.
- To ensure the resource value of rainwater, a sustainable stormwater management approach is imperative.
- Current and imminent runoff management regulations in the United States point toward a full-site green infrastructure approach that manages small flows, especially first flush, in a system of small, dispersed, site-wide interventions.
- To be truly sustainable, stormwater management must be beautiful so that people value it.
- Using ARD as a sustainable stormwater management strategy is an opportunity that designers should seize.

What Does ARD Address?

Projects that incorporate ARD are usually designed to sustainably manage small rain events and the first flush of large rain events (i.e., the initial—and dirtiest—rainfall up to 1½ inches). ARDs do *not* generally manage major flooding from large storms. But rain events up to 1½ inches represent the majority of runoff in temperate climates, accounting for 60 to 90 percent of all rain events, depending on geographic location. Consequently, the ARD approach to rainfall management presents an exciting design strategy in the context of increasingly stringent requirements to manage first flush and small storms. In other words, the opportunity posed by ARD—and presented in this book—is effective, beautiful, and enlightening management of small storm and first flush rainfall.

Our hope is that ARD will become the new normal of runoff management because it addresses so many important issues. ARD provides a strategy to:

- respond to regulatory demands for runoff management, especially of small storms and first flush;
- provide efficient runoff management on urban sites;
- manage runoff in responsible ways that benefit our natural water systems;
- use rainwater as a resource to nourish the landscape;
- transform people's perception of rainwater from waste product to resource;

- add amenity value to a landscape;
- ensure both environmental and cultural sustainability.

In sum, ARD adds up to a significant and timely approach to rainwater management in the twenty-first century.

The Scope of This Book

While some designers across the United States are undertaking ARD, many are wary. They fear it's too expensive, too hard to shepherd through the approval process, not appropriate for their geographic region, or they simply don't know how to do it. This book will provide designers with useful how-to information and ideas on this approach to runoff management.

We began to explore this topic in 2005 with the identification of a robust set of outstanding ARDs from across the United States. Although we admire the extraordinarily innovative ARD work occurring abroad, regulations and aesthetic preferences in the United States differ from those in other countries, so geographic focus was a necessary element of our research. And although our focus is on projects in the United States, we hope that readers in other countries will also find these projects and our points useful and inspirational.

We found exemplary ARD projects initially by sifting through American Society of Landscape Architects and American Institute of Architects award-winning projects, identifying those with an artful approach to sustainable stormwater management, contacting their designers, and asking them for more ARD ideas. Since that time, by talking with folks at our presentations around the country and by developing a network of professionals and students who know of our work, we've expanded our initial set to well over fifty projects nationwide. (See "Artful Rainwater Design Project List" at the back of the book.)

We have visited nearly all of these projects to conduct onsite analyses, and we have obtained and reviewed information from their designers; in other words, each design has undergone our scrutiny before being admitted to our project set. Because ARD is a new and evolving design subject, additional exciting projects undoubtedly have been overlooked simply because they haven't yet received the exposure and popularity of the projects profiled in our book, but we have made every effort to study a wide variety of exemplary projects.

A glance at the ARD project list will show that just about half of the designs are located in Seattle, Washington and Portland, Oregon. A variety of factors have made the Pacific Northwest a virtual mecca of ARD. The consistently wet weather in these states from October to May demands that citizens develop strategies to live with rain, ranging from establishment of very strict stormwater regulations to development of innovative ways to transform rainwater from a nuisance to an asset. And it's important to note that Seattle and Portland aren't mystical, artsy meccas of ARD because of any kind of counterculture creativity. In fact, by the 1990s those two cities were *forced* to act—by calamitous combined sewer overflow issues in Portland and by severe salmon habitat degradation in the Seattle area. Those problems, combined with frequent light rain, simply meant that these cities were first in line to address all the challenges faced by the rest of the country when ARDs are considered, from needing to change regulations to convincing municipal officials. And so our examples from Portland and Seattle, though geographically clumped in the Pacific Northwest, should not be dismissed by designers from other regions. In fact, they offer a particularly rich collection of exciting and potentially transferable ideas to designers nationwide.

This book divides ARD into two components: the amenity of landscape design and the utility of sustainable stormwater management. Within amenity and utility topics, we discuss goals, objectives, and techniques. This format is intended to be user friendly, easy to follow, and easy to use as a reference document.

Part 1 provides background on the subject, from the historically traditional approach to stormwater management (gray infrastructure) to the strategy that manages stormwater with soil and plants (green infrastructure) to recent demand that stormwater management address amenity. The discussion then focuses on the recent history of ARD: where it's being implemented, in what kinds of facilities, and reasons designers are taking this approach.

Part 2 covers each of the amenity goals, objectives, and techniques in depth, and part 3 presents the utility goals, objectives, and techniques of ARD. Both of these sections further encourage readers to consider creative ways to apply these ideas to their own designs by offering a set of questions for each topic.

Part 4 presents a set of twenty case studies: ARDs we've found across the United States that offer some exemplary strategies. For each case study, we first provide basic data and a brief overview of the project background (impetus and intentions for the project, as well as special challenges); then we describe both the utility strategies and the amenity strategies, concluding each with a section we call "Of Note": a few interesting facts about that design worth considering in your own ARD design.

Part 5 presents some final thoughts on ARD, including the most common reasons people say "We can't do Artful Rainwater Design in *our* stormwater management" and useful rejoinders. We conclude the book by giving you information and encouragement as you embark on your own ARD efforts.

From rain scuppers shaped like salmon to sculptures inspired by palmettos, river rocks that show a "rain trail," and water plants that create habitat—and much, much more—the ideas in this book will help you design better, more ecologically sensitive stormwater management systems that celebrate rain. ARD is a rewarding approach that honors water as a precious, life-giving, and inspiring resource.

Notes

1. Tom Liptan, Personal communication with authors, 2013.
2. Elizabeth Meyer, "Sustaining Beauty: The Performance of Appearance," *Landscape Architecture* 98, no. 10 (2008): 92–131.

1. The History of Stormwater Management and Background for Artful Rainwater Design

Although rainwater has been considered a resource in agricultural contexts for millennia, in urban contexts it has historically been considered a waste product. With some exceptions in historical management strategies, urban rainwater was treated as a problem to be mitigated, a waste product to be eliminated or controlled.

However, recent innovations in stormwater management have catalyzed a transition from treating urban runoff as undesirable to appreciating it as a natural resource that must be managed with great care. Management strategies have shifted in past decades, from simple flood control levees and combined storm and sewer systems to onsite detention systems intended to control excess flow rates, and later to infiltration and rainwater harvesting systems intended to reduce runoff volumes and non–point source pollution. Since the 1990s there has been greater interest in treating rainwater as a resource for groundwater and surface water recharge, especially through infiltration and biofiltration. In the late 1990s, authors of some regulations and publications began to call for stormwater management to include the goal of creating amenity in addition to reducing runoff quantity and quality. And since the early 2000s, some designers have begun to effectively address all three goals and celebrate rainwater through the creation of Artful Rainwater Designs (ARDs). This part presents background understanding of this transition in stormwater management and how it has evolved into ARD.

Addressing Stormwater Runoff Quantity: Traditional Flood Management

For thousands of years, stormwater management focused exclusively on flood prevention. Even in 1760 b.c.e., King Hammurabi of Mesopotamia presented stormwater regulations in the Code of Hammurabi to protect downstream landowners:

Figure 1.1. Historically, stormwater management focused on flood control; the design of systems like this detention basin considered neither beauty nor even visibility, because they were often located out of the public eye (design: unknown; photograph: Stuart Echols).

Figure 1.2. Over time, designers began to realize that stormwater management systems could also provide habitat and amenity, as in the case of this wet detention pond (design: unknown; photograph: Stuart Echols).

Figure 1.3. Today, designers see benefit in locating sustainable stormwater management systems in highly visible spots, making them beautiful, and providing means for the public to learn how the system works, as at this rainwater biotope at the Visitor Center entrance in the Queens Botanical Garden (design: Atelier Dreiseitl and Conservation Forum, BKSK Architects; photograph: Stuart Echols).

> Section 53. If anyone be too lazy to keep his dam in proper condition, and does not keep it so; if then the dam breaks and all the fields are flooded, then shall he in whose dam the break occurred be sold for money and the money shall replace the crop which he has caused to be ruined.
>
> Section 55. If anyone open his ditches to water his crop, but is careless, and the water floods the field of his neighbor, than he shall repay his neighbor with crop for his loss.
>
> Section 56. If a man lets out the water, and the water overflows the land of his neighbor, he shall pay 10 gur of crop for every 10 gan of land flooded.[1]

Controlling the quantity of water was the exclusive goal. From earliest times the emphasis was on protecting property from flood damage by moving the water offsite; more recently, the focus expanded to protection of natural water bodies from the impact of erosion caused by flooding. In both, the basic strategies were conveyance and detention.

Flood Management Tools: Basins, Channels, and Pipes

As stated earlier, the historic underpinning of urban stormwater management was the simple desire to convey runoff away from structures and protect local property from flooding. As Roesner and Matthews, whose engineering firm specialized in "integrated solutions in water," explained in their often-cited article "Water Management in the 1990s,"

> Historically, stormwater management has been limited to planning, designing and implementing storm drainage improvements. For the most part, planning and design have focused on protecting only the site being drained, with little consideration of the downstream effects of resulting increases in volume and peak flows.[2]

But the inherent problem with this focus on localized flooding, as Roesner and Mathews explained, was that flooding impacts on the downstream natural drainage system were literally out of sight and out of mind.

Stormwater flood management by conveyance was historically achieved by drainage systems that would quickly move a storm's peak flow downstream (consider, for example, the array of combined sewer conveyance tunnels in ancient Rome that disgorged from the mighty Cloaca Maxima into the Tiber River). The primary focus on managing stormwater was to dispose of the water as quickly as possible; there was no concern for preservation of stream flow rate, volume, frequency, duration, or water quality; management techniques focused simply on safely moving water away. For millennia, this entailed sizing pipes and drainage ways large enough to efficiently move the water away from a site. The common convention was to look at the size of a pipe in a comparable drainage situation and replicate that size in the hope that it would be adequate. This worked well enough if the pipe was, for example, conveying stormwater under a rural road, but once piped sewer systems were developed to handle urban runoff, the possibility of overflow from inadequately sized pipes became a real danger.

The first effective method to estimate flood flow was developed by Irish engineer Thomas Mulvaney in 1851 and made popular in the United States by Emil Kuichling. Mulvaney assumed rainfall was naturally disposed of in three ways: evaporation, infiltration, and runoff. He reasoned that evaporation and infiltration were constant throughout the year and that only daily runoff would vary with rainfall amounts. As a result, the "rational method" of runoff calculation was developed to focus specifically on predicting peak runoff flow rates resulting from the largest storm in a completely impervious urban situation. The rational method gave designers a means to predict stormwater runoff in urban areas so that pipes could be sized to dispose of the water and thus prevent local flooding. This method proved so simple that it is still used today to calculate surface water flow. But one of the inherent problems in this approach is that it ignores evapotranspiration and infiltration as useful stormwater management strategies.

Another problem with the historical approach to piping stormwater offsite lay in the fact that as these peak flows were successfully conveyed away, downstream land was still subject to increased flooding (Strom & Nathan, 1993, p. 87). In all of these approaches, stormwater in the urban environment was seen not as a resource but as a forceful enemy. According to Tourbier, a pioneer in sustainable landscapes and author of *Best Management Practices for Stormwater*,

> Stormwater management had its origin in what was known in legal language as the common enemy rule: draining runoff away from houses and backyards as fast as possible. As populations grew, this practice proved to be detrimental because one person's backyard drained into someone else's front yard. The runoff then accumulated, resulting in flood damage downstream. For many years the [United States] federal government was heavily involved in flood control, only to discover an ever-increasing spiral of expenditures, but still mounting flood losses.[3]

As if flooding weren't problem enough, stormwater too often caused even more damage when combined with sewage. Since ancient times, pipes in cities often carried both stormwater and sewage. Rome's Cloaca Maxima, mentioned earlier, remains a famous example, an engineering marvel that discharged not only rain runoff but also sewage directly into the Tiber River. Despite resulting quality degradation of rivers and other surface waters on the receiving end of combined sewer systems (CSSs), for centuries they were considered an efficient means of discarding unwanted urban liquids, and in fact CSSs were seen as a clever way to use stormwater both to move and to dilute sewage. Cities everywhere, including those in the United States, commonly built CSSs as late as the early twentieth century. But what happens when large rain events flood CSS pipes? At worst (and far too often) they fill and backflow, sending sewage backwards to its original source or simply letting the sewage overflow into streams, rivers, lakes, sounds, and bays. This unfortunate occurrence is known today as a combined sewer overflow (CSO), and it is a problem that cities worldwide seek to prevent. Most cities stopped building CSSs, but many still struggle with CSOs in their older piping systems. In sum, managing stormwater by piping it offsite arguably created more problems than it solved.

Note that Section 53 of Hammurabi's code demanded maintenance of dams, which raises the subject of detaining stormwater on site, another historical management strategy to prevent runoff from resulting in flooding. The detention basin is simple in concept. First, create a basin into which stormwater runoff is directed. Second, ensure that water is released slowly enough from the basin that local downstream damage from flooding is prevented. Much like a bathtub, detention basins must be large enough to store the volume of water resulting from a large storm, and, like the bathtub drain, an outlet is sized to control the peak flow rate of the water released from the basin. Although codes to this day state that detention must control postdevelopment peak water discharge at a predevelopment rate, downstream problems still occur because of two errors in reasoning. First, stormwater detention methods fail to recognize that when water is simultaneously released from a large number of basins, each at the maximum legal flow rate, these flows combine downstream and cause flooding once again. But because this flooding is caused by legal basin drainage and occurs so far downstream, it's hard to blame a specific landowner for the cause.

The second error is the assumption that release of water from detention basins has no negative impact on stream channels: Because water flows from each basin at predevelopment rates, streams should be fine. Once again we see a failure to recognize the cumulative impact of discharge from many detention basins simultaneously. The result is that natural streams endure bankfull (i.e., "to the brim") flows for unnaturally long periods of time, leading to scouring and stream bank erosion. Solutions to this problem were not addressed until the 1980s, when issues of stream bank erosion from detention basin discharge were more fully recognized.

In sum, traditional stormwater management practices generally addressed only excess runoff as a hazard to be contained, conveyed, and discarded as an unwanted byproduct of land development. Historical stormwater flood management practices were developed to control local urban flooding and protect local property, and they were never intended to emulate natural evapotranspiration, infiltration, and runoff processes. As a result, far from emulating natural hydrologic processes, these traditional management methods further destroyed healthy ecosystems, because the true environmental problem created by urban development was excess runoff volume created from reduced infiltration and evaporation. Treating rain as a waste product in some ways resulted in more problems than it solved.

The Detention Basin Saga Continues: Stream Channel Protection from Detention Basin Discharge

As stated earlier, for centuries detention basins managed local stormwater flooding but caused unintended downstream impacts.

Things changed with the release of Technical Release 20 by the Soil Conservation Service (TR-20) in 1982, which provided a particularly useful means to compute the stormwater runoff rate and volume for an entire watershed, effectively combining the downstream impacts of runoff from many sites. The TR-20 allowed improved modeling of the downstream flow levels and frequencies, including the downstream impacts of bankfull flows. This modeling program made it much easier to evaluate the combined effects of detention facilities located throughout a watershed and gave designers a better understanding of how these facilities affect flow rates at specific points in system. As a result, the location, size, and design of detention systems could be adjusted to release runoff at a much slower rate and thus reduce the downstream bankfull flows. This required regional stormwater planning and design. More importantly, it also required implementation on a regional scale, which seldom occurred before SCS-TR-20. The most common local stormwater facilities, however, remained on site detention, as required by most local land development regulations. This simple approach was, and still is, the easiest and most common.

A Different Tack: Addressing Stormwater Quality

By the mid-twentieth century, regulators and researchers in the United States recognized that flooding wasn't the only problem caused by stormwater moving downstream. Unfortunately, water also picks up pollutants in its path, so water bodies downstream can be polluted by stormwater carrying a wide range of toxins, from animal feces to hydrocarbons. And so quality joined quantity as a stormwater issue to be managed. Early strategies included a range of filtration methods, and by the 1980s and 1990s, biofiltration and infiltration began to be recognized as useful tools, which in turn led to promotion of green infrastructure as a strategy to effectively manage stormwater.

The Prelude: Point Source Pollution

As early as 1948, the US federal government decided to address the diminishing quality of the country's lakes, rivers, and streams; every one should be swimmable and fishable, they reasoned. The Federal Water Pollution Control Act of 1948 mandated that states identify water bodies polluted beyond a "tolerable" level and that they locate and suppress the polluting discharge. Because of the difficulty of eliminating point sources of pollution, this act was not well enforced. According to Andrew Dzurik, emeritus professor of environmental engineering at Florida State University,

> As a result of the inefficiency of such procedures, rivers were being turned into open sewers, the aquatic life of the Great Lakes was threatened with extinction, and the purity of water used for drinking, irrigation, and industrial uses was endangered.[4]

It wasn't until the 1960s, considered a watershed moment in environmental awareness in the United States, that a set of significant demands regarding prevention of water pollution were introduced.

From Rachel Carson's *Silent Spring* (1962) to Ian McHarg's *Design with Nature* (1969), publications, experts, and activists sounded the alarm to warn Americans of the dangers of environmental pollution. Stormwater management research and design began to focus on controlling point source pollution. In 1972, the Clean Water Act was modified so that discharge of pollutants to any navigable waters in the United States from any point source was *unlawful*, unless the polluter had an authorized discharge permit from the Environmental Protection Agency (EPA). These point source pollution regulations paved the way for non–point source pollution laws some years later.

Non–Point Source Pollution Control

Experts on stormwater and water pollution had known for some time that stormwater runoff is polluted by the surfaces it runs across, picking up everything from oil and antifreeze to fertilizer nutrients. But the prominent thinking was that "the solution to pollution is dilution," that is, that the water's pollution is diminished when the contaminant levels are lowered by the cumulative quantity of water as it flows downhill. Experts recognized that stormwater could also be managed to reduce pollutants; for example, literature of the 1980s speaks of settling ponds and wetlands as pollutant mitigation strategies, and infiltration of stormwater had been used for some time for water disposal in the form of French or Dutch drains (known in the United Kingdom as soakaways). But until the 1990s, these management strategies were seldom mandated or implemented as means to decrease runoff pollution.

The demand to clean stormwater runoff ramped up with the recognition of urban stormwater pollution hot spots in the 1990s: places with high pollutant levels, such as fertilizer storage facilities and gas stations. Such hot spots came to be regulated based on use and perceived hazard, with mitigation strategies including the Delaware sand filter (a gravity flow system that catches hydrocarbons). As of this writing, such strategies are still not uniformly mandated.

With revisions to the Clean Water Act, municipalities were required to document the amount of pollution they discharged in stormwater. This documentation requirement soon led to a regulatory requirement, which in turn led to the demand that municipalities set targets to reduce urban non–point source pollution.

As urban areas grew, attention was redirected away from agriculture to urban runoff as the leading non–point source pollution generator. Municipalities started focusing on reduction of non–point source pollution in stormwater runoff. It was obvious that cleaning all stormwater runoff was impractical and probably unnecessary, because simple sampling of stormwater runoff revealed that most pollutants are carried in the first flush. In other words, sampling the runoff generated by a storm over its duration revealed that the first samples (during the first ½ to 1½ inches of rainfall) held the most pollution (e.g., silt, pollen, metals, oils, nitrogen, phosphorus). The truth of this concept can be seen in the oily sheen visible on asphalt at the beginning of a rain event but not always at the end.

The result was the development of regulations across the United States to capture and treat the first flush, usually the first ½ to 1½ inches (the exact amount varies from one region to another). Most early technologies to treat first flush were examples of gray infrastructure (engineered solutions), such as filters, oil grit separators, and settling tanks. Unfortunately, many were poorly installed, resulting in all the water from a storm event flowing through the system without treatment. Maintenance was problematic also, especially because the entity responsible for maintenance (e.g., municipality, landowner) was often subject to debate.

In the 1980s and 1990s, certain experts became proponents of green infrastructure strategies to mitigate stormwater pollution. They recognized a self-evident opportunity by observing what was already known from many agriculture treatment designs: that water drained into a grassy swale is cleansed by the vegetation and soil. They thought, "Why not harness those natural cleansers as a cost-effective alternative to engineered urban management systems?"

The concept is simple: Reduce impervious surface on a site and increase landscaped areas. The design should direct runoff into the landscaped areas just enough to capture the first flush, which is cost-effectively treated for pollutant load. Initially this green strategy became popular simply as another way to address pollution mitigation, but over time, green infrastructure came to be recognized as a stormwater management strategy with multiple benefits that can address not only water quality but also water quantity through infiltration, biofiltration, and bioretention, and it provides other benefits such as wildlife habitat, open space, and landscape amenity.

Infiltration

Simply put, runoff infiltration is the movement of surface water into the soil through adsorption (adherence to plants and soil) or absorption (water taken into the plants or soil). Water that infiltrates can be held in the topsoil and taken up by plants, it can flow laterally and discharge nearby, or it can flow down into the soil, into groundwater aquifers. Infiltration is important to water ecology because it puts the water in a location where it is useful in nurturing plants, in restoring stream base flow, or in groundwater recharge. Infiltration is also one of the most efficient methods of cleansing water. Because infiltration requires land area, it has often been used when no viable alternative exists or when dwindling water levels make water recharge more desirable. Infiltration is often considered most efficient in highly porous, sandy soils and has consequently been used most often for runoff management in places such as Florida and Long Island. But Bruce Ferguson, internationally recognized stormwater expert, argued,

> Unlike any other approach to stormwater management, infiltration is capable of solving all the problems of urban runoff: peak flow, base flow, stream bank erosion, ground water recharge and water quality.[5]

Indeed, Ferguson made a large number of contributions to infiltration ideas in the 1990s and 2000s. With increasing urbanization, infiltration wasn't happening at predevelopment rates, with the consequence that groundwater levels were dropping, exacerbated by groundwater pumped out for human use. Ferguson and others were interested in trying to track and potentially restore infiltration to predevelopment levels based on annual water levels rather than storm size. This led to researching and developing an understanding of water balance, essentially an equation addressing a watershed; it demands that water coming into the watershed (through every means, from all forms of precipitation to water flow) and water going out (that infiltrates, evaporates, or flows) must be equal. This concept is central to preserving the low-level base flows in streams and understanding the impact on basin design and function.

Ferguson also developed the concept of an overflow splitter, proposing that some runoff be sent downstream but that excess runoff could sometimes be split off to an infiltration area. This idea of splitting runoff into different volumes for different treatment will come back as an important development later in this book.

Biofiltration and Bioretention

The basic idea recognized from many agriculture treatment designs—that water drained into a grassy swale is cleansed by the vegetation and soil—developed into what we now call biofiltration and bioretention. Biofiltration is a stormwater management strategy that filters pollutants out of the water by means of plants and soil; bioretention both holds and cleans runoff using plants and soil in shallow depressions. Contemporary ideas of using such natural systems to manage urban stormwater pollutants evolved from methods used in the 1970s to protect streams from agricultural pollutants (feces, pesticides, fertilizer): If it works for agricultural pollutants, why not use it to mitigate suburban runoff from impervious surfaces?

Biofiltration and bioretention are commonly considered effective sustainable stormwater management strategies. However, it's worth noting that some early bioretention designs had inherent flaws: Many of these early systems were flow-through designs that captured and temporarily held pollution in the first flush, only to have those temporarily retained pollutants pushed out and downstream by subsequent large storms. In contrast, infiltration systems most often trapped the first flush pollutants, allowing cleaner, subsequent runoff to overflow.

How Focus on Pollution Set the Stage for ARD

Regulation of pollution carried by stormwater runoff remained a challenge for decades. The number of stormwater runoff sources, the scattered nature of urban runoff, difficulties in treating and controlling non–point source pollution, financial constraints, and numerous legal challenges impeded progress in achieving the goals of the clean water programs developed by the EPA. In response to these difficulties, the 1972 amendments to the Federal Water Pollution Control Act, known as the Clean Water Act, provided the basis for the National Pollutant Discharge Elimination System (NPDES) permit program and the basic method for regulating the discharge of pollutants from point sources. But in the late 1980s, a landmark regulation redefined some stormwater as *wastewater with a pollution point source.*

Because major sources of water pollution, including stormwater, are treated as point sources, entities generating this pollution must obtain a permit regulating discharge of pollutants into the waters of the United States.

To address this problem of pollution, over the course of the 1990s and early 2000s, a predominant stormwater management objective in the United States became treating the first flush: Capture the most polluted ½ to 1½ inches of runoff through retention, infiltration, biofiltration, or bioretention, remove pollutants from the water, and permanently remove the water or temporarily detain it from the downstream discharge. Although runoff from major storm events bypasses first flush systems, as stated earlier this strategy actually controls about 60 to 90 percent of annual rainfall events (depending on geographic location). Once captured and cleansed, the runoff can then be used for irrigation or used in toilets, it can be infiltrated to replenish groundwater, or it can be detained and slowly released into surface water bodies.

The concept of using natural systems, or green infrastructure, to mitigate stormwater runoff quantity and quality began as an alternative to gray infrastructure simply to meet regulatory demands. But soon experts recognized that green infrastructure could accomplish more: While cleansing and accepting rainwater, planted areas could also reduce urban heat islands and convert carbon dioxide to oxygen; they could provide amenity, adding curb appeal to properties. If green infrastructure could be used to capture and hold most pollutants on the surface, the maintenance cost for the entire system could be reduced substantially. Green infrastructure even came to be recognized as environmentally symbiotic with the rain, treating and controlling rain while using the rain as a resource to water the plants and recharge surface and groundwater systems.

The first flush stormwater management strategy to address pollutants virtually demands that designers conceive of systems that are dispersed around a site rather than centralized. A group of small, shallow basins that capture first flush while allowing flooding stormwater to pass by or through is a much more effective way to capture pollutants than a single, deep basin. This strategy of managing stormwater on site using small, dispersed facilities also addresses most rain events, at least in temperate climates. Because the idea of small, dispersed facilities across a site is a fundamental basis for ARD, emphasis on first flush management in many ways paved the way for the ARD approach.

Another important impetus for environmentally responsible management of rain has come from voluntary assessment systems, including Leadership in Energy and Environmental Design (LEED) and SITES (formerly the Sustainable Sites Initiative). In each, designers strive for points in various categories of sustainable design to achieve a certified status for the work, and both offer points for management of quantity and quality of stormwater on site, again creating an opportunity for ARD.

In all of this, a sustainable stormwater management commitment has emerged, with each new technique striving to address postdevelopment runoff in ways that approach the predevelopment state. We're not there yet: Each human-controlled management technique has flaws that make it less effective than the natural hydrologic cycle. But increasingly stringent regulations, voluntary sustainability assessment systems, and burgeoning urban development will continue to push creative designers toward increasingly sustainable stormwater management.

Increasing Demand for Amenity in Stormwater Management Systems

Once rainwater was recast from enemy to friend, it was perhaps inevitable that someone would up the ante of expectations of its management: Why shouldn't the systems offer amenities in addition to rainwater cleansing and control?

Many creative designers had already found amenity potential in certain stormwater management strategies: Stormwater retention basins became beautiful duck ponds, and dry detention basins came to be used for playing fields. And a few trailblazing "big idea" designers had already begun to seriously rethink stormwater in the nature-conscious 1970s: Consider Ian McHarg (especially in his natural systems-focused community design for The Woodlands) and Michael and Judy Corbett (designers of Village Homes, where rain infiltration commingles with community spaces).

But, as mentioned earlier, the opportunities for amenity in stormwater management changed most dramatically with the focus on treating first flush. First flush stormwater treatment demands onsite management; regional or centralized systems to treat first flush don't work. To clarify the problems, consider the following: First, a centralized collection basin would need to be huge; second, the water in that huge basin, including not only first flush but also water from the extended storm event, would dramatically dilute the pollutants, making pollutant collection more challenging than it needs to be. Unlike centralized systems, local, onsite stormwater management systems need only hold and filter a small amount of water (the first flush ½ to 1½ inches). Additionally, the small, distributed, onsite management approach is much safer because the pollution management is distributed between multiple systems on different sites. If one small system fails, the other ones still work, and smaller water volumes are inherently safer to control. Onsite management also shifts maintenance responsibility clearly to the landowner and away from the municipality.

Since the 1990s, thanks to the recognition that site design that starts with sustainable stormwater management may hold the solution to effective stormwater management, some authors and designers have recognized that new onsite stormwater treatment methods—including bioretention, vegetated swales, and rain garden systems—have the potential to add various and distinct amenity values to projects.[6] Although specific techniques for creating, restoring, and protecting aquatic habitats have become common in stormwater management,[7] no current manuals for stormwater design specifically present best management practices as a means to enhance the aesthetic, experiential attributes of urban landscapes.

A few exceptions stand out. Peter Stahre's research showed how new stormwater management facilities in Malmö, Sweden, have added "positive values": In his 2006 book *Sustainability in Urban Storm Drainage: Planning and Examples*, Stahre classified the values as aesthetic, biological, cultural, ecological, economic, technical, educational, environmental, historical, recreational, and public relations—the last value being a result of the others. Another example of amenity demands in stormwater management is found in literature from the United Kingdom based on Sustainable Urban Drainage Systems (SUDS) regulations. Indeed, the United Kingdom has introduced policies that include amenity factors in stormwater management as a key part of the Sustainable Urban Drainage Triangle (CIRIA, 2007). There, regulations now require amenity to be evaluated along with quality and quantity for all new drainage plans.

Originally the amenity designation focused often on creating wildlife habitat and open space; however, the Sustainable Urban Drainage Systems regulations revised the definition to include "community value, resource management (e.g., rainwater use), multi-use of space, education, water features, habitat creation, biodiversity action plans" (National SUDS Working Group, 2003). But although Stahre and SUDS presented the amenity potential inherent in stormwater management, neither articulated ways that designers can actually achieve it. Probably the most inspiring examples of ARD to date are provided in Nigel Dunnett and Andy Clayden's book *Rain Gardens* (2007). Their research described and illustrated examples of projects from around the world that capture, divert, and reuse rainwater in beautiful and unconventional ways. Using photographs and drawings, the book explains how different elements of the stormwater treatment chain can be integrated into typical residential and public or commercial landscapes.

By the early 2000s, experts from various parts of the globe were calling for stormwater best management practices (BMPs) to include creation of amenity as a component of management systems but were not offering clear information on how to create that amenity. However, some designers were ahead of the curve and began experimenting with ARD.

The Emergence of ARD

Although beautiful detention ponds and other attractive stormwater management facilities certainly predate 1990, an idea took root that year in the site design of a museum parking lot in Portland, Oregon that has been blossoming ever since. Tom Liptan, recently retired environmental specialist for Portland's Bureau of Environmental Services, describes the parking lot design for the Oregon Museum of Science and Industry (OMSI) as an experimental idea: The city was trying to determine how to comply with impending federal stormwater regulations under the Clean Water Act to improve the quality of the Willamette River. Review of OMSI's traditional parking lot landscape island design led to an idea to cleanse and retain parking lot storm runoff. As Liptan explained to us in a personal conversation in 2013, the crazy notion was this: Why not make everything "opposite" to the norm by crowning the paved parking surface and sinking the landscape strips to accept runoff from the parking lot? The OMSI parking lot strategy, by Murase Associates, became one of Portland's first large-scale, onsite stormwater biofiltration and infiltration systems, and it proclaimed its purpose (through signage) within an attractive landscape of perennials and shrubs. It also became an early example of

ARD: sustainable stormwater management that is not only visually appealing but also informative about the way it manages rain.

Public appreciation for OMSI is one factor that led Liptan and others to find more opportunities for aesthetically pleasing and informative strategies to manage stormwater. This has resulted in numerous urban bioretention basins and small surface detention curb extensions (including Northeast Siskiyou Green Street, the 12th Avenue Green Street, and Southwest Montgomery, to name only a few) and innovative retrofit projects at schools (including the award-winning Mount Tabor Elementary School and Glencoe Elementary School). The high public profile of these aesthetically pleasing and educational projects has provided residents and visitors the opportunity to see, appreciate, and learn about the resource value of rainwater—the very strategy that we call Artful Rainwater Design.

At the same time, other Portland designers recognized the value of the ARD approach and applied it to their projects, including two case studies that appear in part 4: the Oregon Convention Center (2003, by Mayer/Reed) and 10th@Hoyt, an apartment building in the Pearl District by Koch Landscape Architecture (2005). Greenworks is another Portland firm that has not only created many built ARDs (including Washougal Town Square, in part 4) but also produced the very informative *Low Impact Development Approaches (LIDA) Handbook* in July 2009.

Meanwhile, in Seattle, Washington, the Seattle Public Utilities (SPU) was developing a strategy to tackle an alarming increase in urban stormwater runoff between the 1970s and the 1990s. According to the SPU, they were motivated not by legislation but by salmon—the impact of polluted water on Puget Sound and its prized endangered species. In 2001, the SPU created SEA (Street Edge Alternative) Street, the redesign of a residential street right-of-way as a bioretention swale pilot project. That was followed, in 2002, by the 110th Cascade project, a set of stepped basins (planted bioretention cells) to detain and filter rainwater draining along the right-of-way of another residential street. Seattle soon went large-scale, with the ambitious redevelopment of the West Seattle community of High Point. Here, the SPU and Seattle Housing Authority teamed to create a large-scale natural drainage system in an urban environment. (For more information on this project, see part 4, "Case Studies"). As with Portland, Seattle designers embraced the ARD approach, and innovative projects multiplied throughout the city.

The cities of Seattle and Portland adopted an ARD approach because of an urgent need for dramatically improved stormwater management combined with an ethos and creativity that led a group of designers to not only manage stormwater in sustainable ways but take the opportunity to teach and engage visitors, primarily on public projects. By this means, these cities not only managed their rainwater responsibly but also showed the public that they were doing so—a clever and very successful public relations strategy. Some early successes in each city led to more efforts and successes in ARD. ARDs are now abundant in both of these cities, which explains why a large number of the case studies in this book address designs in Seattle or Portland.

Those of us in the rest of the United States shouldn't view Seattle and Portland as "out there" and irrelevant to our own contexts; those cities simply faced major challenges with CSOs and regulatory mandates that were ahead of the national curve. As Steve Law wrote in the *Portland Tribune*, "Across the nation, more than 700 other cities have combined sewer overflow problems, largely communities that developed a century or more ago, like much of Portland."[8] So nearly all major municipalities in the United States are headed in the same direction, and they would be wise to take the creative approach of their peers in the Northwest. Philadelphia, for example, recently embarked on a 25-year agreement with the EPA to address all CSOs with green infrastructure. In 2013, Chicago launched a 5-year, $50 million plan to make green infrastructure upgrades. The list goes on, and we feel the key is that these exciting efforts must be undertaken with all the creativity and skill in celebrating rain with ARD that we see in Portland and Seattle.

Additional outstanding ARDs are found all across the United States. Though far more dispersed than in the fecund ARD region of the US Northwest, noteworthy ARDs have been created in every region of the country and in project types from residential to institutional and municipal facilities. In the case studies in this book (part 4), we present twenty ARDs nationwide that we consider the most inspirational of the more than fifty we've explored to date. Of course, many more ARDs already exist, and, grounded in our hope that ARD will become a new normal for sustainable stormwater management, we expect that there will soon be too many ARDs to count.

Conclusion

In our lifetime, we have seen dramatic changes in attitudes toward and management of rainwater runoff. Stormwater—a waste product and common enemy blamed for property damage through flooding and for surface water and aquatic system damage through pollutant conveyance—has morphed into rainwater, a valued natural resource beneficial to our water cycle. Experts believe that our environmental responsibility is to adopt an integrated, holistic approach that addresses rainwater management in ways that emulate and contribute to the natural hydrologic cycle as closely as possible; furthermore, a growing number now believe that rainwater management systems should be conceived for their resource value, becoming amenity landscapes that engage, educate, and entertain visitors through celebration of the rainwater.

Clearly the ARD approach to stormwater management entails more complex goals and a more challenging design and implementation process than traditional gray infrastructure strategies; so why do it? The following responses come right from some of our country's most prolific artful rainwater designers.

Warren Byrd, Nelson Byrd Woltz

Why wouldn't we? Why do we practice this fine complex art called landscape architecture? Because we are committed to making this world a better, healthier and more beautiful place.

Stormwater will always be "managed" in some way or the other in most civilized societies. We choose to incorporate artful and intelligent ways of harnessing rainwater in order to make such environmental systems front and center in landscape designs of every scale. We choose to think of most of our projects, whether public or private, as working landscapes that embrace and honor living systems.

Water is one of our most fundamental elements and essential to every living system: it needs to be celebrated and revealed in as many productive ways as possible. Since we have always understood landscape architecture as a synthesis of artistic, scientific and cultural values (ideas, endeavors, intentions), it seems that taking an "artful" approach to designing with (rain)water should not really even be a choice, it should be an expectation.

* * *

Kevin Perry, Urban|Rain

For me it has always been a question of function rather than expression. Creating designs that best replicate the function of natural systems demands that stormwater facilities be made simple, shallow, decentralized, and of course, beautiful. It is a design approach that can be applied to any type of climate/environment: wet, dry, urban, suburban. The result is a high-performance landscape that is engaging and very cost-effective.

* * *

Joan Nassauer, Professor of Landscape Architecture, University of Michigan

For me, the motive for taking an artful rainwater design approach was to make environmentally beneficial design last. My design strategy was to align a culturally desirable landscape appearance with environmental benefits that might be invisible or would otherwise look objectionable. I used what I had learned in my research about the aesthetics of everyday landscapes to propose patterns that were intended to win the affection of the public for those early green infrastructure designs. This reduced the risk that innovative landscape patterns would disappear with the next land owner or new manager.

* * *

Steve Benz, OLIN

Personally, as an engineer I am not content to design green infrastructure at the expense of the place. Rainwater adds a unique dimension and design opportunity that is not available with traditional landscapes. I look at Artful Rainwater Design as a way of creating incredibly rich places that are highly efficient "working landscapes" and improve life at all levels. For this reason I always team with creative and talented landscape architects and designers!

* * *

Stacy Levy, environmental artist

As a kid, I spent hours playing in a drainage ditch at the edge of an urban park, watching the rain-swelled stream erode its banks. Back then I did not think much about the destructive power of the stormwater,—but I loved how the stream's flow changed over time: sometimes a trickle, sometimes a torrent. Bringing this kind of changeability back into our landscapes is my job as an artist. I want to make a site that works like a verb: active, encompassing changes and solutions; rather than a noun: a static picture that does not interact with nature.

* * *

To achieve high-functioning, multitasking ARDs, rainwater management designers need more than regulations and inspirations. They need ideas: concrete information on ways to transform stormwater management into sustainable rainwater management that is perceived as a value added in the landscape. With this information, designers can move ARD forward as a multifaceted approach to sustainable stormwater management. The next two parts of this book provide specific information to address these needs: Part 2 presents landscape amenity goals, objectives, and design techniques, and part 3 presents sustainable stormwater management goals, objectives, and design techniques that you can consider in the creation of your own ARDs.

Notes

1. Asit K. Biswas, *History of Hydrology* (Amsterdam, The Netherlands: North Holland Publishing, 1970), 20–21.
2. L. Roesner and R. Matthews, "Stormwater Management for the 1990s," *American City and Country* 105 (1990): 33.
3. J. T. Tourbier, "Open Space through Stormwater Management: Helping to Structure Growth on the Urban Fringe," *Journal of Soil and Water Conservation* 49 (1994): 14.
4. Andrew A. Dzurik, *Water Resources Planning* (New York, NY: Rowman and Littlefield Publishers, 1990): 56.
5. Bruce Ferguson, *Stormwater Infiltration* (Boca Raton, FL: Lewis Publishers, 1994): 3.
6. Significant resources on this topic include the following, listed in the References section of this chapter: Göransson (1998), Wenk (1998), Niemczynowicz (1999), Thompson and Sorvig (2000), Dreiseitl, Grau, and Ludwig (2001), and Dreiseitl and Grau (2005).
7. See, for example, Coffman (2000), Hager (2001), and Urbonas et al. (1989) in the References section of this chapter.
8. Steve Law, "River City's Pipe Dream," *Portland Tribune*, November 9, 2011, accessed January 5, 2014, http://cni.pmgnews.com/component/content/article?id=15327.

2. Achieving Amenity with Artful Rainwater Design

Overview of Amenity Considerations in Artful Rainwater Design

As we discussed in the Introduction, there are two components of ARD, amenity and utility. This section of the book presents the amenity side of ARD: the goals, objectives, and techniques a designer might use to make a sustainable stormwater management system into a landscape amenity that celebrates rain, encouraging visitors to learn about, be entertained by, or otherwise enjoy the rainwater-focused landscape.[1] Our hope is that, armed with the cumulative information from this section and part 3, augmented by real-world details from the case study section, designers will have abundant ideas and strategies for their own creation of ARDs.

In this book, the definition of *amenity* is a synthesis of our definition of ARD and definition 3 of *amenity* offered in the *American Heritage Dictionary*: "A feature that increases attractiveness or value, especially of a piece of real estate or a geographic location."[2] In the context of ARD, amenity is understood as a feature focused on the experience of rainwater in a way that increases the landscape's attractiveness or value.

Our use of this definition has a few inherent limitations, which are important to recognize. First, in this book a design's "attractiveness or value" is measured only by human appreciation (as opposed to wildlife—or any other life form, for that matter). Second, we acknowledge that our measure of "attractiveness" in this book is based on what could be called conventional aesthetics, based on our understanding of mainstream American taste in landscape beauty. We think this focus on conventional American aesthetic preferences is useful for designers working in the United States.

To appreciate the content of this chapter it is important to clarify that, before our ARD work began in 2005, there were no established goals, objectives, or techniques to accomplish amenity intentions in sustainable stormwater management. We had to begin our effort by developing those important referents. To do this, we carefully reviewed the ARD case studies to derive themes. The process we used is sometimes known as grounded theory method. In this approach, a researcher begins with the data (in our case, the ARD projects) and, by examining and reexamining those data, discovers a set of points or themes that can cumulatively add up to a theory.[3] In our study, repeated scrutiny of the projects led us to develop not a full-fledged theory but a useful set of amenity goals, objectives, and techniques for ARD.

Our first step in the process was to develop a set of ARD amenity goals. We began with a list of general landscape amenity goals gleaned from published land development literature (Beyard, 1989; Bookout, 1994a, 1994b; Kone, 2006; O'Mara, 1988), amenity goals often addressed in landscape design:

- Convenience: location, ease, or comfort
- Education: provision of favorable conditions for learning
- Recreation: provision of favorable conditions for play or relaxation
- Safety: freedom from exposure to danger or risk
- Social interaction: the commingling of individuals or groups
- Public relations: semiotic expression of values of the designer or owner
- Aesthetic richness: beauty or pleasure experienced as a result of design composition

We then looked to our data—the ARD projects—comparing these general landscape amenity goals with the amenities we found in the designs. We found that nearly all were relevant, although the ARD projects did not reveal significant achievement of convenience or social interaction through focus on rainwater (admittedly, these goals might be accomplished in ARD projects not on our list). So the amenity goals most clearly achieved in our list of ARD projects, and used as the foundation for this book, are as follows:

 Education

 Public relations (PR)

 Recreation

 Aesthetic richness

 Safety

Once we established these amenity goals, we returned to the data to see what amenity objectives we could glean from the ARD projects. After a lot of examining and categorizing, we developed a short list of useful objectives for each amenity goal found in more than one ARD project (although no objective was found in every project).

The last step was identification of design techniques that could be used to achieve each amenity objective. Once again we returned to the data, looking for all the ways we found in the ARD projects to accomplish each one of our objectives. The result was a short list of numerous techniques that a designer can use to fulfill each amenity objective.

Although explanation of the process is ponderous, the method itself is quite useful; it's a great way to derive fruitful patterns of information from (in this case) a set of designs. We think it's an especially useful research method for landscape architects, and we're gratified that Elen Deming and Simon Swaffield chose to include an explanation of our research method in their 2011 book *Landscape Architecture Research: Inquiry, Strategy, Design*.

The following sections of the book are organized according to the five amenity goals: education, recreation, safety, public relations, and aesthetic richness. Each goal is briefly explained, and then key recurring objectives and design techniques from the projects are outlined in a one-page table. Each table is followed by brief presentation, in text and image, of noteworthy project examples for each amenity objective.

We offer a suggested reading strategy to guide you through this part of the book: Choose a goal that interests you, skim the table of objectives and techniques to accomplish that goal, then go to the examples, which helpfully illustrate the ideas. When you're ready to undertake an ARD of your own, use the tables of goals, objectives, and techniques as resources, along with the "Things to Consider" sections; these should provide effective inspiration and ideas for your own creation of ARDs.

Notes

1. This chapter expands on an article that appeared in *Landscape Journal* (27:2/ISSN 0277-2426), published by the University of Wisconsin Press.
2. http://education.yahoo.com/reference/dictionary/entry/amenity accessed August 12, 2013.
3. Corbin and Strauss (2008).

PART 2.1

Education in Artful Rainwater Design

In the context of ARD, the education goal is understood as creating favorable conditions to learn about rainwater or related issues. Examples include presenting opportunities to learn about the site's sustainable stormwater management systems, the site's historical water condition, riparian plant associations, and so on. In some cases, these ideas may be gleaned from the design as specific lessons learned; in other cases, the design may tell a story of water in that place through a landscape narrative. Education-oriented ARDs may also entail programming educational opportunities through tours, games, and the like.

In the ARD case study projects we discovered three different education objectives accomplished through a variety of techniques, described in table 2.1.

The following pages describe ways that specific ARDs use each of the education objectives and various techniques. Three projects provide ideas to learn by telling a rainwater story, and one project teaches about its rainwater treatment systems while also providing an exemplary way to learn through the best signage we've seen. Another project provides an effective context for learning by placing the treatment systems in very visible spots where people congregate, and a final project creates an interactive experience of ideas to learn in a context that invites people to explore and discover the stormwater management strategy.

Education Objective: Provide ideas to learn about the hydrologic cycle
Technique: Create a narrative of stormwater or the hydrologic cycle
Projects: New Seasons Market at Arbor Lodge, Portland, OR, Lango Hansen Landscape Architects PC, Ivan McLean, artist; "Ridge and Valley," Penn State Arboretum, University Park, PA, Stacy Levy, artist, with MTR Landscape Architects, Overland Partners; Rain Garden at the Oregon Convention Center, Portland, OR, Mayer/Reed

Sometimes the story of rain and its importance to the hydrologic cycle is most effectively told through a landscape narrative, or visual storytelling, from which the viewer gleans meaning. A simple but highly effective example of this educational strategy is found at the New Seasons Market at Arbor Lodge in Portland, Oregon (figure 2.1). Here Lango Hansen Landscape Architects and artist Ivan McLean transformed rain scuppers into eye-catching sculptures that tell of the relationship between rainwater and the most prized fish species of the Northwest, the salmon. McLean draped lilting tendrils of stainless steel from the ends of the scuppers and attached stainless steel salmon silhouettes in such a way that they seem to be swimming upstream toward the water source. When rainwater pours down, the effect is complete: The salmon face water cascading from the scupper, apparently fighting their way "upriver." But even when dry, thanks to the salmon and those seemingly liquid steel tendrils, the sculpture encourages a viewer to become aware of the impact rainwater has on the downstream environment.

Table 2.1. Education goal: Create conditions to learn about rainwater or stormwater runoff-related issues

Objectives: Provide	Design Techniques
Ideas to Learn	
Hydrologic cycle	Make stormwater trails visible and legible. Create a narrative of stormwater or the hydrologic cycle. Use expressive hydrologic symbols.
Historical water condition	Make stormwater trails visible and legible. Integrate stormwater-related site artifacts into the design. Create a narrative of the historical water condition. Use expressive symbols of historical water conditions.
Water treatment types	Make stormwater treatment systems visible and legible. Make stormwater treatment systems playful, intriguing, or puzzling. Include variety of stormwater treatment systems in design.
Treatment system impact	Create systems that visibly collect and store trash or pollution.
Riparian plant types	Provide a variety of visible plant types and communities.
Riparian wildlife	Provide a variety of interesting wildlife habitat by: Using plants that provide wildlife food. Providing different water depths. Creating shelter for wildlife such as bird and bat houses.
Ways to Learn	
Signage	Provide simple signage or exhibits including: Brief text. Clear graphics. Location, color, or motion that attracts people.
Programming	Design treatment systems to invite educational games or activities.
Context for Learning	
Visibility	Create treatment systems that are visible and legible. Create visual interest by varying the appearance of different parts of the stormwater treatment systems.
Gathering	Create a variety of spaces for groups to explore, gather, or sit near the stormwater treatment systems.
Interactivity	Create treatment systems that are touchable. Create designs that encourage people to explore near or in the treatment systems.

Figure 2.1. Scuppers with stainless steel salmon silhouettes at Seven Corners Market allow viewers to mentally connect rainwater to river (design: Lango Hansen Landscape Architects, Ivan McLean; photograph: Eliza Pennypacker).

Figure 2.2. "Ridge and Valley" tells the story of rain and runoff in the Spring Creek Watershed (design: Stacy Levy with MTR Landscape Architects, Overland Partners; photograph: Frederick Weber).

"Ridge and Valley" casts a wider narrative net. This is a work of environmental art that tells the rainwater story of an entire watershed in the Ridge and Valley physiographic province of Pennsylvania (figure 2.2). Here, at the Penn State Arboretum Visitor Pavilion, artist Stacy Levy incised a bluestone terrace with a map of the rivers and tributaries of the local Spring Creek Watershed; long slabs of sittable limestone represent the region's iconic ridges lining the watershed map's "valleys." When rain falls from a scupper cascading roof runoff onto the relief map, the incised rivers and tributaries go to work, directing water into a rain garden at the terrace's edge. This popular terrace provides visitors a miniaturized view of surface water movement in the local landscape.

At the Oregon Convention Center Rain Garden in Portland, landscape architect Carol Mayer Reed designed a metaphorical landscape that (with a bit of creative observation by the viewer) presents the hydrologic cycle. Here five huge scuppers protrude from the Convention Center building, conveying rainwater from its 5-acre roof into a detention, biofiltration, and infiltration system designed as an abstraction of a regional river. Native basalt columns punctuate a tiered channel of sequential runnels, pools, and weirs; native plants are elegantly arranged in and along the channel, a sophisticated version of riparian and wetland volunteers. This entire design presents a river metaphor, and like "Ridge and Valley," it tells the story of the rainwater journey from rooftop to river (figure 2.3).

Figure 2.3. In the Rain Garden at the Oregon Convention Center a river abstraction tells the story of water's journey from rooftop to river (design: Mayer/Reed; photograph: Eliza Pennypacker).

Education Objective: Provide ideas to learn about water treatment types
Technique: Make stormwater treatment systems visible and legible; include a variety of stormwater treatment systems in the design

Education Objective: Provide ways to learn through signage
Technique: Provide simple signage that uses brief text, clear graphics, location, and color that attract people
Project: Pierce County Environmental Services, Chambers Creek, WA, Bruce Dees & Associates, SvR Design Company, The Miller|Hull Partnership

Making the stormwater treatment system visible and legible encourages visitors to notice the treatment strategy and either instantly grasp it or (perhaps even more intriguing) piece the puzzle together to comprehend how the site manages runoff. A visible stormwater management system often combines effectively with signage to maximize the educational opportunity: A visitor reads a sign that explains the system and then sees it functioning in the design. (In part 4, the case study of Pierce County Environmental Services Facility in Chambers Creek, Washington, provides more detail on this combined educational strategy.)

Figure 2.4. The water trail at Pierce County Environmental Services begins with water falling from a scupper into a concrete basin incised with a spiral runnel (design: Bruce Dees & Associates, SvR Design Company, The Miller|Hull Partnership; photograph: Stuart Echols).

The water trail begins on a corner of the building (figure 2.4), where runoff falls from a scupper into a concrete basin incised with a spiral runnel. When it rains, water spirals from that basin into an adjacent wetland that visitors are invited to view from an elegantly meandering boardwalk (figure 2.5). At the end of the wetland the water disappears briefly under a roadway to reemerge in a bioswale designed to indicate its function: The bioswale is lined with river pebbles and riparian plants interspersed with pieces of driftwood, to drive home the water theme. The bioswale forms a 270-foot-long axis, edged on one side by the employee parking lot and on the other by a neighborhood walking trail, which ensures maximum visibility of the stormwater management system (figure 2.6). At the end of the bioswale the water again disappears briefly under a roadway, to end in a particularly intriguing piece of the system: a plaza that contains three visible valve heads, on axis with the bioswale (figure 2.7). Signage explains that this is a "flow splitter plaza" channeling runoff into two different conveyance and infiltration swales, one grass lined and one wetland plant lined, while a third diverter awaits development of future treatment strategies. Throughout the linear system, multiple water "lessons" and a high level of craft and care reflect the designer's effort to call the visitor's attention to the multifaceted rainwater treatment system.

The educational impact of the complex rainwater design at Pierce County is enhanced by

Figure 2.5. A meandering boardwalk at Pierce County Environmental Services invites visitors to view the wetland (design: Bruce Dees & Associates, SvR Design Company, The Miller|Hull Partnership; photograph: Stuart Echols).

Figure 2.6. A 270-foot-long bioswale at Pierce County Environmental Services lines a parking lot and a recreational trail, ensuring maximum visibility of the water treatment system (design: Bruce Dees & Associates, SvR Design Company, The Miller|Hull Partnership; photograph: Stuart Echols).

Figure 2.7. The axial bioswale (background) terminates in a "flow splitter plaza" (foreground) where signage explains different strategies used to convey and infiltrate runoff (design: Bruce Dees & Associates, SvR Design Company, The Miller|Hull Partnership; photograph: Stuart Echols).

particularly effective signage located at strategic spots. Signage is undeniably a useful means to offer education in the landscape, and our ARD projects reveal a range of signage strategies, some more effective than others. We found that signs presenting dense blocks of edge-to-edge text lack eye appeal and can seem too much like a lecture in the landscape to pique a person's interest. In fact, we found some signs so daunting in their dense paragraphs of text that we photographed them for future reference rather than reading them on site. But at Pierce County Environmental Services a clever signage system seems intended to cajole visitors into learning through some simple strategies. First, each sign presents a small, digestible tidbit of information that can be read at a glance, providing an intriguing bit of knowledge rather than thorough but daunting paragraphs (figure 2.8). Next, because signs are located throughout the site, these discrete bits of information each contribute to an extensive cumulative educational system. Additionally, the signs are strategically placed along the walking trail next to the stormwater treatment system; in other words, one can't walk the trail without encountering the small signs and their intriguing info-bites. Finally, every sign in this system is bright yellow, making it impossible to miss. The overall impact of this set of strategies is very effective: Once drawn by the color to discover the interesting information on one sign, we found ourselves looking for the "yellow tags" along the stormwater treatment trail—and thus learning a lot about the system and having fun doing it (figure 2.9).

Figure 2.8. At Pierce County Environmental Services, numerous signs each offer a digestible tidbit of information, carefully balancing text and graphics (design: Bruce Dees & Associates, SvR Design Company, The Miller|Hull Partnership; photograph: Stuart Echols).

Figure 2.9. Eye-catching yellow signs are strategically located along the walking trail (design: Bruce Dees & Associates, SvR Design Company, The Miller|Hull Partnership; photograph: Stuart Echols).

Education Objective: Provide a context for learning and gathering
Technique: Create a variety of spaces for groups to explore, gather, or sit near the stormwater treatment systems
Project: Swarthmore Science Center, Swarthmore, PA, ML Baird & Co.; Einhorn Yaffee Prescott

The Swarthmore Science Center has two stormwater management systems next to outdoor public spaces: one at an upper level of the building, a second at a lower level. A person standing at the large glass walls of Eldridge Commons, a public space inside the upper level of the science center, can easily see both systems. At the upper level, a waterfall wall dramatically spills runoff from the roof into a 2-foot-high raised concrete channel that runs along the building; the channeled water then drops and disappears into a square river rock–filled basin at grade. All of this rainwater action is placed right next to a public patio with plenty of tables and chairs (figure 2.10), edged by Eldridge Commons's huge glass wall. The water movement is clearly visible to those sitting in the patio space and in the commons, although the water's destination is a mystery. A tiny sign near the waterfall wall explains that the water trail leads to an underground cistern and is pumped into nearby gardens. The water trail is legible without the signage, making an intriguing rainwater focal point for those in the patio area, but the sign definitely satisfies the curious (figure 2.11).

On the other side of the building, students and faculty can move from the upper to the lower level outdoors by walking through a building underpass, then descending a wide stone stairway. The pedestrian steps are edged on one side by rainwater steps that allow runoff from an invisible source to tumble down to the lower level; at the bottom of the rainwater steps, a runnel within a perfectly sittable wall conveys the rain along the edge of a patio. At the end of the wall, this system displays the same theme as the waterfall wall: Water falls from the raised channel and disappears into a square river stone–filled basin at grade, again leaving the water's destination a mystery (figure 2.12).

In this project, at both levels the runoff conveyance system's location adjacent to commodious public spaces—both indoors and out—makes it very visible. And at both levels, the water source and destination are unknown without the assistance of signage.

Figure 2.10. The rainwater trail from roof to ground is visible from an adjacent patio at the Swarthmore Science Center (design: ML Baird & Co.; Einhorn Yaffee Prescott; photograph: Stuart Echols).

Figure 2.11. A small sign explains the rainwater treatment strategy of the waterfall wall at the Swarthmore Science Center upper-level patio (design: ML Baird & Co.; Einhorn Yaffee Prescott; photograph: Stuart Echols).

Figure 2.12. The rainwater trail from the stormwater steps to the ground edges pedestrian stairs and a lower-level patio at the Swarthmore Science Center (design: ML Baird & Co.; Einhorn Yaffee Prescott; photograph: Stuart Echols).

Education Objective: Provide ideas to learn about the hydrologic cycle
Techniques: Make stormwater trails visible and legible; create a narrative of stormwater or the hydrologic cycle; use expressive hydrologic symbols

Education Objective: Provide a context for learning and interactivity
Technique: Create designs that encourage people to explore near or in the treatment systems
Project: Southwest Recreation Center, University of Florida, Gainesville, FL, RDG Planning and Design

At the University of Florida Southwest Recreation Center expansion, a number of education objectives and techniques coalesce—in the form of a clear water trail, metaphorical sculpture, bold invitations for pedestrians to enter the system, and a prominent location—to create an ARD that is beautiful, informative, intriguing, and inviting.

First, the location: This is an expansion of the Southwest Recreation Center of the university, located along a busy road near a prominent campus entry. The center expansion designers refaced the old building with a broad, glassy front along a main road. Along that new glass facade, between road and building, the designers placed a long bioswale robustly planted with native perennials. Sidewalks parallel the bioswale on both sides, one along the roadway and one along the glassy building face. Simply put, this stormwater management bioswale is showcased to passing drivers, bicyclists, and pedestrians and to everyone headed into the recreation center.

Next comes the clear idea to be learned, thanks in part to a site-specific art installation made possible by Florida's Art in State Buildings Program. Pedestrians walking between bioswale and building are treated to an intriguing water narrative: At rhythmic intervals along the building, six small, low bronze scuppers discharge roof runoff into river pebble–filled basins; the runoff then cascades into pebble-lined runnels that extend out perpendicularly from the building to water the bioswale. Each of the six runnels crosses the pedestrian path, and an observant pedestrian can clearly see that water from the building is underfoot, headed toward the bioswale; before the runnel spills water into the rain garden, it passes under a brightly colored filigree columnar sculpture (figure 2.13) at the edge of the bioswale plantings.

On the base of the yellow sculpture, near the recreation center front door, is a plaque explaining the art installation, titled *Thirst* by David Dahlquist. The plaque states, in part,

> The sculptural columns suggest a root structure of the palmetto palm, almost like human tissue, symbolic of the common denominators between plant and animal and our shared dependence upon water.

And observant passersby will note that each rainwater runnel runs under a sculpture, suggesting that the organism sucks up the life-giving water (figure 2.14). In sum, this design presents a clear but symbolic lesson about rain and its life-giving quality.

Figure 2.13. Six runnels carry roof runoff from the building across the sidewalk to the bioswale, each encountering a brightly colored columnar sculpture (design: RDG Planning and Design; photograph: Eliza Pennypacker).

Figure 2.14. Each runnel in the design flows under a sculpture, symbolizing the organism's absorption of life-giving rain (design: RDG Planning and Design; photograph: Eliza Pennypacker).

But wait, there's more. Each runnel line extending from the building continues across the bioswale as the top of a checkdam, then reaches all the way to the public sidewalk as a landform-hugging stepped stone pathway. In other words, at six points along the bioswale, this design boldly and clearly invites passersby to enter the stormwater management system from the roadside sidewalk (figure 2.15).

All told, this ARD addresses all the education objectives—ideas to learn, ways to learn, and context for learning—with some great techniques, resulting in an exciting design particularly appropriate on a university campus.

Figure 2.15. A broad stone path extends the line of each runnel all the way to the public sidewalk, inviting passersby to enter the bioswale (design: RDG Planning and Design; photograph: Eliza Pennypacker).

Things to Consider in Your Effort to Achieve an Education Goal in ARD

Both the matrix and the projects provide plenty of opportunities and questions to consider in the design of educational ARDs, summarized here:

- What information about rain would you like visitors to grasp?
- What sustainable stormwater management systems does the design use? Do they provide a learning opportunity if rendered visible?
- Can the rainwater story be told without signage, or even without water (i.e., when dry)?
- Can the rainwater story be told even in freezing winter weather?
- Are the water sources and destinations clear?
- If signage is needed, how can it be designed to be interesting, brief, and clearly part of the ARD design?
- Can part of the stormwater system be located in a public gathering area to promote awareness of, and conversation about, the system?
- In what other ways can people be compelled to notice and learn from the system?
- Would it be possible to promote interaction with the system to enlighten visitors?

PART 2.2

Recreation in Artful Rainwater Design

As a design goal in ARD, recreation means providing conditions that are favorable for interacting with the stormwater treatment system in ways that are relaxing, amusing, or refreshing. In contrast to the education goal, the focus here is on playful interaction, with simple enjoyment as the intent. The distinction between education and recreation is admittedly nuanced, with considerable overlap, but we present them as distinct categories to help designers who want to emphasize one over the other.

Our exploration of recreational opportunities led us to recognize three objectives of recreational interaction with Artful Rainwater Design: view (the opportunity to see water or the water system while relaxing in the landscape, whether moving or seated), enter (the ability to step into the water or water system and come into physical contact with it), and play (the opportunity to engage with or modify the water or water system). These recreation objectives and a variety of design techniques to achieve them are presented in table 2.2.

Table 2.2. Recreation goal: Create conditions for interacting with the stormwater systems in ways that are relaxing, amusing, or refreshing

Objectives: Create Opportunities to	Design Techniques
View	
Pass by	Provide paths in strategic locations that ensure encounters with stormwater treatment systems.
	Connect onsite trails to offsite trail systems and destinations that ensure encounters with stormwater treatment systems.
Pause	Create overlooks with views of stormwater systems.
	Create destination points related to stormwater treatment systems.
Rest	Provide seating using walls, benches, or tables and chairs with views of stormwater systems.
Enter	
Wayfinding	Provide clear points of entry into stormwater systems.
	Make entry points visually inviting or mysterious.
Access	Make entry points easily accessible.
	Provide places to sit in stormwater systems.
Play	
Explore	Provide a variety of small and large places to play in or explore.
	Make areas that invite climbing and physical exploration and that balance perceptions of safety with adventure.
Interact	Create stormwater systems that can be safely modified by the user, such as small movable river rocks and weirs.

Some techniques to address recreation stand out in our ARD cases: Two projects provide views of the stormwater treatment for those strolling or biking on strategically placed paths, one project encourages relaxed viewing of the rainwater conveyance through well-placed seating, one project encourages visitors to leave the sidewalk and enter the stormwater management system, and one project encourages visitors to splash and play in the conveyance system.

Recreation Objective: Create opportunities to view and pass by the ARD
Technique: Connect onsite trails to offsite trail systems and destinations that ensure encounters with stormwater treatment systems
Project: Water Pollution Control Laboratory, Portland, OR, Murase Associates

One way to ensure views of stormwater management systems is to place recreational paths in locations that direct passersby to encounter those systems. Connecting offsite destinations to onsite paths is a good strategy, because it compels people to notice the rainwater treatment as they cross the site en route to their destinations, an approach effectively executed at the Water Pollution Control Laboratory. Here pedestrians and bicyclists traveling to or from nearby Cathedral Park, or the commercial and residential neighborhood directly to the north, or simply along the Willamette River trail, find themselves in this intriguing site, compelled to notice its enormous, artistic stormwater management system (figure 2.16).

Figure 2.16. Trails linking offsite destinations at the Water Pollution Control Laboratory direct passersby to encounter the stormwater management system (design: Murase Associates; photograph: Seth Wilberding).

Recreation Objective: Create opportunities to view or pass by the ARD
Technique: Provide paths in strategic locations that ensure encounters with stormwater treatment systems
Project: Waterworks Gardens, Renton, WA, Lorna Jordan

A second noteworthy example of a strategically placed path system is found at Waterworks Gardens. Here the designer transformed a stormwater treatment system adjacent to a county wastewater treatment plant into an inviting sequence of garden rooms that follow the water trail downhill: the Knoll, the Funnel, the Grotto, the Passage, and the Release. Visitors meander through the garden rooms on a recreational path that presents almost all the characteristics of mystery cited by the Kaplans in their book *With People in Mind* as promoting a "desire to explore," including "the suggestion that there is more to see" through curving paths and vegetation that partially obscures what lies beyond. The circuitous path not only invites exploration but also presents the delightful scenery of retention ponds and wetlands rich with plants and wildlife (figure 2.17).

Figure 2.17. At Waterworks Garden, an enticing trail leads pedestrians past wetlands and water treatment ponds (design: Lorna Jordan; photograph: Stuart Echols).

Recreation Objective: Create opportunities to view/rest by the ARD
Technique: Provide seating using walls, benches, or tables and chairs with views of stormwater treatment systems
Project: Stephen Epler Hall, Portland State University, Portland, OR, Atlas Landscape Architecture, KPFF Consulting Engineers, Mithun

When it comes to encouraging people to view a landscape feature, there's nothing quite as effective as providing a place to sit. Whether wall, bench, or table and chairs, sitting simply invites people to pause and take in their surroundings. In ARD, one typical intention is to encourage people to view some feature focused on rainwater; and the best example we found was a pair of sheltered benches strategically located to view a veritable rainwater show outside Stephen Epler Hall, a dormitory on the urban campus of Portland State University. In this design the water action is particularly dramatic in rain events: Water shoots down five-story downspouts into a set of small rock-filled boxes, then gushes out small scuppers at the boxes' bases into runnels that carry water across the space to fall into "biopaddies" (sunken plant-filled basins, as in figure 2.18). Located under freestanding canopies (important

Figure 2.18. Runoff at Epler Hall travels from downspouts (on columns) into basins at their base, then via runnels across the space to "biopaddies" (design: Atlas Landscape Architecture, KPFF Consulting Engineers, Mithun; photograph: Seth Wilberding).

for use during the rain), two benches face the water action. The benches are backed by a wall, resulting in an effective sense of prospect and refuge and making the sitting space particularly inviting (figure 2.19). In all, this design provides a convenient, comfortable seat to enjoy the rain at Epler Hall, and it apparently works: According to the architects, students emerge from the dormitories during storms to watch the rainwater show (McDonald, 2006).

Figure 2.19. Covered benches at Epler Hall provide a view of the water show during rain events (design: Atlas Landscape Architecture, KPFF Consulting Engineers, Mithun; photograph: Stuart Echols).

Recreation Objective: Create opportunities to enter and access the ARD
Technique: Make entry points easily accessible; provide places to sit in stormwater systems
Project: The Rain Garden at the Oregon Convention Center, Portland, OR, Mayer/Reed

Another type of recreational interaction with ARD occurs when visitors can actually enter the stormwater management system. At the Oregon Convention Center Rain Garden, in Portland, Oregon, the previously described river abstraction allows the adventuresome to participate in the river experience. The linear water trail is disconnected from the nearby sidewalk by a lush lawn and even more clearly separated from passing pedestrians by a border of thick plantings and rocks along its lawn edge, but at certain points the border opens and a flat rock laid flush with the lawn allows visitors to enter the "river" at one of the checkdams (figures 2.20, 2.21).

Figure 2.20. The abstracted river corridor at the Oregon Convention Center is disconnected from the sidewalk (right of photo) by lush lawn and a thick plant border along the "river" edge (left of photo) (design: Mayer/Reed; photograph: Stuart Echols).

Figure 2.21. Occasional flat rocks laid flush with the lawn allow visitors to enter the "river" at a weir (design: Mayer/Reed; photograph: Eliza Pennypacker).

Once in, the adventuresome may clamber across (or even dance on) the rocks (figure 2.22), whereas others may choose to simply sit on one of the rock checkdams and enjoy the lush surroundings.

Figure 2.22. The "river" design celebrates play, permitting visitors to sit or even dance at the checkdams in the system (design: Mayer/Reed; photograph: Teresa Chenney, ASLA).

Recreation Objective: Create opportunities to play in and explore the ARD
Technique: Provide a variety of small and large places to play in or explore
Project: Queens Botanical Garden, Flushing, NY, Atelier Dreiseitl with Conservation Design Forum; BKSK Architects

At the new Queens Botanical Garden Visitor Center, rainwater is the star in a design clearly stating that rain is a treasured asset within a place that showcases plants. To highlight the rain, the designers created a rainwater conveyance system that is the site's linear focal point, and in many spots the water is accessible, touchable, and very enticing, making for a playful interactive presentation.

First, rainwater falls from a scupper extending from the visitor center roof, cascading into a shallow pool at the building's public entrance, where it is biofiltered; that water is further treated with ultraviolet rays in an underground cistern, then pumped to a fountain in another area of the site. Water burbles into the fountain via a semicircular level spreader at the top, then falls in a stepping, shimmering cascade down a set of concentric semicircular black granite steps. The fountain is entirely accessible and touchable: The upper lip is level with a grassy lawn, and the steps are edged by a sittable granite wall. This is definitely a fountain that invites visitors to touch the water. But the water isn't running all the time. As stated on a sign near the fountain, "Just like the streams in nature, when there's lots of rain, water flows from this fountain. But when there's little or no rain, like in a drought, our fountain and the streams around it may run dry." This ephemeral fountain reminds us that we must enjoy the rain while we can (figure 2.23).

Figure 2.23. Treated rainwater fuels the bubbly, shimmering, and very touchable—but ephemeral—fountain at Queens Botanical Garden (design: Atelier Dreiseitl with Conservation Design Forum, BKSK Architects; photograph: Stuart Echols).

At the bottom of the fountain, the rainwater begins its journey back to the visitor center in the form of a meandering stream. Within the fountain plaza, the stream is edged on both sides by low-profile, rectilinear pavers that step down to the water; at the far edge of the plaza, paving on one side of the stream is replaced by riparian plantings. In both areas, running water at the paved edge is completely accessible to visitors; the design encourages them to splash their feet or just reach in a toe, float a toy boat, watch the birds bathe, or simply gaze at the water as it passes by (figure 2.24).

Two bridges cross this shallow stream, providing visitor access to different parts of the botanical garden. At the end of the stream, near the northeastern corner of the site, the rainwater drops along a level spreader into a constructed basin (on the service side of the building), then flows back to the pool at the center's public entrance. Attentive visitors note that the rainwater's movement brings it full circle, across the landscape, through planted zones, and back to its origin, a delightful metaphor of the hydrologic cycle.

Figure 2.24. Easy access invites visitors to splash, float objects, or just watch the water in the Queens Botanical Garden rainwater stream (design: Atelier Dreiseitl with Conservation Design Forum, BKSK Architects; photograph: Stuart Echols).

Things to Consider in Your Effort to Achieve a Recreation Goal in ARD

Both the matrix and the case studies provide plenty of opportunities and questions to consider in the design of recreational ARDs, summarized here:

- Would it be possible to run trails from off site along your ARD?
- Would it be possible to locate seating with a clear view of focal points in your ARD?

- Could elevated areas provide an interesting view down to your ARD?
- Do local regulations permit you to invite visitors to enter your ARD? If so, how and where should access points be located?
- How might you design inviting places to sit in the ARD?
- How might people modify or play with physical objects in the ARD (e.g., water, rocks), and would this hurt or enrich the design?

PART 2.3

Safety in Artful Rainwater Design

The safety goal in ARD focuses on promoting safe interaction with water by mitigating dangers associated with stormwater. This may not be an obvious amenity goal in ARD, but in the currently litigious society of the United States, this goal is central to making ARD possible.

In ARD, standing or running water often forms a central part of the experience, but how do we prevent it from being perceived as a drowning hazard?[1] Our list of ARD projects revealed two objectives to mitigate water-associated danger: controlling access to water and controlling water quantity (both velocity and depth). Table 2.3 presents these mitigation objectives and an array of design techniques to address each of them.

Table 2.3. Safety goal: Promote safe interaction with stormwater treatment systems by mitigating danger associated with water

Objectives	Design Techniques
Control Access	
Vertical barrier	Provide walls, screens, or railings that allow views but prevent access to stormwater systems.
	Provide upland, riparian, or wetland plant massing that allows views but prevents access to stormwater systems.
Horizontal barrier	Use bridges, boardwalks, or platforms to allow users to view stormwater systems from above.
Water containers	Use water-themed aboveground stormwater storage facilities such as rain barrels, water towers, or cisterns.
Control Quantity	
Depth	Do not collect stormwater in large, centralized storage facilities.
	Disperse stormwater into shallow storage facilities using flow splitters or tiered basins.
	Limit stormwater depth by creating horizontal space for water to spread out.
	Limit stormwater depth by adding large river stone to basins where people could have access.
Velocity	Do not collect or move stormwater in large centralized conveyance facilities.
	Disperse stormwater into small conveyance facilities using level spreaders or flow splitters.
	Create “water brakes” to slow stormwater by abruptly changing flow direction.
	Slow stormwater by creating small waterfalls that dissipate energy.

Within the projects, five examples of design techniques addressing safety stand out. Two projects address the objective of access control by limiting physical access to water through different types of vertical barriers: One uses a clever horizontal barrier, and one uses a symbolic water container. To control water quantity, one project addresses water depth using an approach we saw frequently in the ARDs, and another project effectively limits water velocity, again in a frequently used approach.

Safety Objective: Control access with a vertical barrier
Technique: Provide walls, screens, or railings that allow views but prevent access to stormwater systems; provide upland, riparian, or wetland plant massing that allows views but prevents access to stormwater systems
Projects: Historic Fourth Ward Park, Atlanta, GA, HDP and Wood+Partners; Shoemaker Green, Philadelphia, PA, Andropogon Associates Ltd., Meliora Design LLC

These two projects present entirely different safety strategies in their vertical barriers: Historic Fourth Ward Park presents a variety of tall, rigid barriers that permit ample views but clearly say "Keep out of the water!" In contrast, Shoemaker Green's barriers to access are subtle and low.

Historic Fourth Ward Park is a massive, sloping, two-block park along the Atlanta BeltLine in downtown Atlanta. Rainwater in the southern block is conveyed downhill in a landscape designed to look like a natural stream. A winding path follows the "stream" downhill, permitting clear views while saying "keep out" with a combination of two simple strategies. First, the meandering path is edged on both sides by curving stainless steel rails (sometimes—especially on bridges—augmented by steel cables) (figure 2.25); second, the plantings beyond the rail are riotous and exuberant, sometimes even feral-looking. The juxtaposition of thin, elegant steel bordering wild-looking landscape clearly suggests that we stay on the paved path (figure 2.26).

Water from this block plus a larger local watershed is conveyed to a deep, stone-walled detention basin (with walls up to 23 feet tall in spots) in the northern block. Remarkably, this basin has been designed as a beautiful and very welcoming park thanks to a permanent wet pond, a variety of rainwater fountains, and robust riparian plantings. The basic safety strategy here is the same as on the south block: Visitors are confined to a meandering path by a shiny steel railing rendered impenetrable by twelve rows of steel cabling, reinforced by lush plantings. What's remarkable about this safety system is that it's so visually light, and so liltingly meandering, that one experiences the beautiful water landscape rather than any sense of confinement (figure 2.27).

The redesign of Shoemaker Green adjacent to the Palestra at the University of Pennsylvania includes paved seating space close to the buildings, a generous oval quadrangle, and a rain garden at the site's downhill northwestern corner that collects water from the entire area. Visitors can easily grasp the stormwater management system: Grate-covered trench drains direct water from the plaza into the rain garden, where the water then flows along a river rock–lined "streambed." What's remarkable about this project is the subtlety of the vertical barriers: Visitors are discouraged from entering the stormwater management system only by thick, low plantings inside the 6-inch granite curbing surrounding about three quarters of the garden and by sittable granite walls edging major sidewalks around the rest.

Figure 2.25. Thin stainless steel railings backed by wild-looking landscape punctuate the lilting curve of the path while saying "Stay on the pavement!" (design: Wood+Partners; photograph: Eliza Pennypacker).

Figure 2.26. On bridges, the steel railings are augmented by cables to ensure that people stay out of the runoff "stream" (design: Wood+Partners; photograph: Eliza Pennypacker).

Points of possible entry into the rain garden actually exist: Cuts in the granite curbing receive water from the trench drains, and the river rock "streambed," pristinely maintained to be free of invading plants, extends all the way to the curb cut. Additionally, one of the seating walls is edged by a strip of paving on the rain garden side, inviting people to sit facing into the rain garden. What keeps people out of the rain garden is largely a very effective planting plan: If one does step into the garden, the dense, impassable plantings—especially the grasses—leave nowhere to go (figure 2.28).

Figure 2.27. A path along the south block's wet detention pond is edged by visually light but physically impenetrable steel railings plus twelve strands of steel cable (design: HDP; photograph: Eliza Pennypacker).

Figure 2.28. Thick plantings of low grasses and shrubs along the edge of Shoemaker Green's rain garden dissuade potential interlopers from entering the system (design: Andropogon Associates Ltd., Meliora Design LLC; photograph: Stuart Echols).

Safety Objective: Control access with a horizontal barrier
Technique: Use bridges, boardwalks, or platforms that allow users to view stormwater systems from above
Project: Waterworks Gardens, Renton, WA, Lorna Jordan

In the Waterworks Gardens, previously discussed for its recreation amenity (part 2.2), the designer also used a number of effective design techniques to limit physical access to the rainwater while ensuring that visitors are fully attuned to the water that surrounds them throughout the site. A particularly delightful example is found at the garden entrance (the Knoll): Here, visitors are enticed to walk down an allée of basalt columns toward a beckoning overlook. Along that walk, rainwater flows literally right beneath the visitor's feet, safely out of reach yet very noticeable. Steel grating traverses the stone terrace in a stream-like shape; just below that grating runs the babbling water. Visitors can see it, hear it, even smell the bubbling, gurgling flow—they just can't touch it. Moving rainwater is central to that entry experience, yet it is rendered completely safe by the simple walking grate (figure 2.29).

Figure 2.29. Rainwater at Waterworks Gardens is a key part of the entry experience, made safe with a simple walking grate. Note also the railing at the destination overlook (design: Lorna Jordan; photograph: Eliza Pennypacker).

Safety Objective: Control access with water containers
Technique: Use water-themed aboveground stormwater storage facilities such as rain barrels, water towers, or cisterns
Project: Ladybird Johnson Wildflower Center, Austin, TX, J. Robert Anderson Landscape Architects, Overland Partners

The Ladybird Johnson Wildflower Center has a noble mission: to educate visitors about the native landscape of Texas. One of the characteristics of this landscape is that water is a precious resource, and historically, Texans have devised ingenious ways to capture rainwater for human use. At the center, this reality is highlighted in a clear but entirely safe way: Rain falls on the butterfly roof of the auditorium, and the roof's inverted V form funnels runoff into an aqueduct. The aqueduct's channel carries water high above the ground along the top of a Spanish mission–style stone loggia that lines one side of the center's entrance walkway. Water from the aqueduct is then harvested in a huge, traditional Texas-style, above-grade cistern that stands as a 15-foot-tall beacon and welcoming focal point at the center's entrance, bedecked with a huge dragonfly sculpture to suggest the water and nature theme (figures 2.30, 2.31). All this water movement and conservation is clearly legible, but entirely out of reach and safe, thanks to the aqueduct and cistern system.

Figure 2.30. A huge, traditional Texas-style cistern bedecked with a dragonfly sculpture welcomes visitors to the Ladybird Johnson Wildflower Center, making rainwater conservation a center focal point (design: J. Robert Anderson Landscape Architects, Overland Partners; photograph: Pam Penick).

Figure 2.31. An aqueduct high and far from our reach carries water from the roof to the entry cistern (visible in the background), rendering rainwater a safe entry feature (design: J. Robert Anderson Landscape Architects, Overland Partners; photograph: Pam Penick).

Safety Objective: Control quantity and depth
Technique: Limit stormwater depth by adding large river stones to basins where people could have access
Project: Glencoe Elementary School, Portland, OR, Portland Bureau of Environmental Services

The Glencoe Elementary School retention and biofiltration basin presents an excellent example of a very simple technique to limit rainwater depth that we found in many of the ARD projects. The detention basin created on the uphill side of a checkdam is filled to the brim with river rock. The mass of rounded rock creates voids that permit water to collect in the basin, but the rainwater either disappears into the interstices or, at most, rises slightly above the rock surface (figure 2.32). Technically, a designer could use any material that provides adequate voids for significant water retention, but river rocks are particularly appealing in this technique, both for their water-shaped forms and for the extensive voids created by abutting those rounded forms.

Figure 2.32. A detention basin at Glencoe Elementary School is filled to the brim with river rock, allowing stormwater to safely collect in the basin (design: Portland's Bureau of Environmental Services; photograph: Stuart Echols).

Safety Objective: Control quantity and velocity
Technique: Slow rainwater by creating small waterfalls that dissipate energy
Project: Campbell Hall Bioretention Terraces, Charlottesville, VA, Nelson Byrd Woltz Landscape Architects

The 2008 redesign of Campbell Hall, home of the School of Architecture at the University of Virginia, included landscape retrofits to address drainage problems on the hillside site. Here, Nelson Byrd Woltz redesigned a slope along the building into a series of terraced, shallow basins with checkdams and weirs that control both water velocity and depth, a strategy we found in many cases located on sloping sites. Stepped pools created by the checkdams release standing water along the water trail into a sequence of shallow basins thickly planted with colorful natives. At the same time, the vertical drop of water at each weir brakes the water velocity: Water flow energy is dispersed by its drop and impact (figure 2.33). Over the length of the stormwater management system, the checkdam and weir system transforms a potential downhill torrent of stormwater into a series of shallow pools and gently cascading water that pedestrians can safely enjoy from the adjacent sidewalk. And, when dry, the basins simply present a colorful garden edge running up the hill along the sidewalk and service drive.

Figure 2.33. A series of terraced checkdams and weirs at Campbell Hall at the University of Virginia control both water velocity and depth (design: Nelson Byrd Woltz Landscape Architects; photograph: NBW).

Things to Consider in Your Effort to Achieve a Safety Goal in ARD

Both the matrix and the case studies provide plenty of opportunities and questions to consider in the design of safe ARDs, summarized here:

- Would vertical barriers prove useful to keeping visitors from entering your ARD? If so, would manmade barriers be best, or would plantings be more appropriate? And how might you emphasize views of stormwater management systems, over or through the barriers?
- Might visitors stand or walk above the ARD? If so, how should the rainwater be presented to them: visible below their walking surface or from the edge of the platform? Would it be more intriguing for the water to be heard but not seen?

- Could the rainwater be effectively presented in containers decorated with water themes or easily recognized regional vernacular rain barrels, cisterns, or other containers?
- Does the site have enough land area for stormwater management systems to spread out water depth in numerous small basins or in a large shallow zone?
- How can rainwater flowing downhill be slowed? Can it change direction, step, drop, or be controlled by checkdams and weirs?
- Every water brake poses a design opportunity. How might brakes in your ARD reveal an interesting or fun characteristic of rainwater?

Notes

1. Here we focus on the issue of safety from drowning. Other injuries that can be incurred through contact with water (e.g., tripping, slipping, falling) are omitted because they are hazards in any landscape, not exclusive to ARD. Associated danger related to waterborne disease is also omitted, because it has been addressed in common stormwater management design manuals.

PART 2.4

Public Relations in Artful Rainwater Design

As an ARD goal, public relations (PR) means that either a feature or the overall design character makes a clear statement about the values and qualities of those who designed or own the site. Any such design message is inherently a PR gesture, whether overt or implicit. Once again you may find overlap between this ARD goal and others in this part, but we present it as a distinct goal so that you may understand different ARD PR message types and design techniques used to achieve them.

Analysis of the ARD projects led us to recognize four broad PR objectives frequently delivered through ARD: "We care," "We are progressive," "We are smart," and "We are sophisticated." We additionally found it useful to classify these very broad PR messages into submessages that can be expressed alone or in tandem with others. Table 2.4 presents the PR objectives and some design techniques to achieve them, as found in the ARD projects.

Within the cases, we found an array of projects addressing each PR objective. In all, a variety of statements are clearly made through an array of design approaches.

Public Relations Objective: Express "We care, we are environmentally responsible, and we want you to learn about stormwater"
Techniques: Create a variety of highly visible stormwater treatment systems; locate stormwater treatment systems near entries, courtyards, or windows for high visibility; use signage explaining stormwater treatment and intent
Project: High Point, West Seattle, WA, SvR Design Company, Mithun, Bruce Meyers

The PR objective "we care, we are environmentally responsible, and we want you to learn about stormwater" can be communicated through clarity of the sustainable stormwater management mission; that is, the design can overtly exhibit what hydrologic benefits are accomplished and how. Is this a form of education as well? Most definitely, but the focus here is on the PR objective and technique, that is, the values promoted and ways that the rainwater design expresses those values. This "we care" value message comes through loud and clear at High Point, a neotraditional community in West Seattle. This design displays a wide range of sustainable stormwater management systems, from porous sidewalks and driveways to bioswales lining nearly every street right-of-way, all meticulously designed and located in highly visible areas. Brightly colored signs with brief text and graphics are strategically located along community roads and sidewalks, succinctly explaining how different facets of the stormwater management system work (figure 2.34). Indeed, a focus on rainwater pervades the whole community: Select sidewalks are incised with concentric rings reminiscent of a water drop's impact on a pool, decorative concrete castings of dragonflies adorn drain inlets, and even the splash guards at the base of some downspouts are decorated with stormwater-related imagery (figure

Table 2.4. Public relations goal: Create symbolic stormwater statements about the values and qualities of those who created and own the site

Objectives: Express or Communicate	Design Techniques
We Care	
We are environmentally responsible and want you to learn about stormwater	Create a variety of highly visible stormwater treatment systems. Locate stormwater treatment systems near entries, courtyards, or windows for high visibility. Use signage explaining stormwater treatment and intent. Create opportunities for programming educational activities.
We want you to know that you can do this yourself	Use commonly available materials. Create small-scale, replicable interventions. Use common settings such as sidewalks and parking lots.
We Are Progressive	
We are experimental	Use innovative stormwater treatment methods. Use signage that explains stormwater treatment and intent.
We are innovative	Use new forms and materials. Use traditional stormwater treatment methods in new ways. Show how significant sustainable stormwater management can be accomplished even on a small site.
We Are Smart	
We are resourceful and clever	Be opportunistic by using small, leftover, and unexpected spaces. Achieve additional functions such as traffic calming and beautification.
We know you'll notice the treatment if it's fun	Make stormwater trails easy to find and follow. Make stormwater trails mysteriously disappear and reappear. Make stormwater or water treatment systems touchable. Make stormwater audible with plunge pools or downspouts. Make stormwater move in different ways (tumble, run, splash). Run the stormwater through interesting features that proclaim, "Look! Rainwater is a resource!" Encourage walking in or climbing on water treatment systems.
We Are Sophisticated	
We are aesthetically refined	Create elegantly simple composition. Use refined or expensive materials. Use refined or expensive construction methods. Use restraint in diversity of materials and forms. Design for manicured look: clipped, trimmed, and clean.
We are distinctive	Make an unusual line of stormwater trails. Use unusual rainwater presentation forms and themes.

2.35). Through these and other design decisions, two types of PR points are made. First, the sheer range and number of sustainable stormwater management strategies that permeate the community send the message that the developers care deeply; second, the display and design of green infrastructure throughout the community as highly visible, aesthetically appealing amenities show how progressive the developers are, skilled in transforming an act of environmental responsibility into a desirable landscape feature. Together these design moves proclaim the developers' (and, because the developers are Seattle agencies, the city's) forward-looking commitment to celebration of rain as a resource.

Figure 2.34. Colorful, upbeat signage explains the stormwater management "do good" efforts in a bioswale at High Point (design: SvR Design Company, Mithun, Bruce Meyers; photograph: Seth Wilberding).

Figure 2.35. The rainwater theme at High Point carries through all the way down to decorated downspout splash guards (design: SvR Design Company, Mithun, Bruce Meyers; photograph: Stuart Echols).

Public Relations Objective: Express, "We care, and we want you to know that you can do this yourself"
Techniques: Use commonly available materials; use common settings such as sidewalks and parking lots
Project: Queens Botanical Garden, Flushing, NY, Atelier Dreiseitl with Conservation Design Forum, BKSK Architects

Visitors who drive to Queens Botanical Garden pass through the entry gate into a "parking garden" for about 100 cars. What makes it a parking "garden," not a "lot"? As explained in a brochure found inside the Visitor Center, the parking is located on a former wetland, and bioswales between rows absorb a large amount of rainwater. But the real "I could do this!" discovery is in the parking surface itself: Rectangular pavers are separated by about 1 inch of gravel in one of the most obvious statements of porous paving we've seen (figure 2.36). The brochure, titled "Green Parking," states,

> Permeable pavers rest on three tiers of bluestone gravel of increasing size, allowing water to penetrate deeply into the soil. The structure also facilitates the growth of beneficial oil-eating bacteria that break down leaking car fluids and remove them from the environment.

The management strategy is sound, the design is very legible, and the location of this "statement" in the parking lot is extremely clever, providing a first hint and last reminder of an attractive and simple sustainable stormwater management design that the visitor could create at home (figure 2.37). And presenting a brochure on the subject, available at the Visitor Center, adds both information and emphasis to the Botanical Garden's commitment to sustainability.

Figure 2.36. Paving stones separated by gravel in the parking lot at Queens Botanical Garden present one of the most obvious statements of porous paving we've seen (design: Atelier Dreiseitl with Conservation Design Forum, BKSK Architects; photograph: Stuart Echols).

Figure 2.37. This porous parking lot provides a first hint and last reminder of an attractive and simple sustainable stormwater management design that the visitor could create at home (design: Atelier Dreiseitl with Conservation Design Forum; BKSK Architects; photograph: Stuart Echols).

Public Relations Objective: Express "We are progressive, and we are experimental"
Techniques: Use innovative stormwater treatment methods; use signage that explains stormwater treatment and intent
Project: Pierce County Environmental Services, Chambers Creek, WA, Bruce Dees & Associates, SvR Design Company, The Miller|Hull Partnership

The most obvious "We are experimental" statement we've found to date is at the "Flow Splitter Plaza" at Pierce County Environmental Services, described in part 2.1. It presents such a bold and effective statement that the design warrants mention again. At the end of the long, linear bioswale, three valve heads extend the axis into a paved space; signage tells us that this is a "flow splitter plaza" with one valve diverting some stormwater into a grass-lined swale, one valve diverting other water into a wetland plant-lined swale, and the third valve standing ready "for future technologies" (according to the sign), sending the clear message that Pierce County is ever ready to jump on the next useful sustainable stormwater management strategy (figure 2.38).

Figure 2.38. Pierce County's "Flow Splitter Plaza" proclaims the facility's commitment to experimentation and future-oriented thinking (design: Bruce Dees & Associates, SvR Design Company, The Miller|Hull Partnership; photograph: Stuart Echols).

Public Relations Objective: Express "We are progressive, and we are innovative"
Technique: Show how significant sustainable stormwater management can be accomplished even on a small site
Project: Stephen Epler Hall, Portland State University, Portland, OR, Atlas Landscape Architecture, KPFF Consulting Engineers, Mithun

At Stephen Epler Hall, an innovative necklace of biofiltration basins can detain a great deal of stormwater within a tiny paved plaza, clearly proclaiming Portland State University's commitment to sustainability. In fact, this design presents a particularly effective strategy to disperse and manage rain in a green infrastructure system on a very small, very urban site. As briefly described in part 2.1, water drops from the Epler Hall dormitory roof via downspouts into raised concrete containers filled with river pebbles; from those boxes, rain is conveyed in plaza-crossing runnels to a set of sunken "biopaddies," where it is cleansed and detained. Water in the biopaddy system is collected for reuse in the building, with any extra water overflowing from one biopaddy downhill to the next and—if needed—from the last biopaddy into the stormwater system. All this stormwater management is happening in a very small and narrow site. In sum, this complex, interconnected sustainable stormwater management system of multiuse (sittable planters), safe (walkable runnels) conveyance, biofiltration, and water harvesting elements fills this tiny plaza without crowding it, clearly stating that Portland State is committed to doing the right thing, even on a tight site (figure 2.39).

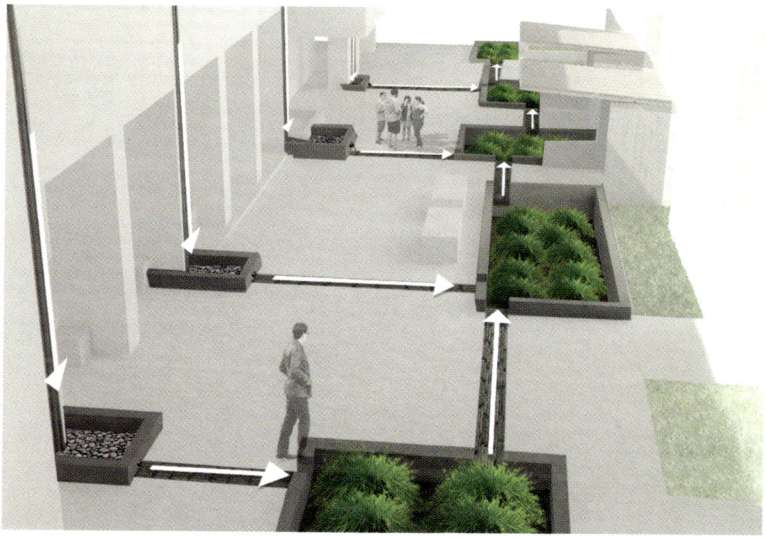

Figure 2.39. This perspective diagram of the Stephen Epler Hall plaza shows the sustainable stormwater management system of runnels and sequential biopaddies (design: Atlas Landscape Architecture, KPFF Consulting Engineers, Mithun; diagram: Stuart Echols and Chris Maurer).

Public Relations Objective: Express the idea that "We are smart, and we are resourceful and clever"
Techniques: Be opportunistic by using small, leftover, and unexpected spaces; achieve additional functions such as traffic calming and beautification
Projects: NE Siskiyou Street Curb Extensions ("NE Siskiyou Green Street"), Portland, OR, Portland Bureau of Environmental Services; Mount Tabor Middle School, Portland, OR, Portland Bureau of Environmental Services

The city of Portland, Oregon was facing major combined sewer overflow (CSO) issues affecting the Willamette River, and the city's Bureau of Environmental Services was exploring opportunities to solve stormwater problems with green infrastructure solutions. On NE Siskiyou Street, a leafy, quiet, residential street in northeast Portland, the bureau saw an opportunity to add curb extensions near the intersection of Siskiyou and 35th Street that would divert and biofilter first flush runoff. The design was simple: 7-foot-wide bumpouts were attached to existing road curbing. In each, an uphill curb cut accepted first flush rain, which was slowed in the planters by river rock checkdams (figure 2.40). The basins were filled with ferns and grasses in soothing shades of green, blue, and gray, and a small sign,

Figure 2.40. The Siskiyou Green Street manages first flush by accepting runoff through a curb cut into a shallow basin, where water is slowed by river rock weirs (design: Portland Bureau of Environmental Services; photograph: Kevin Perry).

with diagram, explained how the system works. This is an example of locating an ARD literally in "found" space, transforming asphalt into a landscape element that not only manages stormwater but also beautifies, calms traffic, and educates the public (figure 2.41).

Another clever example of resourcefulness is found at Mount Tabor Middle School, also in Portland. Mount Tabor had a *U*-shaped, one-story building characteristic of so many 1960s public schools; and, like so many of them, the outdoor space surrounded by that south-facing *U* was an asphalt parking lot that created a problematic heat island, especially for all the classrooms and offices with windows that faced the space. In 2002, Portland's Bureau of Environmental Services needed to address a CSO problem in streets near the school; the bureau and school saw this as an opportunity to showcase sustainable stormwater management systems by replacing the parking lot with a rain garden to biofilter and infiltrate stormwater (along with a number of other stormwater retrofits on the site). Of course the rain garden accomplished much more than stormwater management; today it provides a visual amenity that cools the adjacent rooms, provides a spot to gather or sit, and educates students

Figure 2.41. The Siskiyou curb extensions manage rainwater while educating passersby (through signage), beautifying the street, and calming traffic (design: Portland Bureau of Environmental Services; photograph: Stuart Echols).

about the benefits of green infrastructure. Overall the rain garden design makes a clear statement: "Look how smart and resourceful we are, turning an asphalt oven into a multifaceted, useful amenity!" (figures 2.42 and 2.43).

Figure 2.42. Mount Tabor Middle School's asphalt parking area before its transformation into a rain garden (design: Portland Bureau of Environmental Services; photograph: Portland Bureau of Environmental Services).

Figure 2.43. Mount Tabor Middle School's rain garden (design: Portland Bureau of Environmental Services; photograph: Kevin Perry, City of Portland).

Public Relations Objective: Express the idea that "We are smart, and we know you will notice the treatment if it's fun"
Techniques: Make stormwater trails easy to find and follow; run the stormwater through features that proclaim, "Look, rainwater is a resource!"
Project: Washougal Town Square, Washougal, WA, GreenWorks, Sienna Architecture Company, Inc., Ivan McLean

Washougal is a small town about 25 miles northeast of Portland, Oregon that has undergone a stormwater renaissance: Nearly every street right-of-way in the tiny downtown sports elegantly planted bioswales, while rimless planters on a central plaza collect and filter runoff from that paved surface. In this context of beautiful and extensive sustainable stormwater management, the Town Square stands out. Here, an interior courtyard serves as a focal point for new surrounding retail and office buildings, and the message of this focal point is clearly, "Look at what the rain is doing!" First, water is conveyed from the roof of one building via a long, slender arm of a scupper; rainwater falling from the scupper splashes onto a playful, 15-foot-tall metal sculpture that looks like a burst of splashing water, created by artist Ivan McLean (figure 2.44).

Figure 2.44. At Washougal Town Square, a long, slender scupper sends water out into the courtyard space to fall on a tall metal sculpture that looks like a water splash (design: GreenWorks, Sienna Architecture Company, Inc., Ivan McLean; photograph: Stuart Echols).

But the fun water message doesn't end there. The courtyard is also dotted with "rain trees": tall, metal frames in umbrella-like forms stand in raised flow-through filter planters. Runoff from downspouts clearly flows into these planters. At the base of each structure the filtering plants include *Clematis armandii*, *Jasminum* x *stephanense*, and *Wisteria sinensis* vines that grow up the structures, resulting in a tree-like plant form. Again, the message is clear: Water flows from the building roofs to water the "rain trees." Overall, the rain-related sculptures in this space are both playful and clever at conveying the message that rain is a resource. One other characteristic of this design is noteworthy: The message reads clearly whether rain is pouring or the sun is shining (figure 2.45).

Figure 2.45. Vines planted in raised basins are watered by runoff and will grow up the "rain tree" metal frames, clearly stating that rain is the plants' resource (design: GreenWorks, Sienna Architecture Company, Inc., Ivan McLean; photograph: Stuart Echols).

Public Relations Objective: Express "We are sophisticated, and we are aesthetically refined"
Techniques: Create elegantly simple composition; use refined and expensive materials; use restraint in diversity of materials and forms; design for manicured look (clipped, trimmed, and clean)
Project: 10th@Hoyt, Portland, OR, Koch Landscape Architecture

Accomplishing the "We are sophisticated" message in ARD is largely a matter of design composition and choice of materials to create an aura of elegance or the avant garde. That PR message, along with the submessage "We are aesthetically refined," is very successfully communicated in the design of 10th@Hoyt, the interior entry courtyard of an upscale apartment building in Portland's Pearl District. The courtyard displays a simple and understated orthogonal composition, on axis with the courtyard entry; a restrained palette of materials, colors, and textures creates an aura of subdued elegance (figure 2.46). The stormwater system is both unusual and consistent with the overall courtyard aesthetic: The courtyard axis is marked by a simple copper downspout running down the face of the five-story building. Rainwater takes a fascinating path from the downspout, in a small aqueduct, down a chaddar (a small, stepped waterfall), then drops into a basin brimming with river rocks, to recirculate in Corten fountains (figure 2.47). Other downspout-and-runnel systems in two corners of the space exhibit variations on the same theme. The whole composition is elegantly serene and intriguingly unusual, creating both an appropriate atmosphere for the stylishly urbane citizens of this district of Portland and the visual suggestion that treating runoff as a valuable resource can be hip. And it apparently works: The apartment developer asked Koch to design ARDs for additional projects, based on their assessment that the 10th@Hoyt courtyard rainwater design attracted tenants (Koch, 2006).

Figure 2.46. A crisp axial composition and refined materials create an aura of subdued elegance at 10th@Hoyt (design: Koch Landscape Architecture; photograph: Eliza Pennypacker).

Figure 2.47. The rainwater trail at 10th@Hoyt is both eye-catching and elegant (design: Koch Landscape Architecture; photograph: Stuart Echols).

Public Relations Objective: Express "We are sophisticated, and we are distinctive"
Technique: Use unusual rainwater presentation forms and themes
Project: Southwest Recreation Center Expansion, University of Florida, Gainesville, FL, RDG Planning and Design

The array of education objectives achieved through thoughtful techniques in this project at the University of Florida was discussed previously in part 2.1, but a detail worth mentioning makes an elegant, sophisticated statement about the university's commitment to sustainability. As stated in the earlier section, this project includes fascinating sculptures in eye-catching colors, meant to symbolize the cells of organisms. This is distinctive enough—of our nearly fifty ARD projects to date, fewer than ten include water-themed sculptures—but what makes this project shine is a fascinating night lighting scheme. Inside each columnar sculpture is a tall, opaque LED tube; at night, each tube emits a cool blue light symbolic of the life-giving water sucked up by the organism's cells. Passersby and people on the treadmills inside the recreation center can easily grasp the elegantly presented message (figure 2.48).

Figure 2.48. At night, tubes inside each columnar sculpture emit blue light, symbolizing water absorbed by cells (design: RDG Planning and Design; photograph: Kevin Thompson).

Things to Consider in Your Effort to Achieve a Public Relations Goal in ARD

Both the matrix and the case studies provide plenty of opportunities and questions to consider in the design of clear public relations messages in ARDs, summarized here:

- What are the site owner's values, user or resident values, or your firm's values that the design might express?
- What parts of the stormwater management systems can be used to communicate important values?
- What's the best aesthetic theme or approach to present the value messages?
- Where should visible value statements be located on site for maximum impact?
- Would signage help clarify the message?

PART 2.5

Aesthetic Richness in Artful Rainwater Design

In ARD, aesthetic richness means that the design is composed to create an experience of beauty or pleasure focused on stormwater. One could argue that aesthetic richness is embedded in all the ARD goals, but sometimes richness of experience is created simply by the composition itself through arresting combination of forms, colors, sounds, and so on. We believe that articulation of strategies that encourage attention to rainwater strictly through composition is worth calling out. In the broadest terms, the composition may address visual, auditory, tactile, olfactory, or taste experiences, but because our ARD projects lack examples of olfactory or taste richness, our findings are limited to visual, auditory, and tactile. Table 2.5 presents these three types of experience in terms of the compositional elements and principles most effectively used in the case studies, then states some design techniques by which they can be accomplished.

An array of the ARD projects display notable examples of design techniques to create aesthetic richness focused on stormwater treatment, and because there are so many different aesthetic objectives and techniques, we won't try to characterize each in this paragraph. The following pages highlight some notable aesthetic objectives; let's dive right in.

Aesthetic Richness Objective: Create visual interest or focal point
Technique: Use scuppers, basins, cisterns, splash blocks, or rain chains to emphasize changes in stormwater direction
Project: "Beckoning Cistern at 81 Vine," Seattle, WA, GAYNOR, Inc., Carlson Architects, SvR Design Company, Buster Simpson

Any spot where rainwater collects or changes conveyance mode is an opportunity for the designer to create a focal point that celebrates rain. Of all possibilities, the most creative we've seen to date is a playful cistern designed by artist Buster Simpson as part of the elaborate stormwater management display on Vine Street in Seattle, collectively known as "Growing Vine." Here, water is collected from a rooftop in a playful and clearly legible gesture: A tall, blue corrugated steel cistern in the street right-of-way tilts toward the building. The downspout angles out from the facade of 81 Vine, high above the sidewalk, to "touch" one of five splaying pieces of green gutter connected to the cistern in the form of a giant hand; with this configuration, it appears that the index finger of the outstretched hand gently reaches up to touch the water coming from the roof. The falling water then divides, with some disappearing into the cistern and some conveyed on the gutter "thumb" into a cascading series of detention basins within a water garden. It's a fun piece that suggests to all passersby—on the road or sidewalk—that the water-harvesting cistern and garden both welcome the water. Another feature on the focal point cistern expands the message: A long, red calibrated "dip stick" protrudes from the cistern's lid, registering the depth of water in the cistern. This clever addition tells passersby not only the depth of the water but also the fact that *we care* how much water the cistern holds—rain is a resource we seek to conserve (figure 2.49).

Table 2.5. Aesthetic richness goal: Create an interesting experience of beauty or pleasure focused on stormwater

Objectives: Create	Design Techniques
Visual Interest	
Point	Create water collection basin as a feature or focal point. Create visual emphasis on stormwater direction change using scuppers, basins, cisterns, splash blocks, or rain chains.
Line	Use downspouts, runnels, flumes, bioswales, and so on to draw attention to the line of the rainwater trail, increasing legibility as well as interest and curiosity.
Plane	Stack horizontal and vertical planes such as pools and falls to exploit visual interest of stormwater flowing over surfaces and plunging down planes, through weirs, or over edges.
Volume	Create visual interest or themes with basins that hold plants and water: sunken, raised, orthogonal, curved, organic, geometric, small, or large.
Color / Texture	Contrast natural elements such as plants and rocks with artificial elements, such as clipped lawns, steel, or concrete. Juxtapose river rock and riparian grasses for compositional contrast.
Axis	Create stormwater trails using axial runnels, downspouts, bioswales, and so on. Dramatize an implied axis using aligned treatment systems, basins, and runnels connected by the water trail.
Rhythm / Repetition	Create unified design themes by using multiple bioswales, basins, weirs, ponds, rain gardens, or other rainwater-focused props.
Auditory Interest	
Volume	Create a variety of volumes by allowing stormwater to fall from various heights onto different materials such as stone or steel.
Pitch	Create changes in pitch by allowing stormwater to fall on different forms such as flat blocks, metal tubes, drums, and ponds.
Rhythm	Create different rhythms by varying the amount and rate of stormwater falling and flowing through treatment systems.
Tactile Interest	
Texture	Use a variety of water-related plants within reach, such as rushes and grasses. Use various water-related hardscapes such as river pebbles and driftwood to provide interesting surfaces.
Wetness	Allow people to touch stormwater in different forms such as flowing, falling, splashing, standing, sheeting, or damp surfaces where water can soak in or evaporate.

Figure 2.49. Artist Buster Simpson's "Beckoning Cistern" at Growing Vine is a focal point that emphasizes our appreciation for rain (design: Buster Simpson; photograph: Stuart Echols).

Aesthetic Richness Objective: Create visual interest through line
Technique: Use downspouts, runnels, flumes, bioswales, and so on to draw attention to the line of the rainwater trail, increasing legibility, interest, and curiosity
Project: Cedar River Watershed Education Center, Cedar Falls, WA, Jones and Jones, Dan Corson

One technique often found in ARD is visual emphasis of the rainwater conveyance—almost always a linear system—as it traverses the site. Composition of this "rainwater trail" can take many forms. The line can be straight and entirely visible, making the trail very pronounced, even bold; it can dart or disappear in spots, making the trail puzzling or mysterious; or the line can be composed as a curve that underscores water's captivating liquidity, as is the case in the curving rainwater trail at the Cedar River Watershed Education Center (figure 2.50). The purpose of this facility is to educate Seattle-area residents about the importance of stewardship in their watershed, because this is the source of their drinking water; consequently, water is the focus and theme and is very elegantly presented in the con-

Figure 2.50. The lilting S-curve of this rainwater trail clearly says "water," although running water is never actually visible (design: Jones & Jones, Dan Corson; photograph: Stuart Echols).

veyance of rainwater across one of the center's public spaces, the Heritage Court. Here, runoff drops from the roof via downspout into a sculpted basin; water dribbles out of that basin into a runnel filled with pea gravel; from that point it traverses the terrace in a most elegant meander, dropping into a biofiltration zone when it reaches the terrace edge. This limpid S-curve of the water's trail across the plaza provides particularly seductive eye appeal, and the serpentine rainwater trail is clarified, enhanced, and made safe by a cover of steel grating perforated with lilting curves that extend the liquid theme, alternating with river pebble fill. Noteworthy is the fact that the visitor doesn't need to see the water flowing across the space, because its gently curving conveyance is clear whether wet or dry.

Aesthetic Richness Objective: Create visual interest through planes
Technique: Stack horizontal and vertical planes such as pools and falls to exploit visual interest of stormwater flowing over surfaces and plunging down planes, through weirs, or over edges
Project: The Dell at the University of Virginia, Charlottesville, VA, Nelson Byrd Woltz Landscape Architects with Biohabitats, Inc., PHR&A with Nitsch Engineering

The daylighted stream and detention pond at the Dell display two particularly elegant and revelatory design compositions based on planes. In both cases, water crossing a plane reveals its volume and intensity through the design.

First, the naturalized, meandering, daylighted stream changes conveyance character and direction as it approaches the pool, turning 90 degrees to enter the pond via a straight, channelized runnel. A level spreader at the raised runnel's end drops water into the pond in a planar sheet that changes character with storm intensity: In small rain events, the sheet drops straight down, and in major storms the water sheet arcs away from the conveyance structure (figure 2.51).

Figure 2.51. In small rain events, water drops from the conveyance structure in a vertical sheet, and in larger events it arcs away from the structure (design: Nelson Byrd Woltz Landscape Architects with Biohabitats, Inc., PHR&A with Nitsch Engineering; photograph: Stuart Echols).

Another simple but elegant planar composition is found in the pond's checkdam weir: 2-foot-wide, flat, dressed stone slabs form the top of the checkdam, offering an enticing pedestrian crossing when dry (figure 2.52); the dressed stone slabs step down two shallow levels in the middle, to form a weir. In small rain events, water crosses only the lowest, central slab, and in larger storms, water sheets over the higher stone planes on each side as well. Again, the character of the water changes with intensity, ranging from a shallow, vertical waterfall to a rolling wave of water (figure 2.53). Overall, this design not only presents beautiful planar compositions but also uses the planes as a visual indicator of the rain's intensity.

Figure 2.52. The planar slabs atop the checkdam offer an enticing pedestrian crossing (design: Nelson Byrd Woltz Landscape Architects with Biohabitats, Inc., PHR&A with Nitsch Engineering; photograph: Stuart Echols).

Figure 2.53. The checkdam planes serve as a visual indicator of rain intensity: Small rain events drop water only over the central (lowest) forebay plane, and large events can roll over the entire structure (design: Nelson Byrd Woltz Landscape Architects with Biohabitats, Inc., PHR&A with Nitsch Engineering; photograph: Stuart Echols).

Aesthetic Richness Objective: Create visual interest through volume
Technique: Create visual interest or themes with basins that hold plants and water: sunken, raised, orthogonal, curved, organic, geometric, small, or large
Project: Growing Vine, Seattle, WA, GAYNOR, Inc., Carlson Architects, SvR Design Company, Buster Simpson

We return to Vine Street in Seattle to visit the "Beckoning Cistern" discussed earlier. Immediately downhill from the cistern, four circular basins receive water in sequence, starting with roof runoff that falls from the "thumb" of the Beckoning Cistern "hand" into the first basin. Their consistent shape creates a thematic rhythm as they step down the hill (figure 2.54).

Figure 2.54. The rhythm of circular basins punctuates rainwater movement down the hill of the first block at Growing Vine (design: GAYNOR, Inc., Carlson Architects, SvR Design Company, Buster Simpson; photograph: Stuart Echols).

Aesthetic Richness Objective: Create visual interest through color or texture
Technique: Contrast natural elements such as plants and rocks with artificial elements such as clipped lawns, steel, or concrete; juxtapose river rock and riparian grasses for compositional contrast
Projects: Stephen Epler Hall, Portland State University, Portland, OR, Atlas Landscape Architecture, KPFF Consulting Engineers, Mithun; Rain Garden at Oregon Convention Center, Portland OR, Mayer/Reed; 10th@Hoyt, Portland, OR, Koch Landscape Architecture

Another means of creating visual richness in ARD is the visual contrast in color and texture created by juxtaposing river rock and riparian grasses, especially rushes and sedges. Many ARD projects exhibit this stunning combination. Not only a visually dramatic pair, riparian grasses and river rock also link naturally to the water theme of ARD, because both are water-related materials (figure 2.55). When they are further contrasted with a straight-lined edging of concrete, cut stone, or weathered steel, the effect is even more striking (figure 2.56).

Of all the ARD projects we've visited, the most intensely textural composition is in the apartment courtyard at 10th@Hoyt. First, the courtyard is approximately 9,000 square feet in size, surrounded

Figure 2.55. Striking compositional contrast can be achieved by combining river rock, riparian grasses, and cut stone, as here at Stephen Epler Hall (design: Atlas Landscape Architecture, KPFF Consulting Engineers, Mithun; photograph: Stuart Echols).

Figure 2.56. Another textural strategy that communicates water is juxtaposition of exuberant riparian plants with a crisp edge of weathered steel against mowed grass, as at the Oregon Convention Center Rain Garden (design: Mayer/Reed; photograph: Stuart Echols).

Figure 2.57. Smooth, black stone planters contrast with the filigree and mossy texture of the plants they contain and the wood-slatted surfaces they sit on (design: Koch Landscape Architecture; photograph: Stuart Echols).

by the five-story apartment building; this intimate space ensures that visitors are close enough to the materials to enjoy their interesting tactile qualities. The thoughtful textural composition helps convey the "We are sophisticated" PR message discussed earlier: Smooth, black stone planters contrast with the filigree texture of the sasanqua camellia (*Camellia sasanqua* 'Yuletide') or Japanese holly (*Ilex crenata* 'Convexa') they hold and the wooden-slatted surfaces they sit on (figure 2.57). Elsewhere, the huge, shiny, bristled leaves of dinosaur food (*Gunnera tinctoria*) complement the delicate leaf patterns of sweet woodruff (*Galium odorata*) and liriope (*Liriope muscari*). The rough surface of Corten steel fountains and level spreaders is complemented by colored glass "buttons" that dot the steel sheets and large, gray river stones that fill the basins in which the Corten structures sit (figure 2.58). This space is filled with tactile sensations, initially for the eye and then, almost irresistibly, for the touch.

Figure 2.58. Contrasting textures of dinosaur food (*Gunnera tinctoria*), glass-dotted Corten steel level spreaders, and river rock nearly beg to be touched (design: Koch Landscape Architecture; photograph: Stuart Echols).

Aesthetic Richness Objective: Create visual interest through axes
Technique: Create stormwater trails using axial runnels, downspouts, bioswales, and so on
Project: Salvation Army Kroc Community Center, Andropogon Associates Ltd. and MGA Partners, Inc.

The site of the new Salvation Army Kroc Community Center was a 12.43-acre brownfield. Andropogon's innovative site design captures and reuses the first 1 inch of runoff, and thoughtfully contrived axes in the design suggest the rainwater management strategy. Axial runnels extend from the building's semicircular, concave facade, carrying roof runoff and air conditioner condensate toward a central grassy oval; the visible water trail ends at the walkway surrounding the grass. The suggestion is that runoff from the building is conveyed out into the landscape (figure 2.59). The truth is a bit more complex: The water travels to an underground cistern, from which it is used for irrigation. The concept is revealed in the design, but the specifics are not.

Figure 2.59. Axial runnels extend from the building toward a central grassy oval, suggesting that water from the building is conveyed out to irrigate the landscape (design: Andropogon Associates Ltd., MGA Partners, Inc.; photograph: Stuart Echols).

Aesthetic Richness Objective: Create visual interest through rhythm and repetition
Technique: Create unified design themes by using multiple bioswales, basins, weirs, ponds, rain gardens, or other rainwater-focused props
Project: SW 12th Avenue Green Street Project, Portland, OR, Portland Bureau of Environmental Services

Because the water trail so frequently serves as a focal point in ARD, repetition and rhythm can be an effective design tool that punctuates rainwater's procession across a site. This strategy is not only useful for aesthetic composition; it can also aid the hydrologic function. By repeating a series of small treatment elements on a site (e.g., bioswales, detention basins, checkdams) a designer can create a more effective and extensive "treatment chain" than one limited to a single location. Opportunities abound for visually interesting rhythm created through repetition of stormwater elements, and a notable example is found at the SW 12th Avenue Green Street Project in Portland, Oregon. Here stormwater is diverted from the urban street into retention basins that filter runoff. A sequence of four concrete-edged, rectangular sunken basins, planted with rushes, sedges, and street trees, creates a rhythm in the urban street that is not only visual but also functional. Runoff flows from one basin to the next, so the repetition serves the water treatment system as well as the streetscape composition (figure 2.60).

Figure 2.60. A rhythmic repetition of sunken basins at the 12th Avenue Green Street Project unifies the composition and serves the water treatment system (design: Portland Bureau of Environmental Services; photograph: Stuart Echols).

Aesthetic Richness Objective: Create auditory interest through volume
Technique: Create a variety of volumes by allowing stormwater to fall from various heights onto different materials such as stone or steel
Project: 10th@Hoyt, Portland, OR, Koch Landscape Architecture

The sound of moving water provides an intriguing opportunity for designers to call attention to rainwater in ARD. An excellent example of auditory consideration is found at the previously mentioned urban courtyard at 10th@Hoyt. Here the stormwater movement takes a variety of forms, resulting in a symphony of sounds during a storm: Rainwater runs through flumes, tumbles down chaddars (small, stepped waterfalls) (figure 2.61), dribbles down glass-buttoned Corten surfaces (figure 2.62), and drops into river stone–filled basins. And the sound continues for up to 30 hours after the rain stops—at least the dribbling over two Corten "weir boxes"—thanks to a detention cistern that temporarily recirculates the rainwater.

Figure 2.61. Rainwater at 10th@Hoyt tumbling down a chaddar (design: Koch Landscape Architecture; photograph: Steven Koch).

Figure 2.62. Rainwater at 10th@Hoyt dribbling across Corten surfaces (design: Koch Landscape Architecture; photograph: Steven Koch).

Aesthetic Richness Objective: Create auditory interest through pitch and rhythm
Technique: Create changes in pitch by allowing rainwater to fall on different forms such as flat block, metal drums, and ponds; create different rhythms by varying the amount and rate of stormwater falling and flowing through treatment systems
Project: Cedar River Watershed Education Center, Cedar Falls, WA, Jones and Jones, Dan Corson

As stated earlier, the Cedar River Watershed Education Center focuses on educating Seattle-area residents about their watershed. One facet of this eco-revelatory theme is found in the Forest Court, adjacent to the main welcome center; here, local artist Dan Corson designed a ring of twenty-one drums played by water droplets electronically released in patterns of specific drum beats that represent twenty-one indigenous cultures worldwide (Owens Viani, 2007). The gentle, rhythmic sound of the drums draws visitors out of the welcome center and into the designed landscape and reminds them of the relationship of native cultures to natural systems, subtly suggesting that perhaps we should embrace an indigenous reverence for rain as well (figure 2.63).

Figure 2.63. Artist Dan Corson's twenty-one drums are played by water droplets electronically released in patterns of specific drum beats that represent twenty-one cultures worldwide (design: Jones & Jones, Dan Corson; photograph: Seth Wilberding).

Aesthetic Richness Objective: Create tactile interest through wetness
Technique: Allow people to touch stormwater in different forms such as flowing, falling, splashing, standing, sheeting, or damp surfaces where water can soak in or evaporate
Projects: Cistern Steps Vine, Seattle, WA, GAYNOR, Inc., Carlson Architects, SvR Design Company, Buster Simpson; Queens Botanical Garden, Flushing, NY, Atelier Dreiseitl with Conservation Design Forum, BKSK Architects

Finally, there is the tactile experience of water—accessible, touchable water. In his landmark book and documentary film *The Social Life of Small Urban Spaces* (1980), William H. Whyte argued that touchable water is an asset in urban spaces and that presenting visible water but prohibiting the tactile opportunity is a virtual crime. In fact, not many examples of touchable rainwater are found in the ARD projects, probably because of our contemporary fear of water that isn't made antiseptic by chemical treatment and the perceived liability presented by accessible water. A welcoming example of accessible stormwater is found in the "Cistern Steps" at Vine Street, previously discussed for creating visual interest with volume. Here the small, shallow (i.e., safe), tapered basins cascade down the hill in a playful rhythm, and water is rendered particularly touchable by pedestrian steps wrapped around the basins, allowing passersby to reach out and touch the water as it drops from each sculptural scupper into the basin below (figure 2.64).

Figure 2.64. Steps wrap around the basins at Growing Vine Street, allowing pedestrians to reach and touch the stormwater (design: GAYNOR, Inc., Carlson Architects, SvR Design Company, Buster Simpson; photograph: Eliza Pennypacker).

But the most invitingly, playfully touchable water we found was in the rainwater fountain and stream at Queens Botanical Garden. As discussed in part 2.2, this rainwater invites visitors to splash and play in a bubbling fountain cascade and in a "stream" carrying rainwater from the fountain to another part of the site (figure 2.65). How is this possible in our cleanliness-obsessed American culture? As noted earlier, the runoff is treated in an underground cistern with ultraviolet rays to destroy bacteria before it is conveyed to the fountain, thus rendering it as clean as most natural streams.

Figure 2.65. The rainwater fountain and stream at Queens Botanical Garden provide many opportunities for interaction with the water (design: Atelier Dreiseitl with Conservation Design Forum, BKSK Architects; photograph: Stuart Echols).

Things to Consider in Your Effort to Achieve an Aesthetic Richness Goal in ARD

Both the matrix and the case studies provide plenty of opportunities and questions to consider in creating aesthetic richness in ARDs. To summarize:

- What character of aesthetic composition is appropriate (e.g., playful, elegant, mysterious, peaceful)?
- Because conveyance is so common in stormwater management, consider the line of water trails particularly carefully. What should their aesthetic character be? How can you make them "read," whether wet or dry?
- Would it be appropriate to create sounds with the water? What kinds of water sounds would support the design messages?
- Do local regulations allow people to touch the water, and would that be desirable in this design? If yes, what kinds of water touching experiences might be created?
- Would it be appropriate to create an enticingly touchable landscape through rich textural qualities?

Conclusion to Part 2

We hope this chapter helps you realize that a wide range of possibilities exists for designers to transform sustainable stormwater management systems into fascinating landscape amenities. We also hope that the ideas and examples presented in this chapter not only inspire you but prompt you to think of even more creative strategies for Artful Rainwater Design.

3. Achieving Utility with Artful Rainwater Design

Overview of Utility Considerations in Artful Rainwater Design

This part of the book focuses on an array of sustainable stormwater management options and their potential connection to the amenity options in ARD. Plenty of manuals on sustainable stormwater management illustrate and explain effective management strategies, and we have no intention of replicating those sources in this book, nor do we intend to present every possible stormwater management strategy. Instead, we present a range of sustainable stormwater management strategies that are particularly appropriate to ARD.

In ARD, the function of stormwater management is consistently grounded in sustainability and strives to emulate the predevelopment hydrologic conditions of a site. Consequently, utility in ARD is synonymous with *sustainable stormwater management*.

Before defining ARD utility, it is important to clarify the difference between stormwater management and stormwater treatment, as used in this book. In our lexicon, *management* means that some form of human effort is made to control stormwater in some way, from directing its conveyance to making it infiltrate. Treatment is a subset of management that addresses water quality. So, in this book, all forms of utility in ARD manage rain, and some treat it as well.

With this background, we define utility in ARD as *managing rain in ways that protect and provide for human and natural systems*. This means managing rain with a diverse range of goals, objectives, and techniques with the following characteristics:

- Environmentally responsible, trying to emulate the natural hydrologic system
- Focused on small storm runoff control or first flush pollutant control
- Focused on site scale, not local or regional

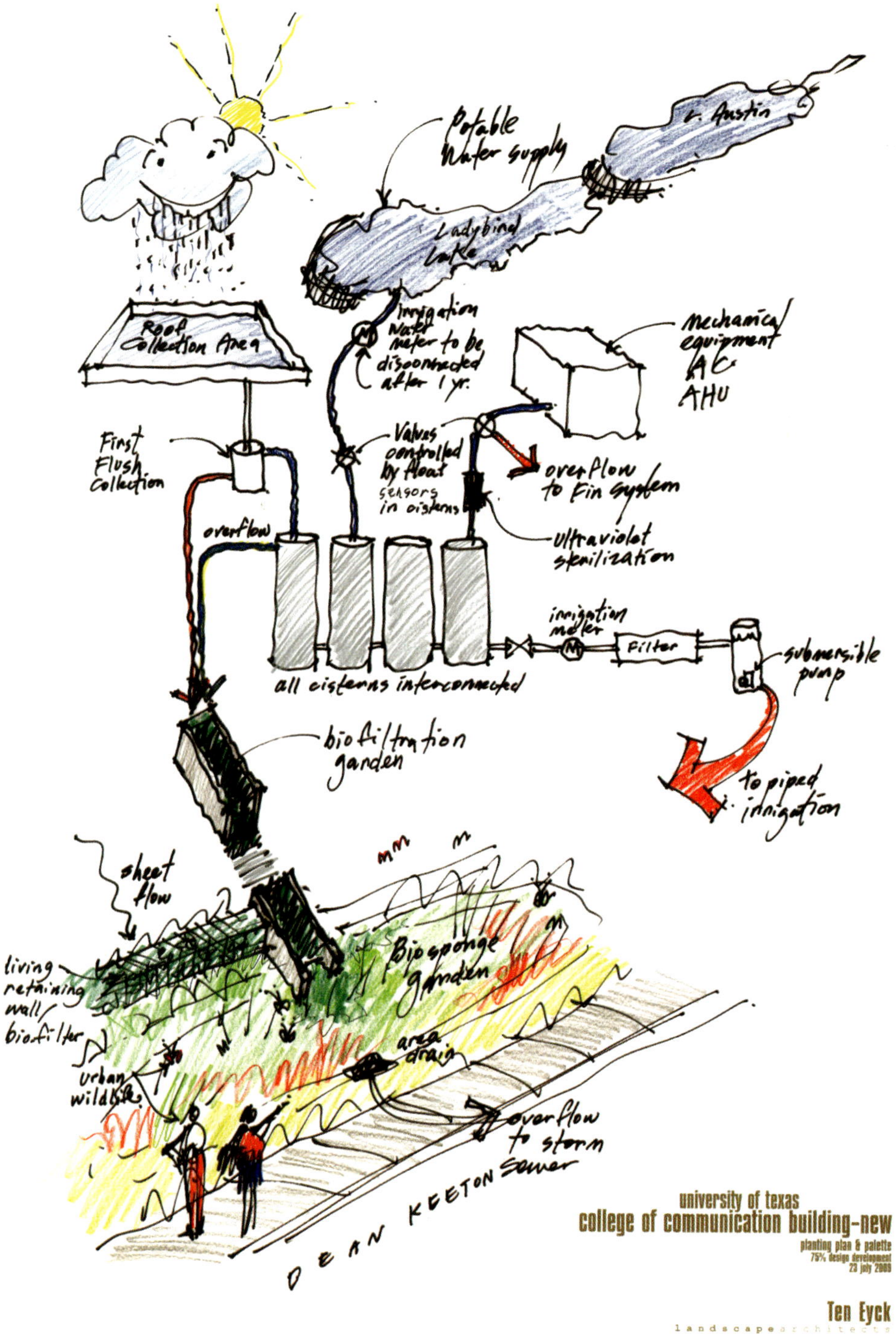

Figure 3.1. Diagram for the University of Texas Belo Center for New Media stormwater management strategy, a system particularly appropriate to ARD (design: Ten Eyck Landscape Architects, Inc.; diagram: Christy Ten Eyck).

And, importantly

- Stormwater management strategies that are appropriate to ARD. In other words, the utility strategies used in ARD are ones that *promote stormwater management that clearly celebrates rain.*

Simply put, sustainable stormwater management in ARD begins with rain-focused site design. Or, to put it a bit differently, the starting point for ARD is site design that begins with consideration of stormwater management and stormwater management that begins with consideration of site design.

> "The more we study stormwater runoff, the more we realize the critical role site planning and design play in our ability to reduce the impacts of development on the quality of our nation's waters."
> —Thomas E. Mumley, Urban Runoff Program manager, California Regional Water Quality Control Board, quoted in *Start at the Source* (Richman, 1999)

> "When I trace back to my early days . . . I'd say stormwater wasn't an issue. . . . This stuff was barely starting up and no one was paying much attention to it. N*ow I think it's a starting point [for site design]* . . . you can almost say it went from a non-consideration to a number one consideration."
> —Warren Byrd, Nelson Byrd Woltz, 2006 interview with authors

It's important to realize how much sustainable stormwater management can be accomplished with site design—before a designer even considers constructing management systems such as infiltration basins or flow-through filter planters. In fact, a fundamental premise of ARD is that sustainable stormwater management begins with site design that considers rain from the start of the process. At the outset of any project, the designer should ask which of the following actions can become "site design commitments" that will, in turn, reduce the need for constructed stormwater facilities:

- Protect natural drainage to slow and hold runoff, collect pollutants, and increase groundwater recharge.
  - Preserve and emphasize natural drainage systems as desirable park-like site features near impervious surfaces.
  - Maintain or restore existing natural drainage ways to keep water discharge dispersed, as it was in the site's predevelopment condition.

- Protect existing vegetation features as assets for rainwater filtration, absorption, and evapotranspiration.
  - Preserve or restore natural vegetative areas that hold water and promote them as site amenities in close proximity to buildings, plazas, entryways, walkways, and play areas.
  - Designate limits of work on site to protect existing vegetation, including understory vegetation and ground cover.

- Grade sites to direct water to small, distributed green spaces that can hold water, in order to mitigate offsite runoff impact.
  - Slope roads, plazas, and roofs toward depressed landscape areas on site that will hold and infiltrate runoff.
  - Grade sites to increase sheet flow and lengthen flow paths by diverting runoff into and through different green spaces.

- Minimize impervious surfaces to limit runoff sheet flow.
  - Where practical, reduce roof area by using multistory buildings instead of single-story buildings.
  - Reduce the length or width of streets.
  - Reduce building setbacks to shorten driveways.
  - Reduce sidewalk widths.
  - Downsize parking stalls and reduce parking aisle widths.
  - Use shared parking lots for adjoining uses.

- Maximize the usefulness of pervious surfaces.
  - Use permeable paving for low-traffic areas, overflow parking, sidewalks, emergency access, and driveways with materials that allow water to infiltrate.
  - Reduce turf areas and add more heavily vegetated areas to reduce excess runoff.
  - Emphasize low-maintenance landscape designs that foster preservation or installation of native plants that minimize the use of water, fertilizers, and pesticides and reduce mowing.
  - Establish extensive vegetated roofs and intensive garden roofs to replace impervious rooftops.
  - Design green roof systems that hold a minimum of ½ inch of rainfall to reduce runoff frequency and volume and filter pollutants.

- Direct runoff away from pipes and disperse it into the landscape to minimize offsite impacts and onsite costs.
  - Remove curbs and gutters from streets, alleys, parking lots, and loading areas where possible so that runoff can flow directly into vegetated areas.
  - Disconnect downspouts and direct stormwater into vegetation or collection systems.
  - Direct runoff across vegetated areas to help filter pollutants and encourage groundwater recharge by using wildflowers, prairie grasses, and riparian plants.
  - Keep runoff dispersed, out of pipe, and on the surface as much as possible to minimize gray infrastructure construction costs and maintenance.

- Promote healthy soils to increase rainwater filtration and absorption.
  - Designate limits of work on site to protect soils that adsorb, hold, and infiltrate rainwater.

  - Restore soil porosity to compacted soils by rip-plowing and adding compost where soils have been degraded.
  - Protect areas that are particularly susceptible to erosion and sediment loss.
  - Select plants that have deep-rooted systems to increase soil absorption capacity.

- Reduce development footprint and increase rainwater-receiving landscape.
  - Use flexible cluster and planned unit development zoning regulations to minimize the development footprint.
  - Preserve undeveloped lands as common open space amenities to reduce imperviousness.
  - Arrange open space parallel to slopes (e.g., contour plowing) to capture rainwater and increase runoff infiltration.

- Plan for safe pollutant storage.
  - Create preventive designs that place common nonpoint pollutant sources (fertilizers, pool chemicals, fuels) in areas that are under roofs or in areas where polluted runoff can be contained and treated.

- Design outdoor recreation areas so that they can receive and manage stormwater, and retrofit existing stormwater management facilities to include educational and recreational features.
  - Design recreation areas in floodplains so that they accommodate occasional flooding.
  - Locate playing fields, running trails, and other amenities in dry detention basins.
  - Retrofit existing detention basins to include educational and recreational opportunities (e.g., paths or boardwalks, bird houses, signage).

These diverse options show just how much sustainable stormwater management can be achieved by using stormwater consideration as a starting point for site design, as Byrd suggested. If we begin with this foundation—site design begins with stormwater consideration, and stormwater management begins with site design—we set the stage for more effectively sustainable stormwater management.

Determining the Utility Goals, Objectives, and Techniques

The five ARD utility goals were derived from many stormwater management manuals and resources. Taken together, these goals address the central intentions in sustainable stormwater management and consider the needs of both human and natural systems:

Reduce pollutant loads in rainwater

Reduce downstream damage from runoff

Safely move, control, and contain rainwater

Capture rain for reuse (of all kinds, human and natural, from irrigation and toilet flushing to groundwater recharge)

Restore or create habitat

The stormwater management objectives used to accomplish these goals are widely recognized in literature and practice:

- Conveyance = move rainwater safely from one place to another.
- Detention = capture and temporarily hold rainwater and control its discharge offsite.
- Retention = capture and hold rainwater on site.
- Infiltration = capture rainwater to recharge groundwater.
- Filtration = reduce pollution carried by rainwater.

A wide range of techniques can be used to design various sustainable stormwater management systems that address these utility goals and objectives. Most of the techniques appropriate to ARDs fall into the category of green infrastructure, which we define as stormwater treatment that includes rainwater contact with nature (plants or soil), but some very useful ARD utility techniques are considered gray infrastructure (i.e., stormwater management using hard-surfaced systems without plants or soil). For the purposes of this book, only *sustainable* gray infrastructure suitable for ARD is presented, omitting a wide range of manufactured devices, from vortex separators to drop-in filters.

Thus, a list of gray and green utility techniques that are particularly well suited for ARD is as follows:

Gray Infrastructure

- Water trails: pipes, channels, runnels, flumes, weirs, ditches
- Water flow controls: entry (presystem) flow splitters and overflow (in-system) splitters
- Water containers: rain barrels, cisterns

Figure 3.2. This runnel conveying rainwater in a plaza at Old Fourth Ward Park is an example of gray infrastructure appropriate to ARD (design: HDR; photograph: Eliza Pennypacker).

Green Infrastructure

- Flow-through filter planters
- Dry detention basins
- Wet detention basins
- Wetlands
- Infiltration basins and trenches
- Rain gardens
- Bioswales

In sustainable stormwater management, we find a complex web of goals, objectives, and techniques, because a variety of objectives can address one goal, and a specific technique can accomplish multiple objectives, thus addressing multiple goals. This complexity can be seen in table 3.1.

Figure 3.3. An example of green infrastructure, using plants and soil, in addition to—or instead of—pipes to manage rainwater at Shoemaker Green (design: Andropogon Associates Ltd.; Meliora Design LLC; photograph: Stuart Echols).

Simply put, the hierarchical sequence of amenity goals, objectives, and techniques presented in part 2 doesn't work well for utility goals, objectives, and techniques. Consequently, we have organized this part of the book in the way we think would be most useful to someone wanting to create an ARD. We first focus on the techniques—the physical actions a designer can take—and then suggest how a variety of these techniques can be used in any design to address a set of sustainable stormwater management goals and objectives. In other words, we present an à la carte menu of possibilities, each clearly explained, from which the designer can choose to develop a useful sustainable stormwater management system.

We have organized all the techniques in the direction of rainwater flow: first, how to move the rainwater to the management system, then how to ensure that the right water goes into the right system. These two parts of management typically rely on gray infrastructure elements. Finally, we address how systems can manage or treat the rainwater, which is generally—although not always—achieved with green infrastructure elements.

Table 3.1. The complex web of ARD utility goals, objectives, and techniques

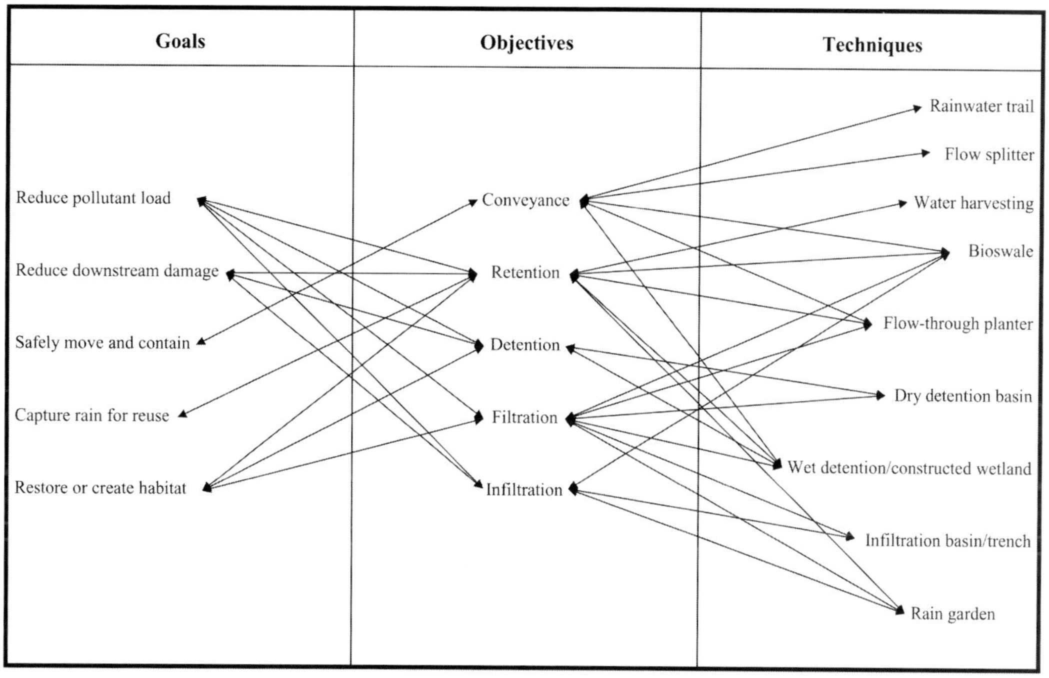

For each technique, we present:

- A matrix of utility objectives and goals the technique can address
- An illustration and description
- Stormwater management or treatment that can be accomplished through this technique
- Some ways rain can be celebrated using this technique
- Some design considerations for this technique

PART 3.1

Gray Infrastructure Techniques for Sustainable Stormwater Management

Our discussion of gray infrastructure techniques focuses only on those we've found most suitable for—and most frequently used in—ARD. As stated in the part 3 overview, we've omitted many commonly used gray infrastructure techniques, but in this section we present three that are often important in ARD. In fact, the first two—the rainwater trail and flow splitters—are extremely important in almost every ARD. The third—the rainwater harvesting container—is optional.

Rainwater Trail

First we'll look at how to move the rainwater to the treatment system, which we call the rainwater trail in ARD. The rainwater trail—the simple movement of runoff away from the place we don't want it—is the oldest of all stormwater management systems. That movement can be accomplished either belowground via pipe or aboveground via channel, runnel, flume, weir, swale, ditch, creek, or stream. When it comes to ARD, "Don't just think pipes!" is the litany of Tom Liptan, retired environmental specialist for the city of Portland, Oregon and ARD pioneer. Try to keep the water trail on the landscape surface.

The rainwater trail is often a form of gray infrastructure and is not typically a true treatment type, but it is central to ARD because it is the means by which we transfer water from the place where it falls to the management system, and it offers a huge opportunity to celebrate the rain.

Table 3.2. Rainwater trail: Creatively moves rainwater from where it falls to where it will be managed

Goal	Objectives
Safely move, control, and contain rainwater	Conveyance Detention Filtration Infiltration

Stormwater Management Accomplished with Rainwater Trails

The rainwater trail is one of the few components of ARD utility where treatment for water quality is an *option*. In other words, a rainwater trail may simply move the water, but it also may manage or treat the water in any of the following ways:

- Oxygenate the rainwater by making it roil (moving across a rough surface, forcing the water to drop or jump).
- Detain the rainwater through complex conveyance holding systems.
- Filter the rainwater through addition of plants and soil in a bioswale.
- Infiltrate rainwater in a bioswale.

Figure 3.4. One of many ways to move rainwater safely from one place to another: here, at Howard Hall, Lewis and Clark College, a simple water trail visibly carries rain from roof to bioretention system (design: Walker Macy; photograph: Stuart Echols).

Some Ways to Celebrate Rain through Rainwater Trails

The aboveground rainwater trail often serves as a focal point in one of the oldest (think gargoyles) and greatest opportunities to celebrate rain by attracting attention to its movement. The rainwater trail often becomes the visual tool that lets people understand the rainwater's movement from sky to earth or from one part of the management system to another. A visible water trail can be presented in almost any sustainable stormwater management system, and it is designed as a well-considered line in nearly every ARD we've seen to date. So for an ARD rainwater trail, think expose, not enclose; think reveal, not conceal.

If we move with the rainwater from roof to ground, we see many opportunities to celebrate the rain, most easily explained through figures 3.5 to 3.18. They are not all-inclusive, but these examples provide a range of options:

- **Visible water dropping vertically:**

Figure 3.5. Rainwater can be made visible in its downspout through clear sections of pipe, as at Springside School (design: Stacy Levy; photograph: Stuart Echols).

Figure 3.6. *(left)* A water chain presents an elegant means to convey rainwater from rooftop to container at grade, here at Penn State's Arboretum Pavilion (design: Overland Partners; photograph: Stuart Echols).

Figure 3.7. *(right)* A contemporary version of the ancient chaddar aerates, activates, and conveys water downhill at 10th@Hoyt (design: Koch Landscape Architecture; photograph: Steven Koch).

Figure 3.8. *(left)* A scupper can dramatize the fall of rain into the management system, as at the Rain Garden at the Oregon Convention Center (design: Mayer/Reed; photograph: C. Bruce Forster).

Figure 3.9. *(above)* Gravel-filled basins rhythmically bounce the rainwater down the hillside, finally dropping it into the planted system at "Growing Vine Street" (design: GAYNOR, Inc., Carlson Architects, SvR Design Company; Buster Simpson; photograph: Stuart Echols).

- **Visible water running horizontally high in the air:**

Figure 3.10. At Washougal Town Center, a long, slender aqueduct carries rainwater from the downspout in mid-photo to fall on an exuberant "splash" sculpture (design: GreenWorks, Sienna Architecture Company, Inc., Ivan McLean; photograph: Stuart Echols).

• **Visible water running horizontally at touchable height:**

Figure 3.11. Rainwater is carried within a long, sittable bench-like structure at Swarthmore (design: ML Baird & Co., Einhorn Yaffee Prescott; photograph: Stuart Echols).

• **Visible water running at grade in a straight, pebble-filled runnel:**

Figure 3.12. Rainwater is conveyed from the building via stone-edged, pebble-filled runnel that is covered by a grate when it crosses the walkway at the Southwest Recreation Center (design: RDG Planning and Design; photograph: Eliza Pennypacker).

• **Visible water running at grade in a visually discontinuous runnel:**

Figure 3.13. Rainwater appears to be conveyed from the building in a runnel that is covered by bluestone in the area of most pedestrian movement, but the axis is so strong that the viewer connects the disconnected pieces at Automated Trading Desk (design: Nelson Byrd Woltz Landscape Architects, Tinmouth Chang Architects; photograph: Stuart Echols).

- **Visible water running at grade in a curving, hard-edged flume:**

Figure 3.14. Rainwater is conveyed via concrete flume from the apartment complex across the street into a series of tiered biofiltration basins at The Headwaters at Tryon Creek (design: Portland Bureau of Environmental Services; photograph: Stuart Echols).

- **Visible water running at grade in a hard-edged "stream" of tiered basins and weirs:**

Figure 3.15. Rainwater tumbles downhill in an elegant abstracted stream sequence of basins at the University of Virginia South Lawn Commons Water Circuit (design: Office of Cheryl Barton; photograph: Eliza Pennypacker).

- **Visible water running at grade in a naturalized stream:**

Figure 3.16. At the Headwaters at Tryon Creek, rainwater is conveyed between apartment buildings in a daylighted tributary stream of Tryon Creek (design: GreenWorks; photograph: Stuart Echols).

- **Visible water running below a walkable grate:**

Figure 3.17. The entry plaza at Waterworks Gardens invites visitors to walk across the meandering grate above babbling water (design: Lorna Jordan; photograph: Eliza Pennypacker).

- **Visible, touchable water lined by one hard edge and one soft:**

Figure 3.18. The rainwater stream at Queens Botanical Garden juxtaposes a sawtooth hard edge on the plaza side with riparian plantings on the other side (design: Atelier Dreiseitl with Conservation Forum, BKSK Architects; photograph: Stuart Echols).

Some Considerations in Designing Rainwater Trails

Engagement

- The rainwater trail is a potent tool to tell a story of the relationship of rain to the site.
- A rainwater trail can create sound and visual interest.
- If the water is clean enough, the rainwater trail can be designed for water play.
- The rainwater trail can become the compositional spine of the entire design.
- Visible rainwater trails can be used to link indoors and outdoors by making a trail run through an exterior wall.

Control

- Changes in flow direction must be carefully considered, modeled, and tested.
- Proper sizing of the conveyance system is essential: Standard pipe and channel sizing methods such as Manning's equation should be used to appropriately size the channel, pipe, runnel, or flume for the drainage site.
- We recommend slightly oversizing the channel as an insurance method. You can also design the channel to accommodate different flow rates (e.g., incise a smaller channel within the main channel to accent variable water volume, as in figure 3.19).

Figure 3.19. A thin, incised channel within the larger concrete system not only ensures water movement at times of low water flow but also makes the conveyance system "read" even when dry, at the University of Virginia South Lawn Commons Water Circuit (design: Office of Cheryl Barton; photograph: Eliza Pennypacker).

- Carefully control the maximum speed of water movement by manipulating slope, length, and size; don't allow water to move so fast that it can't be controlled.
- Avoid moving water down steep slopes because it can pick up too much speed. Instead, move water horizontally down minimal slopes, then let it drop vertically as needed to "brake" the speed; it's always easy to control flow rate with a short vertical drop.
- To safely control water flow while effectively moving it, strive for a flow rate of 3 feet per second, achievable with a slope of about 1 percent.
- Modeling is critical: The designer must understand how water will move in the proposed channel, and water movement is challenging to anticipate. Testing on a full-scale mockup is often recommended.

Maintenance

- Design a backup system for inevitable water clogs. For example, slope the adjacent site so that unintended channel flooding will move water away from vulnerable spots, or use an in-system overflow splitter.

- Determine how the water trail will be cleaned of algae, moss, and lichen, as well as silt and trash.
- Think about the potential impact of long-term water staining and either plan to mitigate or incorporate that aging patina into the design.
- Consider how the rainwater trail system works in subfreezing weather, if applicable. And note that ice can be a strong visual asset during winter in systems that don't involve pipes; think about the aesthetic opportunity presented by ice.
- Open abovegrade systems are easier to observe, monitor, and maintain.
- If water drops vertically, consider the inevitable wetness of the environs (and be especially careful of windows, entries, and walls).
- Design for gusty or heavy wind, if applicable.

Flow Splitters

A flow splitter does exactly what the name states: It splits runoff flow into two or more separate parts. Splitting the runoff addresses two important needs. First, large quantities of runoff that could blow out a typical rain garden are diverted and moved around our green infrastructure systems rather than through them; second, it gives control over which runoff is captured and treated in the system (remember, our focus is on the dirtiest first flush).

There are two basic types of flow splitter:

- Entry (or presystem) flow splitter, which admits only small amounts of runoff into a treatment system
- Overflow (or in-system) splitter, which removes excess water volume from the system

The two must work together in any effective sustainable stormwater management system.

Table 3.3. Flow splitter: Separates runoff into different portions for various treatments

Goal	Objective
Move rainwater safely from one place to another	Conveyance

In sustainable stormwater management, one essential goal is to capture, hold, and treat first flush: the initial, therefore dirtiest, ½ to 1½ inches of runoff from impervious surfaces, which (as clarified throughout this book) includes 60 to 90 percent of annual rain events in temperate climates, depending on geographic location.

It is also important to realize that sustainable stormwater management strategies use primarily biological processes of plants and soil to manage and treat water; sustainable stormwater management neither puts the rainwater in a "tube" or "jar" nor treats it as a waste product.

The combination of these two premises—treatment of first flush and using biological processes—

Figure 3.20. This curb extension combines a variety of entry and overflow splitters to accept first flush and divert or remove large volumes of post–first flush (cleaner) rain (diagram: Stuart Echols and Chris Maurer).

is the essence of green infrastructure. And for biological process treatment of first flush to be most effective, we should distribute the water across the site as broadly as possible, as occurs when rain falls on a landscape, and not concentrate it in large quantities. Therefore, it's important to "divide and conquer" to effectively manage rain, or, as commonly stated, "slow it down, spread it out, soak it in." In this effort, flow splitters prove very useful.

Entry (Presystem) Flow Splitter

The first step in this "divide and conquer" process is to control the rate and volume of water that enters a treatment system. There are two ways to keep the inflow rates low. The first and easiest way is to control the size of the drainage area. A drainage area of one tenth of an acre or less will almost never create a flow rate that could blow out a rain garden. This is because, even with rainfall as high as 1 inch per hour, the surface runoff flow rate would be equal to only about two average garden hoses. That's not to say that you shouldn't drain more than a one-tenth-acre area to a rain garden but rather that the entry points to the rain garden should be distributed as much as practical so that each has a drainage area of one tenth of an acre or less. This combination of limited drainage areas and dispersed entry points will ensure that the rate of water entering the system will be small enough to prevent damage at the entry points, illustrated in figure 3.21.

These multiple entry points should also be designed to prevent erosion damage by including some

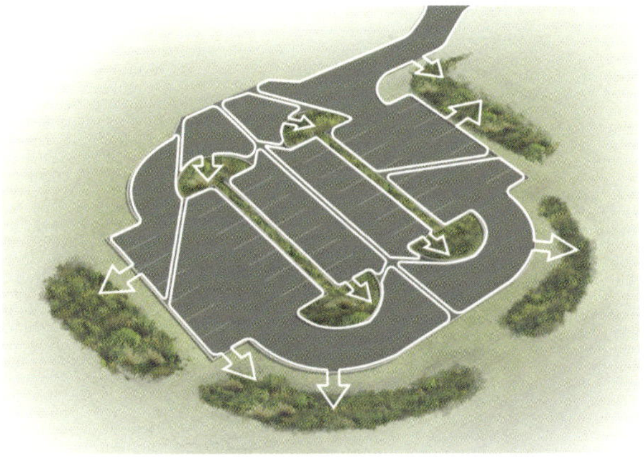

Figure 3.21. This design divides a parking lot into small drainage areas, each with a separate entry point, into eight management areas (diagram: Stuart Echols and Chris Maurer).

Figure 3.22. Inclusion of a hard-surfaced material (river rock, in this case) at the rainwater entry point prevents erosion damage (design: LaQuatra Bonci Associates; photograph: Stuart Echols).

type of hard surfaces that can break up and slow down the flow rate. River rocks function well and present a look appropriate for water, as in figure 3.22. Note that water also can safely drain directly into a treatment system as sheet flow, as long as it is gentle and dispersed.

The second way to control how fast water enters a treatment system is by making the inlet size small enough that it admits runoff slowly. The design can be as simple as a curb with slits cut into it so that runoff only trickles into the treatment system. This inlet strategy really has two functions: to ensure that large volumes of runoff won't blow out mulch, plants, or soil from the green infrastructure system and to admit only the first flush into the system for treatment while diverting the larger and cleaner subsequent flow around the system. Note that it's important to locate entry flow splitters uphill from a drain inlet so that large runoff volumes can flow downhill around the system (figure 3.23).

As of this writing, there are no standard sizing calculations required for an entry flow splitter, but we can assume that entry flow splitters should be small enough to limit flow rates to levels that will not disturb or destroy the treatment system but large enough to capture the first flush. Again, it may be useful to think about the flow rate from a garden hose, because we know from experience that the flow from your average garden hose would not damage the common rain garden. The average garden hose

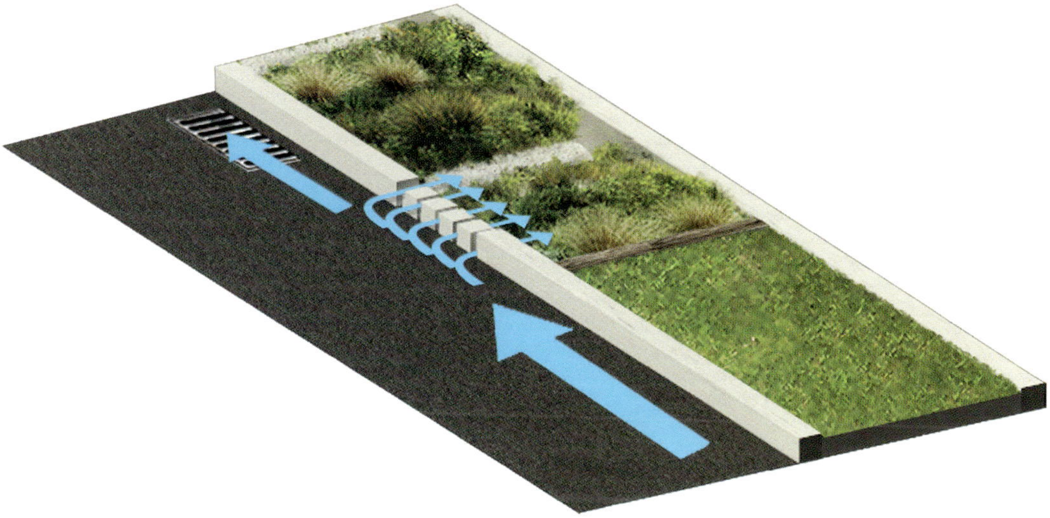

Figure 3.23. A set of narrow slits controls water access into the system: First flush trickles in, and swifter (and cleaner) large subsequent storm volumes flow past this first flush management system (diagram: Stuart Echols and Chris Maurer).

flow rate is between 10 and 20 gallons per minute, so we can be confident that a nondamaging inflow rate would be about 15 gallons per minute.

Another type of flow splitter is needed to ensure that the dirty first flush is held for treatment in the system (not simply pushed out downstream), while excess volume is removed. This is the function of an overflow (or in-system) splitter.

Overflow (In-System) Splitter

The overflow (or in-system) splitter limits the volume of water treated in the system. Designing the overflow splitter requires knowing how much water quality volume, or first flush, must be managed. This volume is derived by a simple equation:

Drainage area × runoff depth to be managed (check with your municipality)

For example, if we need to capture and treat 1 inch of first flush runoff from a 1,000-square-foot runoff area (a typical residential roof area), our equation would be:

1,000 square feet × 0.083 cubic feet (1 inch converted to decimal feet) = 83 cubic feet of runoff volume

So, in this context, we could use a treatment area about half the size of a parking space (8.3 feet × 10 feet) and 1 foot deep to manage 83 cubic feet of first flush. Note what a small area that actually is: A rain garden that size could probably fit into any landscape area required by a local development ordinance, and it offers a great way to make the landscape *work*.

The in-system overflow splitter functions as its name implies: If there is more runoff volume in the treatment system than it can hold, the overflow is diverted out of the system. This diversion can be accomplished in a number of ways. First, the treatment system (let's use a rain garden again) can be sized so that it can only hold the first flush and graded so that when it is full, water will back up through the entry flow splitter, forcing excess runoff to be diverted around the rain garden (figure 3.24).

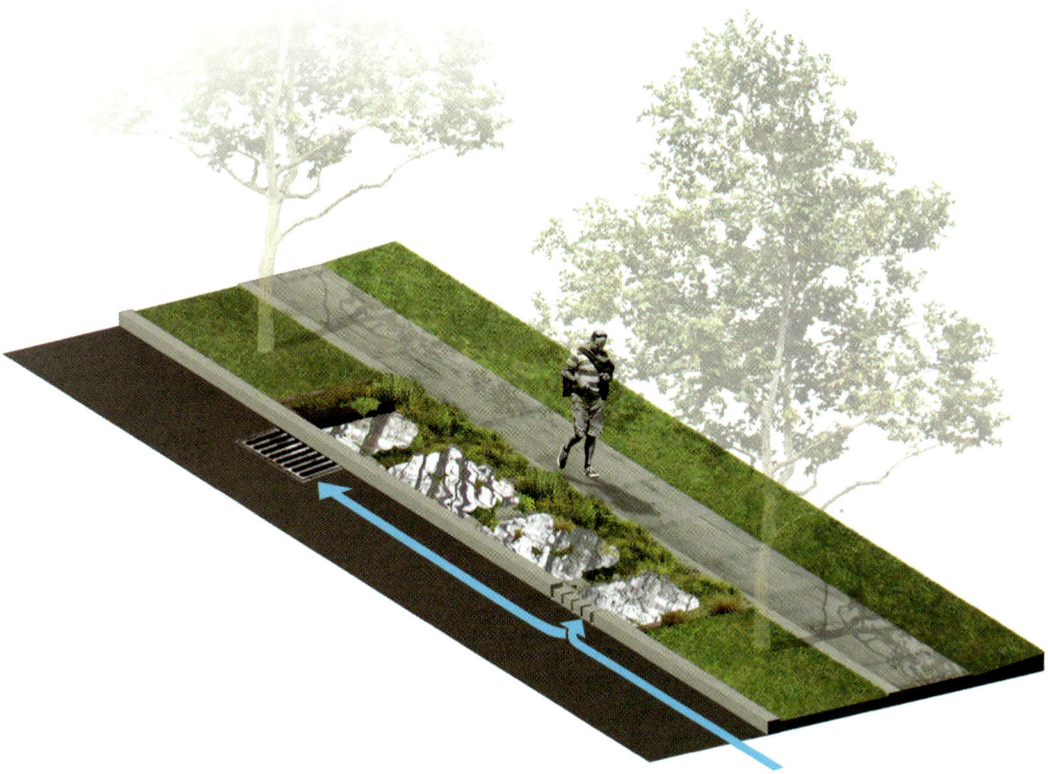

Figure 3.24. One type of in-system overflow splitter simply backs up water out of the entry flow splitter when the system is full so that large flows don't enter (diagram: Stuart Echols and Chris Maurer).

Another overflow splitter strategy entails creating one or more curb cuts downhill from the entry flow splitter, so that excess water can leave the system after entering, as in figure 3.25. Be careful to avoid placing those exit cuts at the low end of the system, because doing so would simply push the first flush right out.

Another option is to place raised drop inlets in the treatment system, ensuring that the treatment system holds the first flush volume of runoff and allows its sediment load to settle while diverting subsequent water out of the system and downstream. These raised drop inlet overflow splitters allow greatest design flexibility because they can be placed in a variety of locations and contexts. This is especially helpful when the site configuration makes it difficult to grade treatment systems to make water back up to, and bypass, the entry flow splitter.

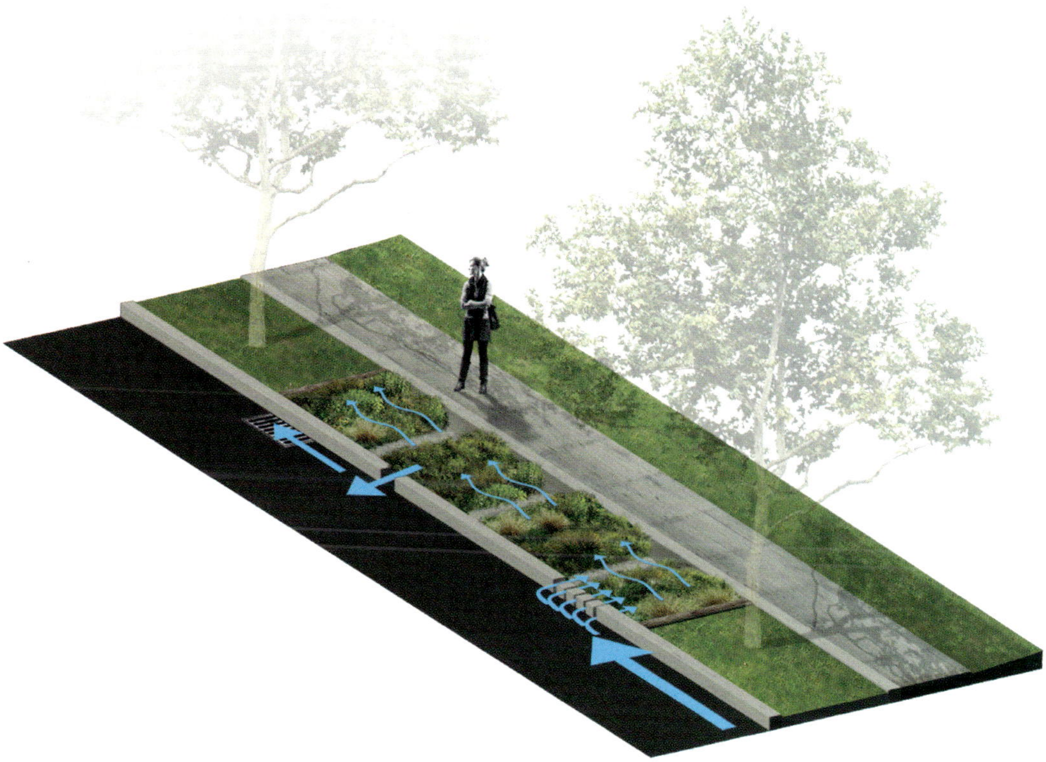

Figure 3.25. Overflow splitters can be curb cuts located downhill from the entry cuts, discharging water after it has entered the system (diagram: Stuart Echols and Chris Maurer).

Figure 3.26. A raised drop inlet accepts water above the ground level of the management system to retain first flush and its sediment load while taking subsequent volume out of the system. The grate prevents debris from entering the piped system (design: LaQuatra Bonci, Associates; photograph: Stuart Echols).

Stormwater Management Accomplished with Flow Splitters

These two types of flow splitter—entry and overflow—work together to control both the rate of water coming into the system and the volume of water held and treated in the system. This ensures that the treatment system is protected and that the first water in stays in the treatment system, while later flows are diverted around or out of the system.

Some Ways to Celebrate Rain with Flow Splitters

The design of entry flow splitters can tell the story of the treatment system by clearly displaying how water enters the system and revealing the way excess water is diverted around the system. In green street design in Portland, Oregon, for example, it's easy to see how water gets in (through a series of curb cuts), then how an internal weir with narrow slits admits some water but forces excess out of the system through other curb cuts (figure 3.27).

Figure 3.27. An early flow splitter designed for SE Ankeny Street in Portland. Runoff enters the gravel forebay via the large curb cut in foreground, then first flush trickles into the bioretention system through slits in the weir. Larger subsequent volume exits through the overflow splitter curb cut at left. Note that this design was ultimately not successful because the first weir is much lower than the curb, which allowed large volumes to "hop" the weir (design and photograph credit: Portland Bureau of Environmental Services).

Overflow splitters can make the water trail visible and help visitors better understand the water treatment story by clearly showing how excess runoff is intentionally moved from one treatment system to another. The in-system overflow splitters at Epler Hall create a water trail out of stone runnels that show the rainwater's playful progression downhill from one biopaddy to the next throughout the pedestrian courtyard (figure 3.28).

Some Considerations in Designing Flow Splitters

- The overflow splitter (such as a raised drop inlet) should be placed at an elevation that will allow the treatment facility to hold the first flush while allowing additional runoff to overflow out of the

Figure 3.28. Rain from large storm events can overflow the sunken biopaddies in this design. This overflow is directed downhill to the next biopaddy. This system retains first flush and offload overflow. It is also highly visible, thanks to the granite set runnels carrying overflow from one biopaddy to the next (design: Atlas Landscape Architecture, KPFF Consulting Engineers, Mithun; photograph: Stuart Echols).

system. Don't allow the inlet to be constructed at grade; there's a reason it's called a raised drop inlet! The idea is to allow first flush to pool in the system before excess water is removed.

- To ensure that runoff entering the system won't push first flush through and out before it's treated, locate a raised drop inlet overflow splitter near the point where runoff enters the system, not (as too often happens) at the other end. This ensures that first flush moves into the system, dropping pollutants at the "low end" of the system (away from the entry); subsequent volume backs up and escapes by way of the inlet.

Rainwater Harvesting Container

Once the runoff has arrived at its management destination, what is the nature of the system, and what kind of treatment does it provide? As stated earlier, in ARD sustainable stormwater management, most systems are green infrastructure, in which the rainwater is treated using plants and soil, but the first management technique presents one last instance of gray infrastructure: the rainwater harvesting container. A rainwater harvesting container is a fabricated tank designed to hold a prescribed volume of runoff. It can be above grade (rain barrel) or below grade (cistern).

Table 3.4. Rainwater harvesting: Collect and store rainwater from impervious surfaces for reuse

Goals	Objectives
Reduce pollutant loads in rainwater	Conveyance
Reduce downstream damage from runoff	Filtration
Safely move, control, and contain rainwater	

Figure 3.29. At the Ladybird Johnson Wildflower Center, one rainwater harvesting structure not only holds rain but also serves as an observation tower that shows visitors how much rain it contains at any given time (design: J. Robert Anderson, Overland Partners; photograph: Pam Pennick).

Stormwater Management Accomplished with Rain Harvesting Containers

Rainwater harvesting containers can accomplish a surprising number of sustainable stormwater management goals. First, by capturing the runoff in a container, the system can hold the rainwater for reuse (typically irrigation or toilet flushing). Second, by this retention, the system also reduces the frequency of negative impacts on downstream systems caused by excess runoff, such as combined sewer overflows and non–point source pollution. Depending on the system's design, it can also clean the rainwater, by disinfecting (using ultraviolet radiation, which destroys bacteria) or by simple deposition of sediments at the bottom of the container.

Some Ways to Celebrate Rain with Rainwater Harvesting Containers

If the container is below grade, the design can cleverly clarify its important sustainable stormwater management role, thus educating visitors, as at the Rigler Community Garden (figure 3.30).

If the container is above grade, it is easy to make the rainwater harvesting tank highly visible and enlightening; multiple tanks can be connected in playful ways to gather both more water and more attention. Systems can be designed to provide educational opportunities if they clearly show how much water is captured at a given time; they can also be used to make PR statements about

Figure 3.30. An outdoor educational and rainwater harvesting pavilion at Rigler Community Garden shows, through its roof, how rainwater funnels, then drops down a rain chain into an underground cistern to be used for irrigation (design and photograph: Liz Hedrick).

rainwater that can be playful and informative. In various regions of the United States, for example, traditional forms of rainwater harvesting containers can show the resource value of rain in that culture and place. Whatever the strategy, the designer has the opportunity to creatively proclaim the owner's and community's focus on, and commitment to, environmental responsibility. Figure 3.31 shows a particularly playful example.

Figure 3.31. In "the Beckoning Cistern," artist Buster Simpson made tongue-in-cheek reference to Michelangelo's painting of God's life-giving touch of Adam's outstretched finger—but here, roof runoff is the life source. Passersby can also get a sense of water depth in this above-grade cistern, thanks to the floating "dipstick" visibly protruding from the top (design: Buster Simpson; photograph: Stuart Echols).

Some Considerations in Designing Rainwater Harvesting Containers

- By harvesting rainwater for reuse, we can reduce municipal water use.
- Rainwater harvesting containers can be used in small, constrained sites (rain barrels).
- A "rainwater is resource" statement can be made through signage at the spot where the water is used.
- Designers can control which runoff, and how much, is harvested. For maximum use and harvesting:
  - First determine monthly usage needs and average monthly rainfall depth.
  - Determine monthly runoff harvesting goal based on capture area and monthly rainfall data.
  - Systems are often sized for 1 to 2 months' usage needs and can always be supplemented with municipal water as needed.
  - Design a filtration system: Commonly a system either filters water before it enters the container or allows sediment deposition at the bottom of the container.

  - Locate the outflow valve high enough to permit sediment deposition and ensure that reused water is as clean as possible.
- Or if the goal is only first flush harvesting and filtration:
  - Size a container just large enough to hold first flush (runoff area × first flush runoff depth). This container can drain into a larger storage facility to increase the storage capacity.
  - Add an overflow splitter to divert later, bigger runoff volumes.
  - Choose the filtration system: Filter water before it enters the container or allow sediment deposition at the bottom of the container.

PART 3.2

Green Infrastructure Techniques for Sustainable Stormwater Management

As stated earlier, every green infrastructure system uses natural processes to manage rain rather than simply piping water and pollutants offsite. According to the Environmental Protection Agency, "Green infrastructure uses vegetation and soil to manage rainwater where it falls."[1] ARD designers have many options, and can accomplish many goals and objectives, by manipulating two basic variables in the green infrastructure system: what happens below the surface and what happens at the surface.

What happens below the surface?

Depending on the context and intentions, green infrastructure can filter, detain, retain, or infiltrate through manipulation of the subsurface design, and these management objectives can also be combined effectively (figures 3.32–3.35):

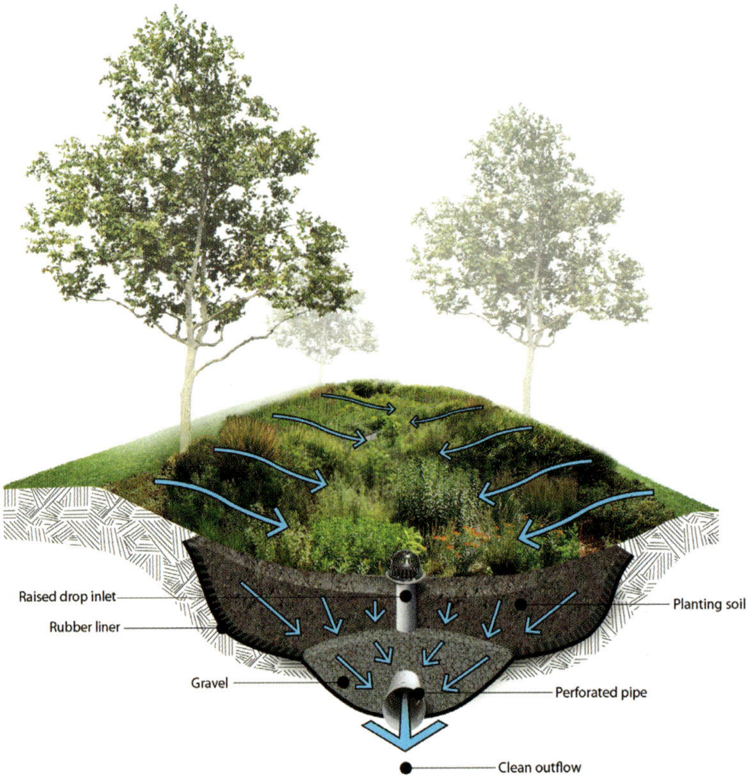

Figure 3.32. This system filters and detains, then sends all overflow downstream. Note the liner (prevents infiltration), perforated pipe (admits, then carries, detained water), and raised drop inlet (removes overflow, while first flush drops sediments and irrigates plants) (diagram: Stuart Echols and Chris Maurer).

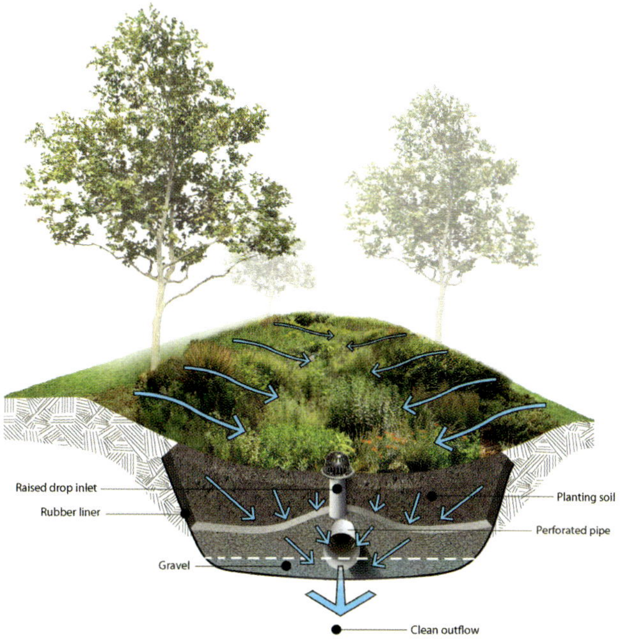

Figure 3.33. This system filters all rainwater, detains some, and retains some (below dashed line) in a soil–gravel medium (diagram: Stuart Echols and Chris Maurer).

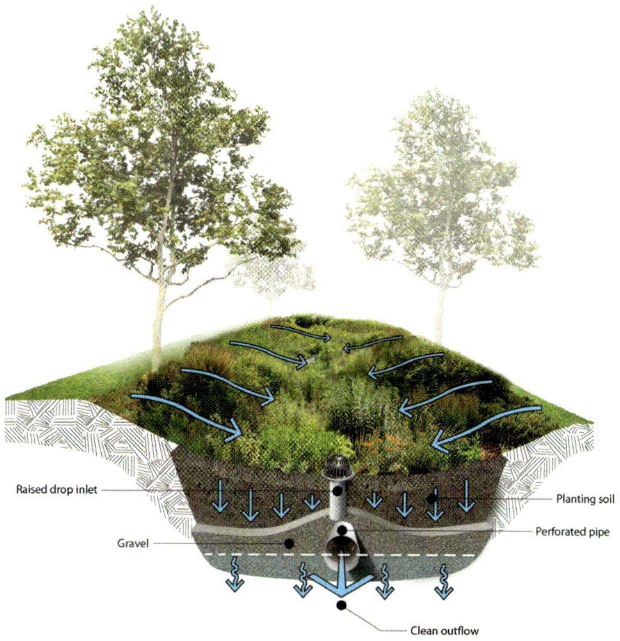

Figure 3.34. This system filters all rainwater, detains some, and infiltrates the rest to recharge groundwater (diagram: Stuart Echols and Chris Maurer).

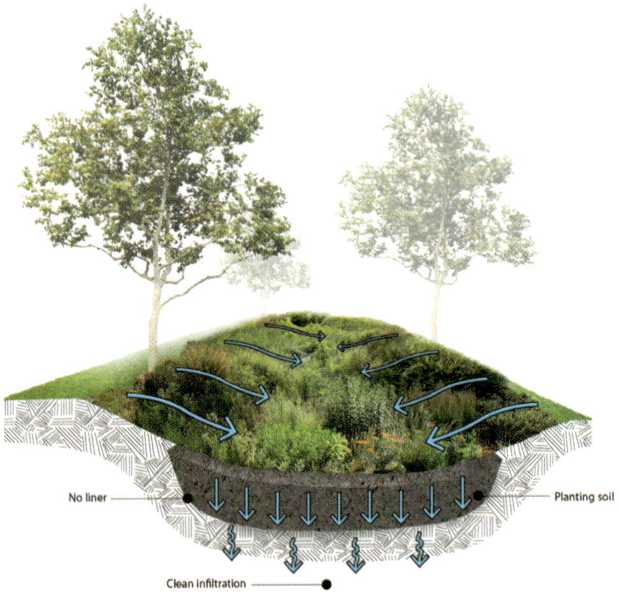

Figure 3.35. This system filters and infiltrates all rainwater (diagram: Stuart Echols and Chris Maurer).

What happens at the system surface?

There are two ways to characterize the surface of a green infrastructure system: wet and dry. Four basic variables result:

- Wet surface that is a pool
- Wet surface that is a wetland (plants and water)
- Dry surface that is vegetated
- Dry surface that is paved

Figures 3.36–3.38 illustrate these variables:

Figure 3.36. Green infrastructure with a wet surface can be a pool or a wetland, both of which are found in this detention basin at State College, Pennsylvania (design: Sweetland Engineering; photograph: Stuart Echols).

Figure 3.37. Green infrastructure often has a dry surface that is vegetated, as in this bioswale at the Glencoe Elementary School parking lot in Portland, Oregon (design: Portland Bureau of Environmental Services; photograph: Stuart Echols).

Figure 3.38. Green infrastructure can also have a dry surface that is paved, as in the porous paving system in the parking lot at Automated Trading Desk. Although this surface isn't "green," the filtration of water through soil and gravel and extensive evaporation of runoff on the surface qualify this stormwater management strategy as green infrastructure (design: Nelson Byrd Woltz Landscape Architects; photograph: Stuart Echols).

Table 3.5. Basic variables for green infrastructure systems

	Filter	Detain	Retain	Infiltrate	Dry Paved	Dry Vegetation	Wet	Wet Vegetation
Flow-through filter planter	•	•				•		
Dry detention	•	•	○	○		•		
Wet detention	•	•	○	○			•	
Wetland system	•	○	•	○				•
Infiltration system	•	○	○	•	•	•		
Rain garden	•	○	•	○		•		
Bioswale	•	○	•	○		•		

• Always ○ Sometimes

Once we understand all these possibilities, both below and at the surface, we can understand that every green infrastructure stormwater management system combines a particular set of these variables, with possibilities shown in this matrix:

In the following pages, we discretely present each of these techniques because each is commonly recognized as a sustainable stormwater management design strategy. One might argue that some of these techniques are variations on others (rain gardens and bioswales, for example), but we present each separately for purposes of clarity.

Now we can look at each technique individually to understand its potential use in ARD.

Flow-Through Filter Planter

A flow-through filter planter is a structured (boxed) planter at grade or above grade that does what the name states: It allows runoff to flow through plants and soil, filtering and detaining it. Eventually, the water flows though to discharge downstream.

Stormwater Management Accomplished with Flow-Through Filter Planters

Most importantly, a flow-through filter planter cleanses rainwater by moving it through plants and soil. It also acts as a small detention system, preventing water from moving too quickly into the down-

Table 3.6. Flow-through filter planter: Planting bed within structure that collects runoff and filters out pollutants

Goals	Objectives
Reduce pollutant loads in rainwater	Conveyance
Reduce downstream damage from runoff	Retention
Safely move, control, and contain rainwater	Filtration
Restore or create habitat	Infiltration

Figure 3.39. This fully lined flow-through filter planter filters and detains, then conveys overflow downstream via raised drop inlet and perforated pipe (diagram: Stuart Echols and Chris Maurer).

stream system. A flow-through filter planter retains some rainwater through absorption, adsorption, and filling the voids in the soil medium, but because flow-through planters are usually lined, there is no infiltration of rainwater into the ground.

Some Ways to Celebrate Rain with Flow-Through Filter Planters

A flow-through filter planter presents a great opportunity to proclaim that rain is a resource by making the water trail to the planter very clear (e.g., this water is coming from a roof via a downspout) and making it obvious that this water is irrigating plants (figure 3.40).

The discharge design can also be used to help people clearly understand where the water is going after it is filtered.

If presented in a linked series, flow-through filter planters can create an interesting rainwater trail rhythm, whether down a hill or throughout a space (figure 3.41).

Figure 3.40. At RiverEast, roof runoff falls from a spout in the building wall (at right) into the raised, pebble-filled splash box. Main overflow from the box sheets across the stainless steel level spreader in the concrete wall and drops into the infiltration basin (center); overflow from that zone is discharged via the grate-covered runnel (left foreground). A secondary infiltration basin catches additional overflow from the splash box (far right) (design: Greenworks, Group MacKenzie; photograph: Stuart Echols).

Figure 3.41. At the Cistern Steps, a tiered sequence of trapezoidal flow-through planters rhythmically steps down the hill. At the bottom, overflow goes to the city sewer system (design: Carlson Architects, GAYNOR, Inc., Carlson Architects, SvR Design Company, Buster Simpson; photograph: Stuart Echols).

Some Considerations in Designing Flow-Through Filter Planters

- They are useful in almost any context and at any grade (in-ground or above). Because they don't allow rainwater to infiltrate, flow-through filter planters are especially well suited to locations where infiltration is precluded: adjacent to buildings, or in subsoil problem spots (polluted subsurface soils that would harm groundwater recharge quality).
- They can be a useful tool on steep slopes, especially where infiltration could cause slope slippage. They slow water by terracing the planters, creating a functional and visible rainwater cascade series.
- It is easy to design them to serve as seating.
- Flow-through filter planters can fulfill some of a project's landscape requirements and add project value.
- They can treat water from any impervious surface, from roof to street.
- They must be planted with species that tolerate both dry and wet conditions.
- Waterproofing should be absolute; if this isn't possible, the design must allow water seepage without damage to surroundings. Location on a roof, for example, may not be wise because of the potential for leakage over time; in contrast, location on the side of a parking garage poses less risk.

Dry Detention Basin

A traditional dry detention basin is a grass-lined depression that holds runoff briefly, then discharges completely at a controlled rate into off site pipes or water bodies. One of the problems that can arise with this approach is that volume or speed of discharge from multiple basins can overwhelm downstream surface water bodies.

There are some basic ways to address this problem. The first is an extended detention basin, which slows the rate of discharge by enlarging the basin volume and using a smaller outlet pipe. Second, one can modify the basin further by increasing the basin depth below the outlet to permit some ponding. This approach reduces both discharge volume and frequency because not every rain event sends water downstream. A third useful modification is to plant the basin with deep-rooted native plants rather than turf, providing habitat, beauty, and increased rain retention.

Table 3.7. Dry detention basin: Shallow depression that collects, holds, and discharges runoff

Goals	Objectives
Reduce pollutant loads in rainwater	Conveyance
Reduce downstream damage from runoff	Retention
Safely move, control, and contain rainwater	Filtration
Restore or create habitat	

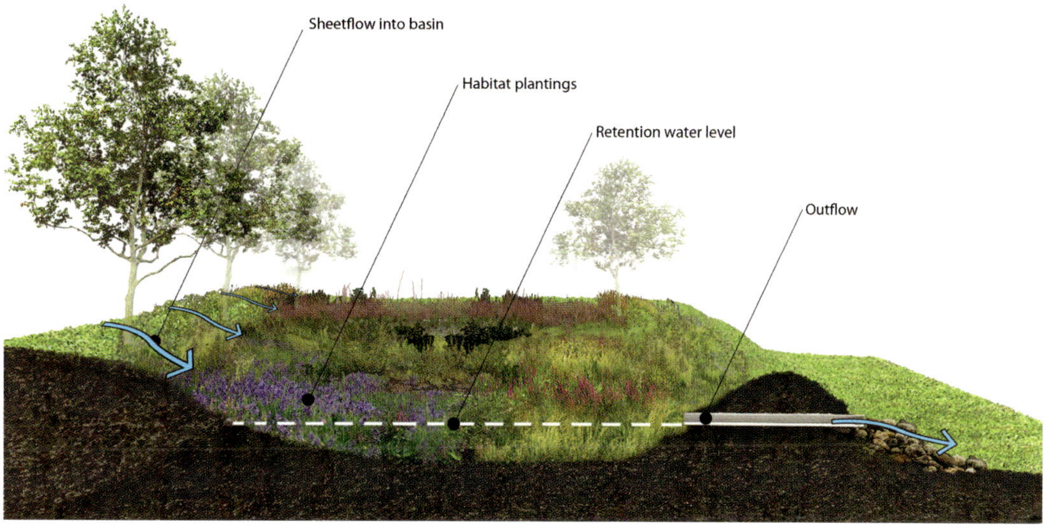

Figure 3.42. Traditional dry detention can be modified to create a robustly planted depression that permits some ponding, which controls discharge volume and frequency. This approach also beautifies, provides habitat, and retains more water than a grassed basin (diagram: Stuart Echols and Chris Maurer).

Stormwater Management Accomplished with Dry Detention Basins

A dry detention basin collects and holds runoff for a period of time and can therefore slow downstream discharge and prevent downstream erosion and combined sewer overflows (CSOs). Additionally, pollutants can settle or can be filtered by plants and soil. An extended detention basin can be robustly planted to provide more biofiltration than turf-lined detention and to provide habitat.

Existing dry detention basins also can be retrofitted to allow some water ponding and infiltration. A common technique is to excavate or rip-plow the bottom of the basin to allow a few inches of water ponding and then plant the basin with deep-rooted vegetation. This modification can be used to retain the first flush, provide infiltration, and create habitat.

Some Ways to Celebrate Rain with Dry Detention Basins

A dry detention basin can proclaim that rain is a resource through planting with colorful or riparian vegetation and an obvious water trail to clarify that the plants are irrigated with rainwater. Bird, bat, and bee structures can be added to help proclaim the environmental benefits (figure 3.43).

Boardwalks or stepping stones can be added for access to the detention basin for educational opportunities focused on rainwater (figure 3.44).

Some Considerations in Designing Dry Detention Basins

- This kind of basin requires a large area.
- They can be lined or unlined depending on the objectives and site conditions.

Figure 3.43. At Glencoe School the two-tiered detention basin displays the water trail from inlet to checkdam weir through use of large river rocks (foreground). Thickly planted sedges and rushes in both basins make the rainwater's irrigation function clear. This design also incorporates bird houses (not visible in photo) (design: Portland Bureau of Environmental Services; photograph: Stuart Echols).

Figure 3.44. At Manassas Park Elementary School, a boardwalk "stage" hovers over a planted detention basin, embraced by tiered amphitheater seating, providing a context for many activities, including discussion of the environmental significance of rain (design: Siteworks LLC; photograph: Stuart Echols).

- Vegetated dry detention basins may contribute to project landscape requirements.
- They may be designed to serve as recreational sports fields when dry.
- They can treat runoff from all impervious surfaces, from roof to street.
- Extended dry detention basins should use plants that tolerate periodic wetness, and the lengthy wetness precludes turf because mowers are easily stuck when grass is wet.
- Consider creating a multicell basin system, where a forebay captures first pollutants and sediments and facilitates maintenance (only the forebay needs to be dredged to clean out deposited sediments).
- Consider offering educational or experiential opportunities by providing access to a lushly planted basin via boardwalk or stepping stones.

Wet Detention Basin and Constructed Wetland

A wet detention basin or constructed wetland is a permanent water body designed to hold more water after rain events. Most stay wet because of a natural water source (constant or ephemeral stream or spring) that prevents water stagnation.

Wet detention basins and constructed wetlands differ in geometry and vegetation: Wet detention basins are often deeper and smaller with little or no vegetation, whereas constructed wetlands are vegetated, shallow, and broad. But hydrologically their function is similar: Fundamentally, they store water.

Table 3.8. Wet detention basin and constructed wetland: Wet vegetated depression that collects, holds, and discharges runoff

Goals	Objectives
Reduce pollutant loads in rainwater	Conveyance
Reduce downstream damage from runoff	Retention
Safely move, control, and contain rainwater	Filtration
Restore or create habitat	

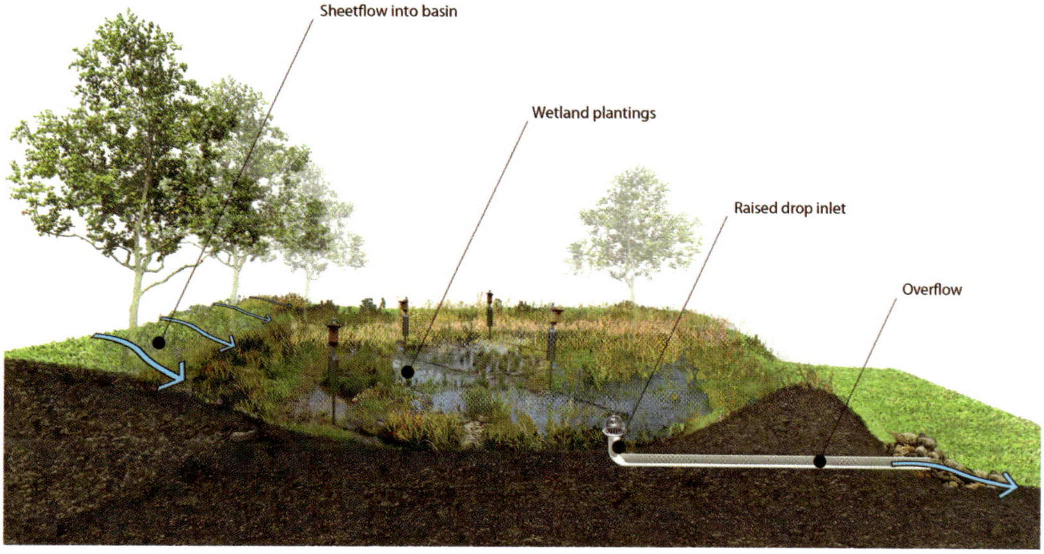

Figure 3.45. A wet detention basin or wetland is a permanent water body designed to hold more in rain events (diagram: Stuart Echols and Chris Maurer).

Stormwater Management Accomplished with Wet Detention Basins and Constructed Wetlands

Wet detention basins and constructed wetlands detain runoff, which can reduce damage to downstream surface water bodies, flooding, and CSOs. Some filtration occurs naturally through sedimentation, but it can be increased through riparian plantings and the creation of more complex flow paths and micropools. A wet detention basin or constructed wetland can also allow some infiltration as water tables fluctuate. And a richly planted constructed wetland can provide habitat.

Some Ways to Celebrate Rain with Wet Detention Basins and Constructed Wetlands

A wet detention basin can display its function by showing the volume of water it can contain, proclaiming its ability to mitigate flooding. It can also be an aesthetically rich water body for public use and enjoyment (figure 3.46).

A wetland can invite visitors to observe its flora and fauna habitat by providing viewing access via a boardwalk. The viewer's awareness of both riparian habitat and rainwater treatment can be further enhanced by signage (figure 3.47).

The ephemeral nature of rain can be emphasized by artful outflow from the basin. At Automated Trading Desk, for example, the detention basin stepped weir releases lots of noisy rainwater in high rains, a trickle in small rains, and no discharge at all when there's no rain, allowing an observant visitor to notice the rain-driven variability (figure 3.48).

Figure 3.46. The Old Fourth Ward wet detention basin is the focal point of a park that invites walking both around and within the basin. Note two horizontal lines of river stone in the wall in the right foreground; these mark the 100-year storm and the 500-year storm levels manageable within this basin (design: HDR; photograph: Eliza Pennypacker).

Figure 3.47. A curving boardwalk invites exploration of the constructed wetlands at Pierce County Environmental Services; and the sign (visible in left foreground) explains that this is "Not Just Another Pretty Garden" (design: Bruce Dees & Associates, SvR Design Company, The Miller|Hull Partnership; photograph: Stuart Echols).

Figure 3.48. The wet detention outflow at Automated Trading Desk emphasizes the ephemeral nature of rain (design: Nelson Byrd Woltz Landscape Architects; photograph: Stuart Echols).

Some Considerations in Designing Wet Detention Basins and Constructed Wetlands

- These techniques require a large area.
- Include a backup system to safely ensure that rainwater volumes larger than the design storm bypass the system.
- If a wet detention basin or constructed wetland is unlined, it must be located away from buildings, but with proper waterproofing, it can also be carefully located near a structure to create a "waterfront" appearance.
- These techniques can contribute to project landscape requirements and project value.
- A wet detention basin or constructed wetland can treat runoff from all impervious surfaces, from roof to street.
- Aeration or water movement in a wet detention basin or constructed wetland is sometimes needed to prevent stagnation.
- Consider creating a multicell basin system, where a forebay accepts first pollutants and sediments and facilitates easier maintenance (only the forebay needs to be dredged to clean out deposited sediments).
- Place wet detention basins where people will appreciate their aesthetic and recreational value.

Infiltration Basin or Trench

An infiltration basin or trench is an amended surface or subgrade system where groundwater is recharged by runoff. Importantly, when groundwater is recharged, pollutants must be filtered out through adsorption to soil, absorption by plants and soil, and settling. Pollutants that cannot be filtered out by these means must be diverted away from infiltration systems. *Basin* and *trench* are simply qualifiers of shape, responding to site design conditions: A trench is long and thin, and a basin is broader.

Infiltration systems can also detain rainwater as well as retain it. In these cases, surface drainage is diverted first into an underground infiltration system to filter and slow it, with subsequent release at a determined rate.

One type of infiltration basin has a hardscape surface at grade: porous paving. Porous paving most basically functions as a downward conveyance system for rainwater into an infiltration system. The hardscape paving medium can itself be porous (e.g., specially designed porous asphalt, concrete), or one can achieve the desired porosity by setting impervious pavers in a porous bed (planted soil or gravel) or using a load-bearing cell system with gravel- or plant-filled holes. Whatever the porous paving system, the simple intent is to mitigate sheet flow and send the runoff downward directly into the infiltration system. And in this version of infiltration, the all-important filtration occurs typically through sediment and pollutant retention in the voids of the porous paving or subsurface medium.

Alternatively, an infiltration basin can have a vegetated surface. In this case, it is often known as an infiltrating rain garden. Infiltrating rain gardens can be designed to hold water on the surface or underground. Either way, the surface vegetation can create many design opportunities.

Table 3.9. Infiltration basin or trench: Facility that collects, holds, and infiltrates runoff

Goals	Objectives
Reduce pollutant loads in rainwater	Retention
Reduce downstream damage from runoff	Filtration
Capture rain for reuse	Infiltration
Restore or create habitat	

Stormwater Management Accomplished with Infiltration Basins

Infiltration basins fulfill two important stormwater management functions: They capture water to reduce CSO frequency and other downstream impacts, and they recharge groundwater, which is a critical tool in our efforts to restore the site hydrology to predevelopment conditions as closely as possible. But, as stated earlier, if we're recharging natural water systems, we must first reduce pollutants, achieved by contact with plants and soil. Finally, note that infiltration basins can always include an overflow splitter that detains and then discharges excess runoff.

Some Ways to Celebrate Rain with Infiltration Basins

If planted, an infiltration basin can tell the story of rain as resource for flora and fauna (figure 3.50); this message can be clarified and enhanced through signage.

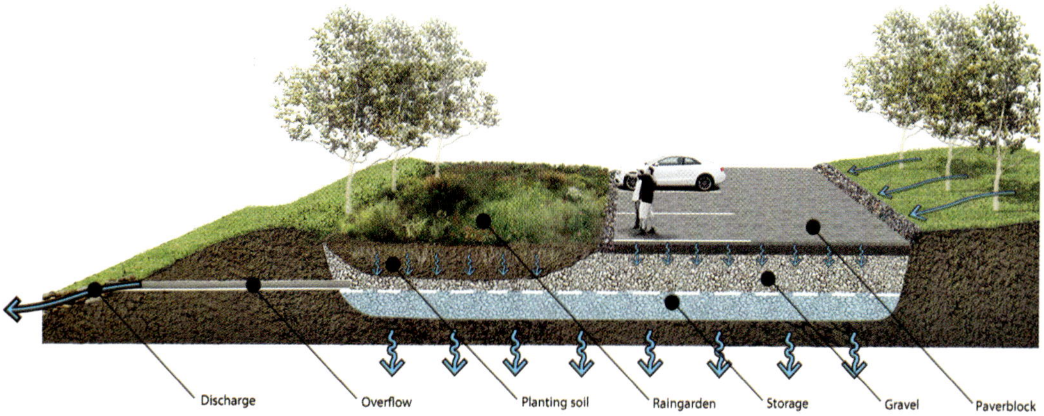

Figure 3.49. An infiltration basin or trench can have a vegetated or a hard surface (diagram: Stuart Echols and Chris Maurer).

If topped with a hard walking or parking surface, an infiltration basin can make many public relations "we care" proclamations. The idea of water infiltration can be clarified even further if the paving material visibly absorbs rain (figure 3.51).

Figure 3.50. At Penn State's arboretum, visitors are invited to cross the lushly planted infiltration basin on a boardwalk bridge; this bridge suggests the basin's task of recharging groundwater (design: MTR Landscape Architects; photograph: Stuart Echols).

Figure 3.51. At the Gwinnett Environmental and Heritage Center, a porous asphalt driving aisle and parking spaces made of pavers set in gravel proclaim the facility's environmental focus, clarified by signage at the parking lot edge (design: The Jaeger Company; photograph: Eliza Pennypacker).

Some Considerations in Designing Infiltration Basins

- Because of their variability in shape, surface treatment, and potential to be located underground, infiltration basins can fit into many sites. They can appear as broad zones or thin strips that can be either planted or paved.
- Because the runoff must be clean, avoid infiltrating in high-pollution zones.
- Make the systems as broad and shallow as possible to disperse recharge effectively.
- Because rain is infiltrating, keep infiltration basins away from structures.
- Take careful note of the subgrade and soils; for example, avoid high water tables, avoid impermeable clays and bedrock, avoid karst, and ensure filtration in highly porous sandy soils.
- In freeze–thaw zones, the subgrade, gravel-filled infiltration basin must be located below the frost line (typically 3 to 4 feet deep).
- Porous paving can clog, so maintenance is essential to keep the voids open.
- Porous paving may be used on sidewalks, parking lots, or driveways and is permissible in some municipalities for public roadways.
- Parking lots are typically responsible for the most runoff volumes in urbanizing areas; therefore, infiltrating parking lots can make a vast difference in fostering sustainable stormwater management.

Rain Garden

A rain garden is a catchall term for a planted, in-ground basin that can fulfill almost all the goals and objectives of sustainable stormwater management, depending on its design and context. Design and construction of a rain garden can be as simple as digging a depression and planting it, or can entail considerable engineering. It all depends on site conditions and design intentions.

Table 3.10. Rain garden: Richly planted depression that collects runoff

Goals	Objectives
Reduce pollutant loads in rainwater	Retention
Reduce downstream damage from runoff	Filtration
Safely move, control, and contain rainwater	Infiltration
Capture rain for reuse	
Restore or create habitat	

Stormwater Management Accomplished with Rain Gardens

A rain garden always retains and biofilters rainwater. If the basin has an in-system overflow splitter (raised drop inlet or perforated pipe), it can detain and filter some or most of the first flush, then discharge subsequent cleaner runoff. If it is unlined, a rain garden can allow rainwater to infiltrate,

Figure 3.52. At its simplest, a rain garden is a "dish" of exuberant plants that accepts runoff from adjacent grass or paving and infiltrates the rain (diagram: Stuart Echols).

and rainwater gathered in a rain garden can even be harvested in a rainwater container for reuse. In addition, the plants and soil can provide microhabitat.

Some Ways to Celebrate Rain with Rain Gardens

Rain gardens are often designed simply to look like colorful, lush gardens; the fact that those plants are in a slightly depressed basin may be the only clue to the rainwater management function of a rain garden (figure 3.53).

Figure 3.53. Rain gardens in the central entry space at Buckman Heights Apartments appear simply as lush plantings edged in boxwood, their rain-holding sunken basins completely hidden (design: Murase Associates; photograph: Stuart Echols).

One way to ensure that people understand the rainwater aspect is to make the water trail to the rain garden very visible, for example, showing that the water is arriving in the rain garden via a noticeable runnel or flume.

Another rain celebration strategy is to convey runoff to a very clear point of entry in the rain garden and plant the garden thickly with rich color and texture so that it tells a clear story of the rain's resource quality for flora and fauna. To emphasize the habitat function, choose plants to attract bees, butterflies, and birds; to emphasize the water function, choose plants that emulate species that grow in or near water (figure 3.54).

One of the strengths of celebrating rain with rain garden design is that it's very easy to express a "we care and want you to know you can do this at home" message; however, one of the challenges is to ensure that viewers realize that this beautiful garden treats rain.

Figure 3.54. Liberty Lands Park demonstrates many rainwater celebration strategies. A cobble runnel carries runoff from the street corner into the park's lushly planted detention basin, delineated by granite edging. This makes a clear statement that street runoff nourishes the garden plants, which in turn provide habitat (designer: Pennsylvania Horticultural Society and CH2MHill; photograph: Stuart Echols).

Some Considerations in Designing Rain Gardens

- A rain garden can be placed in almost any site context, from smallest to largest, most private to most public, and if the native soil infiltrates appropriately, a rain garden can even be created with little or no soil amendment.
- For maximum function, a rain garden should be located in a place where rainwater can be easily collected: near a downspout or in a place that will receive runoff (e.g., near a paved surface to catch sheet flow, at the bottom of a slope).
- Certain rain garden locations should be considered cautiously. If it is close to a structure or in unstable or contaminated soils, for example, a rain garden should be lined.
- Choose plants carefully based on at least two wetness zones. The basin bottom (wet zone) should be planted with vegetation types that tolerate wet, saturated soils; the edges and rim

(upland zone) can be planted with vegetation suitable for moderate to dry conditions with short-term saturation.

- Ensure that the planting is thick and robust. A rain garden with wimpy, intermittent plants won't compel viewers to want one on their own sites, and it will offer too much room for weeds, necessitating more maintenance.
- Consider massing plant types, limiting the diversity of plant types, or planting on a grid to make weeds obvious and the system easier to maintain.
- Consider creating a habitat garden that will attract pollinators.

Bioswale

A bioswale is a gently sloping, planted channel that carries rainwater to a storm sewer, water body, or wet or dry basin, and sometimes additionally into an infiltration system.

Table 3.11. Bioswale: Gently sloped vegetated channel that collects, moves, slows, and filters runoff

Goals	Objectives
Reduce pollutant loads in rainwater	Conveyance
Reduce downstream damage from runoff	Filtration
Safely move, control, and contain rainwater	Infiltration
Capture rain for reuse	

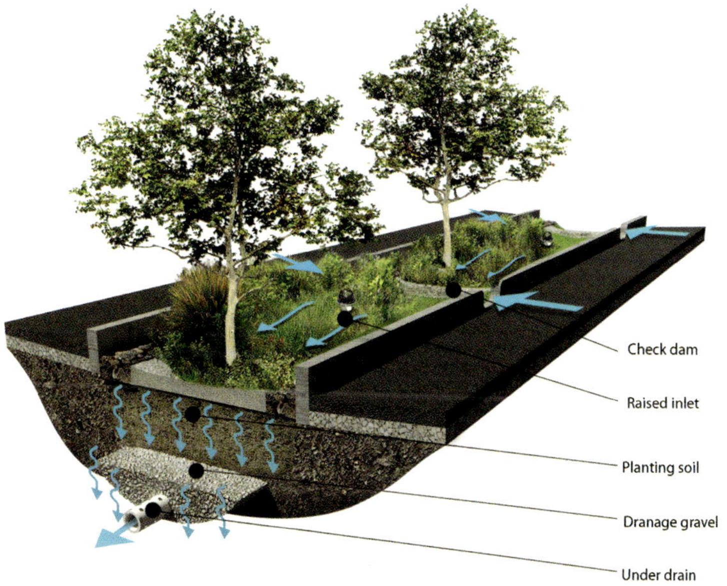

Figure 3.55. A bioswale has the same concept and range of functions as a rain garden, with the addition of moving the water to a destination (diagram: Stuart Echols and Chris Maurer).

Stormwater Management Accomplished with Bioswales

A bioswale is mainly a slow-moving conveyance system, but plantings, soil, and checkdams add pollutant filtration.

A bioswale can be designed to infiltrate, resulting in groundwater recharge and a diminished amount of water discharged downsystem. Overall, a bioswale's primary intent is to capture, hold, filter, or infiltrate first flush. The main difference between a robustly planted bioswale and a rain garden is simply that a bioswale is a linear system that gently slopes to move surface runoff to another destination.

Some Ways to Celebrate Rain with Bioswales

A visible bioswale can contribute to the clarity of the rainwater trail in a stormwater management system. That long conveyance system can tell viewers both where the water is coming from and where it's going (figure 3.56).

Locating bioswales throughout a site design, especially along highly visible, well-traveled routes, can make a statement of commitment to environmental stewardship (figure 3.57).

They can also visibly display the use of rainwater to nourish landscapes and create habitats (figure 3.58).

Figure 3.56. At Pierce County Environmental Services, a 270-foot-long bioswale is lined with river pebble and dotted with driftwood. Community members walking or biking the adjacent path can easily understand this rainwater conveyance and infiltration system and its origin at the building (background) and destination at public playfields (design: Bruce Dees and Associates, SvR Design Company; photograph: Stuart Echols).

Some Considerations in Designing Bioswales

- Space is needed for the bioswale's linear management system. Locations along street rights-of-way, paths, and other high-traveled linear zones are particularly effective for combining effective management with high visibility.
- The functionality of a bioswale is improved if runoff can enter the system along its length, not simply at one end. Accomplish this either by promoting sheet flow or by creating specific points of water entry (e.g., curb cuts along a parking lot).
- A bioswale can be designed to include a series of depressed landscape areas combined with overflow splitters to maximize the capture of first flush runoff.
- The amount of planting in a bioswale can vary from sparse to lush; the more lush the planting,

Figure 3.57. *(left)* At Broadview Green Grid in Seattle (NW 107th Street), a bioswale consisting of tiered basins edges a residential street, proclaiming its function to passersby (design: Seattle Public Utilities; photograph: Stuart Echols).

Figure 3.58. *(right)* Rainwater flows from the left in this photograph through the dark, grate-covered runnel, under the "palmetto cell" sculpture, then falls into the lushly planted bioswale in the foreground (design: RDG Planning and Design; photograph: Eliza Pennypacker).

the more habitat is created and the more biofiltration and evapotranspiration occur.

- A bioswale may contribute to project landscape requirements and project value.
- A bioswale can treat water from all impervious surfaces, from roofs to streets.
- Bioswales must be lined if infiltration is precluded by polluted or urban subsoils.
- Bioswales that are unlined to promote infiltration should not be located directly adjacent to or uphill from structures.
- To control the rate of water movement, bioswales should have checkdams that allow runoff to briefly pool in one area and be filtered before proceeding to the next. Bioswale slopes should be kept low (ideally less than 5 percent); needed grade changes can be easily addressed by vertical water drops to slow and control flow rates.
- Standing water should be limited to about 6 inches and not allowed for more than a few days. Consult local regulations.

Notes

1. U.S. Environmental Protection Agency, "Green Infrastructure," accessed June 7, 2014, http://water.epa.gov/infrastructure/greeninfrastructure/index.cfm.

PART 3.3

The ARD Utility Axioms

Sustainable stormwater management is a complex process and requires both creativity and accurate quantitative analysis. We offer a set of axioms to keep in mind as you plan and design artful rainwater sites.

Axiom 1: Always Slow It Down, Spread It Out, Soak It In

Create designs that use every opportunity to slow runoff movement across a site, disperse it, ideally into many shallow holding areas, and promote infiltration and groundwater recharge. These techniques cumulatively provide a strategy to return site hydrology to predevelopment conditions as much as possible. The designer's goal is to put every site surface to work to mimic what happens to rain in a natural vegetated landscape.

Example Project: High Point, a 120-Acre, New Urbanist, Retrofitted Residential Community in West Seattle, Washington

The stormwater management system for each neighborhood block at High Point is site-specific and entirely focused on the axiom "always slow it down, spread it out, soak it in." On each block a variety of runoff management strategies respond to the developed and natural site context. Cumulatively, they intercept the rainwater in sequence to slow and minimize the runoff; the management types are spread throughout the block, and all of them emphasize both filtration and infiltration.

If we begin at the roof downspout, we find two alternative strategies to move the water into the landscape, each used in a different context. In some spots, conveyance furrows take runoff to rain gardens; in others, below-grade perforated pipes send rain to pop-up emitters that water rain gardens. Any remaining runoff that sheet flows between building and sidewalk on the block is directed to dispersal trenches along the sidewalks. Some of the sidewalks and driveways are porous; sheet flow from many of the nonporous surfaces drains to the natural draining swales that line 4 miles of street right-of-way.

In sum, an array of stormwater management strategies on every block carries rain in different directions, both slowing it and spreading it out, and ensures maximum infiltration. An illustrative graphic by the civil engineering and landscape architecture firm clarifies the concept (figure 3.59).

Axiom 2: Combine Different Management Systems

In any given project, the designer should consider the value of combining a variety of stormwater management techniques to accomplish as many utility goals as possible. Through thoughtful combinations (and backup strategies), the designer can mitigate most, or even all, offsite runoff quantity and quality problems.

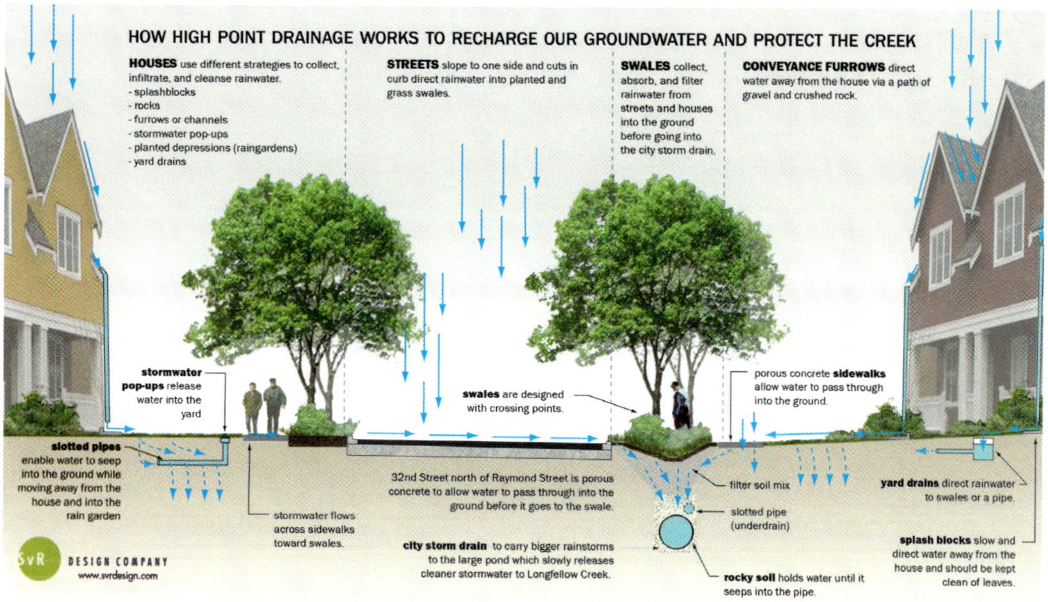

Figure 3.59. This diagram shows the many ways that the High Point stormwater management strategy slows, spreads, and infiltrates rain (design: Mithun; diagram: SvR Design Company).

Example Projects: Stata Center Outwash Basin at MIT, Cambridge, Massachusetts; and Pierce County Environmental Services Facility, Chambers Creek, Washington

We present two examples of this axiom because the first—Stata Center—is highly engineered, and although it remains one of the most complex and fascinating systems we've encountered, such an elaborate gray infrastructure approach may not be appropriate in every context. Pierce County Environmental Services offers a more traditional green infrastructure combination set of management techniques that is also exemplary. The two together suggest the range that is possible in responding to Axiom 2.

At the Stata Center Outwash Basin, a serious CSO problem led to a brilliant, multifaceted stormwater management solution. Rainwater is collected from three buildings via pipes; some goes directly into an underground detention vault after being cleansed by a vortex separator; the rest, along with runoff from surrounding paved surfaces, goes into the landscaped dry detention basin known as the outwash basin. Rainwater in the outwash basin is biofiltered through plants and crushed stone and recirculated by solar-powered pumps, both to continue its cleansing and to irrigate the planted basin. Remaining runoff from the basin joins the other runoff in the belowgrade vault, where a 5-day supply for toilet flushing and irrigation is maintained. Stormwater pumps and level controls send excess water from large storms to the Vassar Street force mains. According to Steve Benz, the lead engineer on the project, this complex system reduces peak rate of flow by 90 percent (figure 3.60).

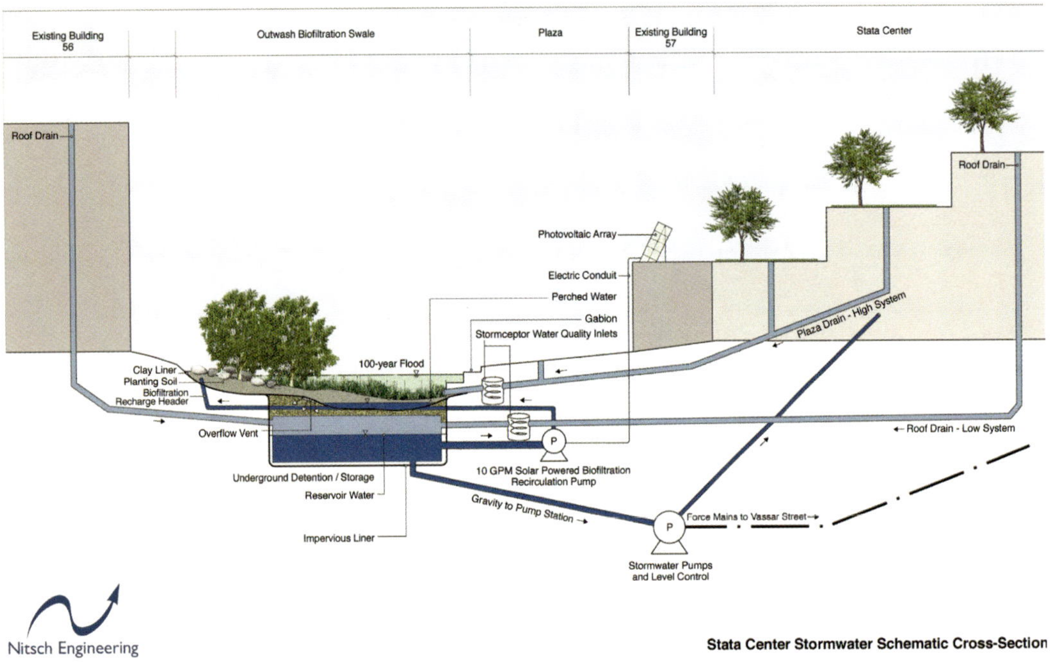

Figure 3.60. This diagram illustrates the technologically complex combination of management systems at work at MIT's Stata Center (design: OLIN and Judith Nitsch Engineering, Inc.; diagram: Judith Nitsch Engineering, Inc.).

At Pierce County Environmental Services, wastewater and stormwater management offices are strategically combined with facilities for public education and recreation. The site design stealthily tells a story to the public about environmentally responsible stormwater management while they have fun. Here, a series of diverse management techniques stretch along a walking, biking, and jogging path, ensuring that community members on their way to the ball fields will encounter all facets of the water system. Roof runoff at the northwest corner of the building falls from a scupper into a basin with a spiral incised in its concrete; rainwater spirals from this basin into an adjacent wetland that biofilters and detains rainwater while providing habitat. Runoff from the wetland then flows into a 270-foot-long bioswale between a parking lot on one side and the major recreation trail on the other. Along its length, curb cuts admit runoff from the parking lot. The bioswale filters and infiltrates much runoff, then conveys the rest to three flow splitters. Here, valves direct some runoff to a grass-lined swale and some to a gravel-lined swale (water quality in both is being monitored to determine which is more effective at mitigating pollutants), while a sign proclaims that a third valve is unused, "awaiting future technologies." From the swales, all remaining runoff flows to infiltration basins near playing fields (figure 3.61).

In both of these stormwater management systems, a variety of techniques are used in sequence to accomplish a wide array of ARD goals and objectives.

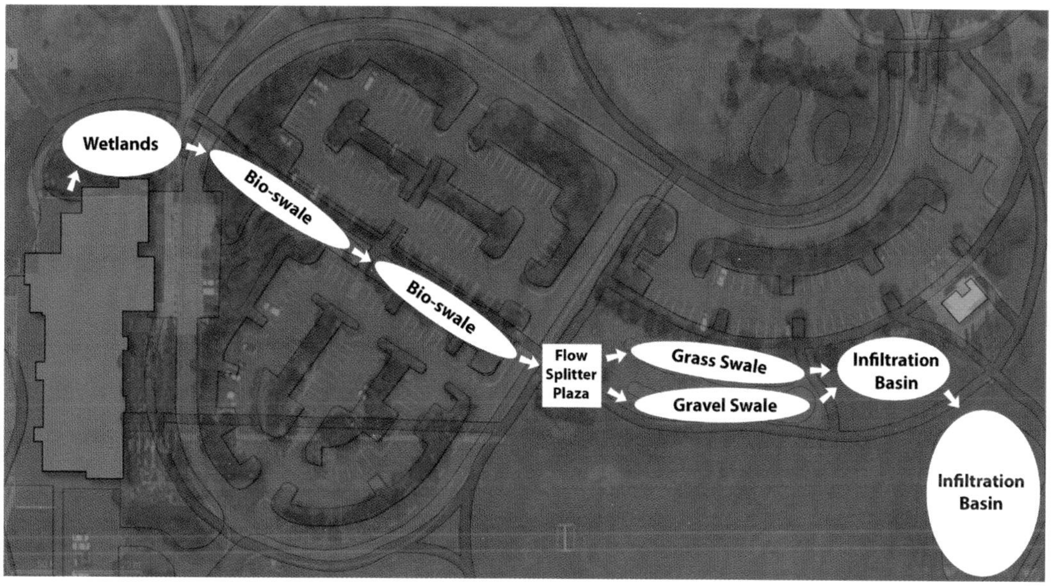

Figure 3.61. At Pierce County Environmental Services, a sequential array of stormwater management systems accomplishes infiltration in various ways (design: Bruce Dees & Associates, SvR Design Company; diagram: Stuart Echols and Lacey Goldberg).

Axiom 3: Build Distributed, Redundant Stormwater Systems

Designers should always remember that multiple and redundant techniques distributed around a site increase the stormwater management system's safety and reliability and reduce the chance of system failure. Many small facilities are more effective than one big facility because if any of the small facilities fails or needs maintenance, others still function while that facility is repaired, rebuilt, or updated. This strategy also creates the opportunity to present a site-wide system of landscape celebrations of rain.

Example Project: Stephen Epler Hall Courtyard at Portland State University, Portland, Oregon

The stormwater management system at Epler Hall presents an effective example of multiple distributed systems. Runoff from 12,000 square feet of roof falls via downspouts into four splash boxes that briefly detain it. Small spouts in the base of each box spill rainwater into runnels that carry it to biopaddies: sunken, planted basins that biofilter the runoff. Perforated pipe in the bottom of each biopaddy sends most remaining rainwater into a belowgrade cistern, where it is treated for bacteria with ultraviolet light. Ten thousand gallons of water at a time are stored in the cistern for reuse in first-floor toilets and for irrigation, while excess water from large storms goes to the combined sewer system. In addition to site-wide distribution of the stormwater treatment, this design offers some useful redundancies. First, if the spouts in the splash boxes clog, pipes below the plaza can carry rainwater to the biopaddies;

second, if the biopaddies overflow in a large storm, runnels extend from one biopaddy to the next, moving excess water to the final biopaddy, which discharges to the sewer system; and, finally, if the cistern fills or fails, excess water goes straight to the sewer system (figure 3.62).

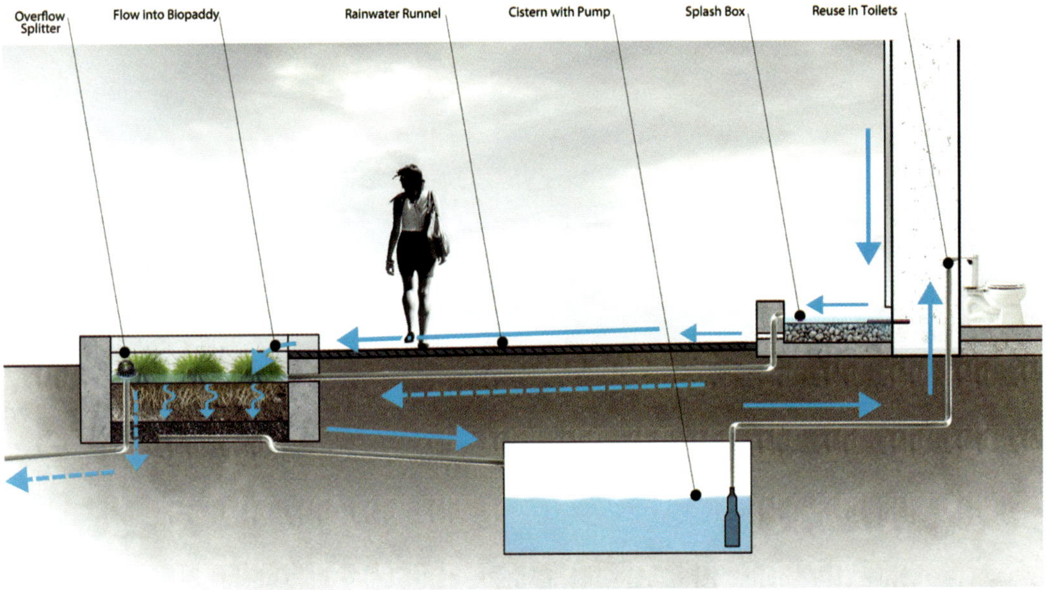

Figure 3.62. At Stephen Epler Hall, the system is layered with backup strategies (shown with dotted arrows) to preclude failure (design: Atlas Landscape Architecture, KPFF Consulting Engineers, Mithun; diagram: Stuart Echols and Chris Maurer).

Axiom 4: Use Landscape, Not Pipes, Wherever Possible

Designers should reduce reliance on pipes. Keeping stormwater systems on the surface in green infrastructure increases the opportunity for evaporation, filtration, and infiltration, creates systems that are easier to monitor and maintain, and provides more opportunities to artfully integrate stormwater management into landscape design.

Example Project: New Seasons Market at Seven Corners, Portland Oregon

Division Street in Portland, Oregon was slated for an upgrade from 12th Avenue to 50th, and in this part of the city, the existing sewer system was undersized, resulting in frequent nuisance flooding and CSOs. Experts in Portland's Bureau of Environmental Services suggested to the city's transportation group that this could be a good opportunity to install and test a green infrastructure demonstration on a heavy arterial road with lots of polluted runoff. At the same time, the existing small supermarket between 19th and 20th avenues was converting to a natural foods store; the supermarket site plan, already well along, used conventional gray infrastructure to manage stormwater. The Bureau of Environmental Services (BES) team convinced the market's owners to shift gears, and the BES undertook the redesign. Throughout, the idea was to make all runoff drain into the landscape, putting the landscape to work with some very simple strategies. Along Division Street, for example, they retrofitted the south side of the street by cutting a series of rectangular holes in the existing sidewalk; the resulting openings were filled with soil and plants, and curb cuts were created to route street runoff to water each of these new planters. Ninety percent of the site landscape was reconceived to manage stormwater. This low-tech green infrastructure approach to stormwater management succeeds in removing significant runoff from roads and lots and putting it into the landscape, where it becomes a resource for the plants (figure 3.63).

Figure 3.63. On Division Street in Portland, the sidewalk was modified to create rectangular planters, with curb cuts directing rain into the planters from the street gutter (design: Portland Bureau of Environmental Services; photograph: Stuart Echols).

Each of these axioms, separately and together, promotes the separation and dispersal of green infrastructure stormwater management systems throughout a site. This is the most effective way to divide and conquer runoff, both to manage first flush and to mimic predevelopment rain management. This is an essential characteristic of sustainable stormwater management: Use the entire site!

Using the entire site may at first seem problematic, especially if the designer is confronted by an urban site without much open space. But we propose that, in fact, "use the entire site" poses an exciting opportunity to make the ordinance-required landscape work as a stormwater management system. Note, too, that if the landscape functions for stormwater management, it won't be "value engineered" out of the project; instead, the landscape becomes a necessity for the project and a means to sustainably manage rain. This is really the key to ARD, because if the stormwater management occurs in green infrastructure distributed around the site, why *not* make it visibly celebrate rain?

Before we end this section, we want to include an important idea from Tom Liptan, retired environmental specialist at Portland's BES.

Axiom 5: Get Your Feet Wet with Small, Nonthreatening, Reversible Interventions

According to Tom Liptan, a great way to begin ARD, whether for you as designer or for a client who's unfamiliar with ARD, is to create "small, non-threatening, reversible" interventions. Rather than waiting for the perfect design opportunity and the perfect client to begin your foray into ARD, try this: Start with something small and inexpensive. You don't always need to shoot for the moon with a complex system—make it simple and nonthreatening (both for you and for the client), and make it reversible, so that it can be easily removed if it doesn't work out.

Example Project: Northeast Siskiyou Green Street

Tom Liptan and Kevin Perry of Portland's BES had an idea: Design curb extensions for a leafy residential street to show homeowners the value of green infrastructure. The lushly planted bumpouts would not only cleanse and infiltrate rain but also calm traffic and beautify the block. But residents were resistant, especially to the idea of losing parking spaces. The result was a humble, inexpensive design (two parallel basins, each 50 feet long and 7 feet wide, costing $20,000 total) that the BES appended to the existing curb so that it could be easily removed if unsuccessful. That never proved necessary (in fact, other neighborhoods now queue up for stormwater curb extensions on their streets), but the admittedly exploratory character of the design created a level of comfort for all—both designers and homeowners. And the remarkable reality is that this humble project has been copied nationwide, because it can really be done anywhere. This "small, non-threatening, reversible" strategy—and this specific design example's remarkable success—make the jump to ARD a hop rather than a leap, for both designer and client (figure 3.64).

Figure 3.64. Note that the old street edge curbing (dark concrete) was retained to facilitate reversion to the old system in case the curb extension experiment (light concrete) proved unsuccessful. The "small, non-threatening, reversible" approach at NE Siskiyou made this ARD a palatable risk for designer and client (design: Portland Bureau of Environmental Services; photograph: Stuart Echols).

Conclusion

We hope that this chapter helps you realize that a wide range of possibilities exists for designers to create sustainable stormwater management systems. We further hope that you will take to heart three fundamental ideas from this section of the book:

- Sustainable stormwater management begins with site design.
- "Use the entire site" is a key starting point for sustainable stormwater management and provides the opportunity for ARD.
- Green infrastructure offers a wide array of stormwater management techniques and the opportunity to make the site landscape *work* and visibly celebrate rain.

4. Case Studies of Artful Rainwater Design

Overview of the Case Studies

Imagine this scenario: You're a designer with a solid regional reputation. One day, the director of campus construction at a local community college calls you with a serious problem: The college and its parking lot sit uphill from a nearby commercial area; the business owners are threatening to sue the college, because in large rain events, storm runoff from the college property floods their building basements. Worse yet, because they have combined sewers in this town, the flooding sometimes results in sewage backup in those buildings. It's a simple enough problem to solve: You could put in one of those turf pits of a detention basin, but then you think, "That's a lot of land to use, probably surrounded by a chain link fence for liability protection, right at a town–gown edge. What kind of a place, and what kind of a town–gown relationship message, would *that* create?" You mull it over for a while, and then suddenly the answer comes: The college doesn't have a stormwater problem, it has a rainwater *opportunity*.

You realize that, rather than a detention basin that treats rain as a waste product to be avoided, you can create an educational rain garden that helps college students—an idealistic group of potential environmentalists—understand that rain is a resource. You can control first-flush-only intake of the runoff by curb cuts; you can mark the rainwater trail that carries water into the tiered sequence of detention basins with white river pebble so that visitors can easily see that there's a path here—a path for *rain*. You can robustly plant the stepped basins so that anyone can realize that the rain waters the vegetation. When the basins fill, a weir in each basin's checkdam can let water overflow to the next level; the sequence of weirs can spiral down to the lowest level, where a raised drop inlet can show that overflow is diverted downstream. And, in this placemaking, you help the college convey a clear "we care" message to the town through a beautiful, educational, stormwater problem-solving landscape. This is Artful Rainwater Design.

Of course, one of the reasons that you realized this design opportunity is that you already knew of some ARDs that had inspired you and made you realize that any stormwater problem is truly a rainwater opportunity.

When we began to study this topic, we realized that an important service we could provide to designers would be to tell the stories of useful precedents to inspire and inform future designs. So we knew that this book had to include a section of case studies. Since we began our study of ARDs in 2005, we've found close to one hundred ARDs in publications and visited more than fifty nationwide. So what distinguishes the twenty presented in this chapter from the rest?

Celebration of rain was our number-one criterion for case study choice: Each of these projects tells a visual story that makes visitors aware of the importance of rain—to life, to regional character, to the earth itself. In fact, this is a fundamental criterion of Artful Rainwater Design: An ARD is not just a beautiful work of green infrastructure; by definition, an ARD *promotes awareness of rain as a resource* through an educational or entertaining experience.

Geographic variety was also important to our selection. As mentioned in the introduction to this book, our study has been limited to the United States because of regulatory and aesthetic preference particulars here that differ from other countries. But within the United States we sought to provide at least one example from a range of regions with different climatic conditions, from the arid Southwest to the frigid Northeast to the balmy Southeast. We did this in response to questions we've heard (which might be running through the reader's mind about now) that we characterize as "Yes, but-isms," as in, "Yes, but that won't work in *my* area." We especially find this reaction to works in the Northwest, often framed as, "Yes, but that's *Portland*!" (see our rebuttal to this doubt in part 5). And so, the reader should know at this chapter's outset that, yes, a large number of the case study ARDs are found in Portland, Oregon and the Seattle, Washington area, but this is with good reason. At the same time, we strive to offer projects that respond to a range of other questions: "Yes, but what about climates that freeze?" or, "Yes, but what about areas that experience drought, then flash floods?" The geographic range is far from all inclusive—there are only twenty case projects in the section, after all—but every effort was made to provide useful variety.

Variety of project type and context was a criterion that proved much harder to meet. Fully half of our case studies are found in educational institutions, with nearly all of them higher education. This is no surprise: Colleges and universities these days often seek to be leaders in sustainability, and the educational opportunities provided by ARDs on campuses are truly exciting. The other largest category of project context is public works by municipalities or public–private partnerships. Although the "Yes, but" crowd may chime in here, we see this trend as heartening: A rapidly growing number of municipal departments and officials are willing to test ARDs as a strategy. And the really good news about the plethora of ARDs in higher education and public works is that these owners are often willing to undertake postconstruction monitoring of the rainwater management efficacy of these ARDs, which is incredibly helpful to designers who want to cajole their clients or municipalities into taking the ARD plunge. A much smaller group of case studies is (not surprisingly) found in private development, where developers are only beginning to realize the public relations value-added benefits of ARD. And although ARDs in residential design may actually be abundant, they're much harder to find; in fact, regrettably, none of the case studies in this book is a private residence (although we hope that this ARD type might be the topic of a later book).

The presentation in this section of our "top twenty" ARDs is organized in a way we hope the reader will find helpful: We've clustered the designs according to achievement of one amenity goal that we find particularly noteworthy in each: education, recreation, safety, public relations, or aesthetic richness. This way, the reader curious about great ways to achieve safety can flip right to that section. Note, though, that our desire to place an equal number of case studies in each of these categories means that the reader can easily take issue with our decisions ("Is recreation really the main amenity goal achieved at the University of Florida Southwest Recreation Center, or is it education?"). In fact, at the beginning of each case study, we offer simple icons to show the full set of both utility and amenity goals achieved in this design. As readers will see, all the case studies accomplish all the ARD amenity goals, at least to some extent.

Before turning the page to enter the case studies, note that each case study presents a consistent set of information:

- An initial photo that illustrates the amenity goal of that case study section, as achieved by this design
- A set of icons that present "thumbnail information" on all the amenity and utility goals achieved by this design
- Basic "fact sheet" data: date, size, location, owner, designers
- Background information on project rationale and intentions
- Brief text explanations of all of the utility goals addressed in this project
- Brief text explanations of all of the amenity goals addressed in this project
- A set of interesting facts about the project
- A brief bibliography of sources

Please know that the thumbnail sketch of each project is far too brief: Each has a much greater story to tell. We simply hope that these abbreviated stories provide useful information and inspiration about Artful Rainwater Design, and we encourage you to use this book as an initial resource for your own work, seeking more detail as you desire.

CASE STUDY

Arizona State University Polytechnic Campus, Mesa, Arizona

- Reduce pollutant loads in rainwater
- Reduce downstream damage from runoff
- Safely move, control, and contain rainwater
- Capture rain for reuse
- Restore or create habitat

- **EDUCATION**
- Recreation
- Safety
- Public relations
- Aesthetic richness

Figure 4.1. This campus design strives to educate about the unique water conditions of the Sonoran Desert in five different manifestations. Here, the Orchard Canal Court recalls traditional irrigation strategies (design: Ten Eyck Landscape Architects, Inc.; photograph: Bill Timmeman).

Date: 2008

Size: 21 acres

Location: 7001 East Williams Field Road, Mesa, Arizona

Owner: Arizona State University

Designers: Ten Eyck Landscape Architects, Inc., Lake|Flato Architects

Background

In 1996, Arizona State University (ASU) established a polytechnic campus at the decommissioned Williams Air Force Base in Mesa, about 30 miles from Phoenix. The existing conditions were less than optimal: acres of asphalt prone to flooding, characterized by the design team in their national American Society of Landscape Architects (ASLA) award submission as having an "oppressive, overpaved ambience." But ASU had aspirations for this campus: Starting with 1,000 students, by 2006 they had more than 6,500, with plans to reach 10,000 by 2010 in forty degree-granting programs. To reach their goals, ASU needed not only more academic space; they sorely needed an attractive, forward-looking campus identity. Although the university's site design budget of $5 million may seem large, it had to cover every aspect of this ambitious project: demolition, utilities, irrigation, hardscape, and planting.

The result of this creative design is a campus of five buildings, four courtyards, and a pedestrian mall that celebrates its unique desert context—and water. As the design team stated in their ASLA award submission, "We reinvented what a campus could be in the unique region of the Sonoran desert which only receives 7" of rainfall a year." Anyone familiar with the desert Southwest knows that rainfall is infrequent, but when it comes, it's a deluge. Consequently, arroyos meander the natural landscape; these riverbeds are most often dry, but locals know to avoid them after rain events because of the likelihood of torrential water flows. And so the resulting design addresses stormwater by creating a campus pedestrian spine along a designed arroyo that gathers and filters rain from buildings; footbridges crossing the arroyo's "tributary" canals provide entry into four academic courtyards of differing character, each based on a different regional landscape and water phenomenon. The whole is a cohesive, vibrant campus that connects students and faculty to each other and to their desert context.

Utility

The stormwater management concept here is capture, cleanse, and infiltrate. When this site was a military base, 14 acres of asphalt road and sidewalks caused significant flooding. The former asphalt road spine has been transformed into a permeable, water-receiving arroyo that manages all onsite rainwater, paralleling a porous, decomposed granite pedestrian mall. Runoff is gathered from rooftops and hardscapes in each of four courtyards along the arroyo: the Orchard Canal Irrigation Court, the Desert Seep Court, the Cottonwood Sponge Court, and the Tinaja Performance Court. This rain is then piped to four acequias (dry, planted canals) that promote infiltration and, in large rain events, feed the designed arroyo. Rainwater is slowed in the arroyo by a series of basins that further promote infiltration, and in torrential rain events, a retention basin at the northwest campus corner holds and infiltrates remaining runoff.

Both the arroyo and the acequias that feed it are planted with native vegetation; consequently, runoff is biofiltered throughout before it infiltrates.

This stormwater management strategy eliminates all offsite discharge for events up to the 100-year storm level by capturing and infiltrating rainwater in the acequias, arroyo, and basins.

This simple system presents some ingenious safety measures. First, rooftop runoff is piped to retention basins adjacent to each courtyard; only basin overflow is conveyed on to the acequia. In essence this system functions as an overflow splitter that manages a great deal of runoff without further conveyance; when a retention basin fills, the extra runoff flows out to the connected acequia. Then, within the arroyo, four detention basins slow rainwater and promote infiltration. And if rainfall exceeds the arroyo's capacity, it is gathered in a retention basin on the west end.

Rainwater both nourishes the native plants in this design and recharges precious groundwater through the site-wide infiltration system.

All plantings (except pistachio trees in the Orchard Canal Court) are native, drought-tolerant plants. The arroyo was planted with salvaged desert trees, native shrubs, and cacti. The result is an indigenous landscape that provides habitat for local fauna and connection to the regional landscape for humans.

Figure 4.2. Concrete chunks recycled from the former Air Force base form the basin edge and channel bottom, creating an abstracted arroyo streambed for ephemeral water (design: Ten Eyck Landscape Architects, Inc.; photograph: Bill Timmeman).

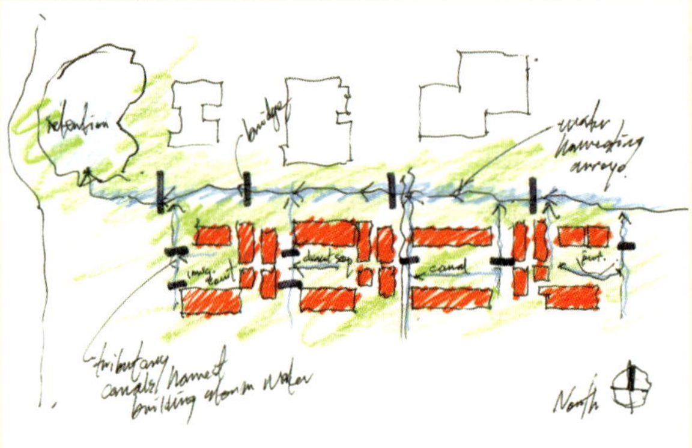

Figure 4.3. Christie Ten Eyck's diagram explains the stormwater system: Water in each court flows to an acequia, which functions as a tributary to the arroyo. Overflow from the arroyo stormwater spine flows to a retention basin at the northwest end of campus (design: Ten Eyck Landscape Architects, Inc.; diagram: Christie Ten Eyck).

Amenity

It may seem odd that this desert landscape uses water as its theme. As the design team explained in their ASLA award submission, "Some might say 'why is storm water important when you get rain so infrequently?' Our response is that it is even more important because the path of ephemeral water in the desert—the arroyo—is the sustaining life force of the desert and urban dwellers that call it their home." In fact, the water theme goes far beyond the arroyo into four courtyards, where a different desert water condition is presented in each. Cumulatively, the landscape offers a varied but unified experience of water in this unique desert environment.

Each building courtyard presents a different desert water theme, most of which relate to the surrounding building functions:

- The Morrison School of Agribusiness surrounds the Orchard Canal Court, where a grid of pistachio trees is watered by traditional irrigation canals, recalling local agricultural heritage.
- The School of Science and Technology is adjacent to the lushly planted, shady Desert Riparian Wetland Court, where a living wall and riparian plantings watered by an irrigation seep recall the wet, green natural environment found in a desert canyon.
- The Cottonwood Sponge Court, planted with its namesake tree and other riparian native vegetation, is designed as a shallow retention basin that illustrates the water-sucking character of these desert-dwelling plants.
- The Tinaja Performance Court, adjacent to the School of Education, Humanities, and the Arts, presents a small abstraction of a *tinaja*, a natural depression in a rock canyon that temporarily holds rain after a storm. This designed *tinaja* discharges its water into a channel that defines the edge of a lawn used for performances.

In all, a variety of water conditions of the desert are presented throughout this campus, providing extensive educational opportunities in this academic environment.

All of the varied Artful Rainwater Design gestures here are front and center, providing many opportunities to see, pass by, sit near, touch, and enjoy. And the design's thematic focus on presentation of water in its varied desert conditions results in many different experiences, from walking along the water-conveying arroyo to finding shady, wet respite in the Desert Riparian Wetland Court.

Footbridges carry pedestrians over the arroyo and acequias, suggesting that these bioswales are off limits (although their gentle slopes and shallow depressions don't pose danger, especially when dry—which is most of the time). Irrigation channels in the Orchard Canal Court are narrow and filled with river pebbles; steel grating at key crossing points renders them even more safe.

The public relations messages here are clear and smart. First is the obvious, "We care; we're environmentally responsible and want you to learn about stormwater." This is achieved not only by the varied desert water theme and focus on water in every outdoor space but also in the design's transformation of a flood-prone, impervious military base into this pedestrian-oriented statement of water management in the desert. This forward-looking campus transformation also proclaims, "We are smart, resourceful, and clever." In addition to repurposing existing buildings, even the old impervious paving was broken up and reused in gabion walls, benches, and other landscape elements.

This design is too complex to effectively explain all the compositional characteristics, but briefly, a small water source becomes a focal point in various courts, appropriately suggesting water's rarity and resource value in the desert. Of course the line of water conveyance is important throughout to recall traditional canals and natural water courses; the texture and color of desert vegetation, rock, rusting steel bridges and grates, all speak of the region; and the variety of water presentations unified by the "water as resource" idea is both compositionally stimulating and thematically consistent.

Of Note

- Ten Eyck's original intent included capturing air conditioner condensate and directing it into the stormwater management system water features, a strategy used frequently by this firm to sustainably address both types of "runoff" in southwestern landscapes.
- The original idea was to harvest stormwater and condensate in cisterns and to pump it to all water features; as Ten Eyck admits, "When parts of the country get no rain it is hard to talk clients into these active [pumped] systems."

Sources

The American Institute of Architects, "ASU Polytechnic Academic District," AIA Top Ten 2010, accessed December 3, 2013, http://www.aiatopten.org/node/34.

ASLA, "Honor Award: Arizona State University Polytechnic Campus—New Academic Complex," 2012 ASLA Professional Design Awards: General Design, accessed December 2, 2013, http://www.asla.org/2012awards/199.html.

Ten Eyck, Christie, 2014, personal communication with the authors.

Ten Eyck Landscape Architects, "Academic Complex at ASU Polytechnic Campus," n.d., accessed December 15, 2013, http://www.teneyckla.com/projects/academic/arizona-state-university-polytechnic-campus-academic-complex/.

U.S. LEED Green Building Council, "Arizona State University Polytechnic Buildings: Made for the Mesa," 2009, accessed December 15, 2013, www.lakeflato.com/documents/asu-leed.pdf.

International Student Center Rain Garden, Kansas State University, Manhattan, Kansas (Flint Hills Ecoregion)

- Reduce pollutant loads in rainwater
- Reduce downstream damage from runoff
- Safely move, control, and contain rainwater
- Capture rain for reuse
- Restore or create habitat
- **EDUCATION**
- Recreation
- Safety
- Public relations
- Aesthetic richness

Figure 4.4. This garden educates about rain not only in the physical design, but also through its engagement of classes in design, construction, and monitoring, as well as in its website full of helpful rain garden information (design: Department of Landscape Architecture/Regional & Community Planning, Kansas State University; presentation board: Lee Skabelund, Jeremy Merrill, Aarthi Padmanabhan).

Date: March–June, 2007

Size: Approximately 2,500 square feet

Location: Claflin Road and Mid-Campus Drive, Kansas State, Manhattan, Kansas

Owner: Kansas State University

Designers: Department of Landscape Architecture/Regional & Community Planning, Kansas State University

Background

The Flint Hills of Kansas form an ecoregion of classic rolling prairies, and they're under duress. At least in urbanizing areas of the state, runoff is typically piped straight to surface water bodies, resulting in erosion as well as sediment and pollution deposition. At the same time, groundwater is tapped for potable and irrigation usage, with little returning to recharge groundwater sources. And so, faced with a micro-version of this statewide problem on their campus, Kansas State decided to be creative. An ambitious partnership of faculty, students, and local professionals collaborated to create a demonstration project that shows Kansans, from homeowners to municipal leaders, how they can address stormwater management in more environmentally responsible ways.

The site-specific problem to be addressed: untreated stormwater from buildings, paved surfaces, and lawns piped straight to Campus Creek, resulting in its degradation. One of the stormwater contributors, Kansas State's International Student Center (ISC), had silt-filled infiltration areas, resulting in roof runoff ponding in front of the building, then eroding a slope and informal pathway on its way to Campus Creek. Associate professor Lee Skabelund and others in the Department of Landscape Architecture/Regional & Community Planning saw this as an opportunity to meld stormwater management goals into a learning experience with a tangible product, because Kansas State has committed to creating a more sustainable campus, including sustainable stormwater management. They took advantage of WaterLINK, a program that provided mini-grants for service learning projects partnering faculty and students at Kansas colleges and universities with local communities to undertake projects addressing water issues. The result is a demonstration rain garden at the ISC, designed, implemented, and managed by faculty, staff, and students (with a lot of assistance from donors and volunteers). As stated in voluminous documentation, the project "strategically addresses a significant hurdle to integrating natural stormwater management systems within the urban fabric—namely, the lack of public knowledge of and appreciation for the function and design of these systems—by integrating art, architecture, ecology, hydrology, and people."

Utility

The basic stormwater management concept at the ISC Rain Garden is capture, cleanse, and infiltrate. Most importantly, the garden is designed to address the two most pressing stormwater management issues in the Flint Hills ecoregion: surface water degradation and the need for groundwater recharge. The resulting system is simple: Roof runoff from the ISC "Taiwan Wing" drops from three scuppers into three artistic bowls sitting on reclaimed limestone splash pads, and water overflows from the bowls into the first basin of a two-basin rain garden. Large limestone planks with gaps between them make up a checkdam and weir system to control rainwater moving from the first basin to the second. During very large storms, runoff also flows from the back of the Taiwan Wing along a wide gravel path into the lower rain garden basin. Rooftop water from parts of two other buildings also flows into the garden on the north side, moving through a permeable pathway made of cut limestone (salvaged from a local stoneyard) and washed gravel. And at the west side of the lower basin, a level spreader disperses any overflow onto a lawn to minimize impact on Campus Creek, roughly 70 feet to the west.

The rain garden's two basins and level spreader slow runoff twice, permitting sediment and other pollutant deposition. Additionally, rainwater is biofiltered everywhere in this design.

To reduce degradation of Campus Creek, infiltration is used as extensively as possible both within the rain garden and within two pathways of porous paving. The design reduces runoff volumes and pollutant and sediment loads entering Campus Creek. Observations indicate that most storm events of 2 inches or less can be captured and infiltrated in less than 12 hours (but this naturally depends on the saturation of the soil in the rain garden at any given time).

The rain garden basins were sized to fit with the site rather than for a specific design storm. Overflow from large rain events gently disperses across the lower portion of the adjacent lawn thanks to the level spreader at the rain garden's west edge.

Visual observations conducted from 2008 to 2013 indicate that the rain garden both collects and infiltrates nearly all runoff from its collection area (the Taiwan Wing roof, portions of two other rooftops, and some surrounding landscape) for storms up to 2 inches in depth. Observations also indicated that, within the first year and a half, all stormwater remaining within the basins infiltrated in less than 24

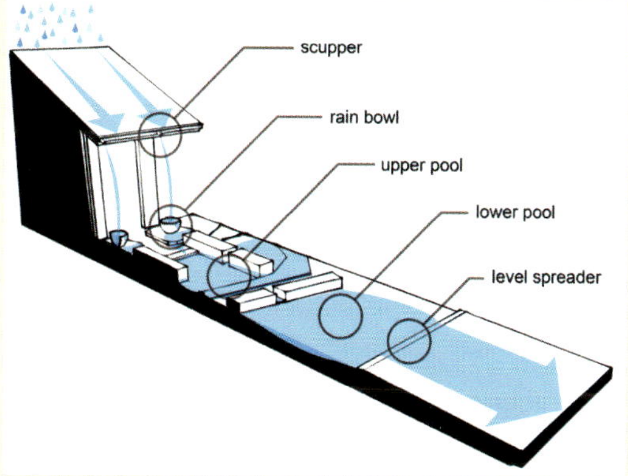

Figure 4.5. *(left)* This drawing explains the system, from roof to scupper to rain bowl to two-celled retention and infiltration system. Overflow from large rain events spreads across the lawn via level spreader (design: Department of Landscape Architecture/Regional & Community Planning, Kansas State University; diagram: Jeremy Merrill).

Figure 4.6. *(right)* Three scuppers spew water into the first infiltration basin (design: Department of Landscape Architecture/Regional & Community Planning, Kansas State University; photograph: Lee Skabelund).

hours, and water is rarely seen in the two basins for more than a few hours. More thorough infiltration testing may be done in the future.

The garden was planted with many species of native perennial flowers and grasses, including those adapted to dry prairie, wet prairie, wetland, and riparian conditions. Green rush, the one true wetland plant used as an experiment, has largely disappeared from the basins. Sedges and wild blue iris (native to eastern Kansas) are abundant in the shady, mesic upper basin. Pollinators are very abundant late spring to fall.

Amenity

This rain garden is so simple yet so enlightening. It is a modest, beautiful garden on a university campus that informs those who see it, those who worked to create it, and others who learn of its many benefits on the "K-State Rain-Garden Design–Build Project" website.

In this particular ARD, education is multifaceted:

- First, there's the garden itself, which clearly communicates that roof runoff is a resource for the Flint Hills ecoregion (visibly nourishing the native rain garden landscape): Roof runoff falls from three scuppers to three bowls, then overflows to the garden's first basin between three limestone planks. The perpendicular limestone checkdam promotes ponding in the first basin, then allows overflow to move into the second basin through gaps between the large, linear limestone planks.
- In both basins, water visibly spreads, ponds, and soaks in. And, if it's not self-evident, a nearby sign explains the basic concept: rainwater collection for reuse in the native garden. In sum, the rainwater trails and garden function are very clear, but in this particular project, there's a great deal more education at work.
- The process was just as important as the garden product: involvement of stormwater experts, local professionals, and faculty, staff, and students in workshops where they could learn from one another; the incomparable student experience of a service-learning design–build ARD project, resulting in their practical knowledge of what ARD entails; and the engagement of faculty and students in at least five different courses (including sculpture, which resulted in the three custom-designed rain-receiving bowls).
- Equally significant are the follow-up products, including postconstruction monitoring that has involved faculty, staff, students, and professionals, and a range of reports, plus a guidebook on rain gardens for homeowners—all found on a project website (http://faculty.capd.ksu.edu/lskab/raingarden.html).

The rain garden is located at the main entrance to the ISC, so it's hard to miss, yet tucked into this enclave of a center, it's not readily visible from the road. To reach the ISC, one crosses Campus Creek via a bridge then continues on axis into the ISC courtyard. In the courtyard, the rain garden is revealed in all its colorful glory. Windows on the Taiwan Wing provide ISC office staff views of the garden's lush flowering perennials from late spring to autumn. In sum, if you are at the ISC, it is hard to miss this ARD's exuberant beauty.

Depth of water in this ARD is kept minimal, thanks to the large, shallow infiltration basin area, and the walkway is separated from the system by plantings.

Although the garden itself is tucked away, its design clearly states that "we care, we're environmentally conscious, and we want you to learn about rainwater." It is worth noting that visitors from local municipal staff to homeowners have left this garden with a new understanding of, and appreciation for, rain gardens; this, coupled with the array of information on the rain garden website, cumulatively conveys Kansas State University's message that "we are forward-looking leaders in teaching and demonstrating sustainable solutions."

The water trail lines in this design, from rooftop to bowls to limestone planks, are fairly subtle; depending on plant growth and weeding regimen, they are sometimes hard to see. But the exuberant colors and textures of the perennials, in combination with the pollinators that benefit, tell this garden's story: Rain from the rooftop serves both flora and fauna.

Of Note

- A university can be an ideal context for innovative ARD. Most schools want to be seen as leaders in sustainability, so many administrators are receptive, and faculty and students can conduct much of the work as research or classroom efforts, whether before project assessment, design and implementation, or after construction monitoring.
- This ARD is a multifaceted "win," especially for a land grant university, combining teaching, service, demonstration, and outreach in a forward-looking campus amenity.
- This project proved that perennial root systems can penetrate and loosen very compacted heavy clay soils and allow rainwater to infiltrate, much to the surprise of skeptical university personnel.

Sources

ASLA Student Awards. 2009. "Honor Award: International Student Center Rain Garden." http://www.asla.org/2009studentawards/264.html. Accessed December 7, 2013.

Skabelund, Lee. 2007. "Kansas State University Stormwater Project—Manhattan, Kansas." Informational poster. http://faculty.capd.ksu.edu/lskab/raingarden.html. Accessed December 7, 2013.

Skabelund, Lee. 2012. "Rain Garden Design & Maintenance." http://faculty.capd.ksu.edu/lskab/raingarden.html. Accessed December 7, 2013.

Skabelund, Lee. 2013. "KSU Stormwater Management Design–Build Project." WaterLINK Minigrant Phase II Report. http://faculty.capd.ksu.edu/lskab/raingarden.html. Accessed December 7, 2013.

Skabelund, Lee. n.d. "Rain-Garden Design and Implementation for Kansas Property Owners, with a Discussion of Lessons Learned from Kansas State University's International Student Center Rain-Garden Design–Build Demonstration Project in Manhattan, Kansas." http://faculty.capd.ksu.edu/lskab/raingarden.html. Accessed December 7, 2013.

CASE STUDY

Mount Tabor Middle School Rain Garden, Portland, Oregon

Reduce pollutant loads in rainwater

Reduce downstream damage from runoff

Safely move, control, and contain rainwater

Capture rain for reuse

Restore or create habitat

EDUCATION

Recreation

Safety

Public relations

Aesthetic richness

Figure 4.7. The Mount Tabor rain garden, located at the school entrance, clearly tells the story of rain: Roof runoff drops via downspouts on three sides against the building, visibly travels across paved surfaces under steel-grated runnels (note the "wavy line" grate pattern, suggesting water), then drops again into the sunken rain garden. On the left, parking lot and play area runoff drops sediment in a forebay before entering the garden (design and photograph credit: Kevin Robert Perry of the Portland Bureau of Environmental Services).

Date: 2006

Size: 2,000-square-foot rain garden within 4,000-square-foot courtyard

Location: 5800 SE 58th Avenue, Portland, Oregon

Owner: Portland Public Schools

Designers: Portland Bureau of Environmental Services; Kevin Perry, ASLA, designer

Background

Mount Tabor Middle School is a traditional one-story 1960s building with multiple wings, some of which enclose a three-sided, south-facing courtyard. The courtyard was paved in asphalt and used for parking, resulting in a heat island so problematic that teachers complained that adjacent classrooms were barely usable in warm weather. At the same time, neighboring homes experienced serious combined sewer overflow (CSO) problems, frequently resulting in sewage backup after large rain events.

In early 2004, the Portland Bureau of Environmental Services (BES) began plans to mitigate the CSO problem with green infrastructure solutions on Southeast Ankeny Street, adjacent to Mount Tabor Middle School. Because the overtaxed sewer lines were in good condition, the BES proposed an idea to the Portland Public Schools: a site-wide green infrastructure system to mitigate CSO problems in a cost-effective array that would also beautify and educate. BES designer Kevin Perry analyzed the entire school property and adjacent streets for the potential to retrofit the campus buildings, parking lot, and expansive asphalt play area. One of the first projects implemented within the overall project scheme was the retrofit of the parking courtyard into a rain garden to avert discharge into the city sewer. Added benefits of the project included reducing the heat island effect, providing an educational opportunity, beautifying a patch of school ground, providing an entry plaza, seating, bicycle access, and more efficient use of car parking.

Secondary green infrastructure elements included a linear rain garden in the parking lot, smaller rain gardens and drywell facilities around the building perimeter, and rain-capturing curb extensions along Southeast 57th Avenue. Although the overall retrofit includes all these elements site-wide, this case study focuses on the courtyard rain garden as an award-winning ARD that serves as an excellent model for future projects. As stated in its project description for the 2007 American Society of Landscape Architects Awards, "1) it is low-cost in its design and execution; 2) it benefits the environment and embodies community livability; and 3) it acts as a model for other sustainable stormwater retrofit projects."

Utility

The basic stormwater management concept at the Mount Tabor Middle School rain garden is capture, convey, cleanse, and infiltrate. The rain garden captures runoff from almost an acre of impervious surfaces (roof, parking, and play areas). Roof runoff drops via existing downspouts disconnected from the storm pipes; this water now discharges from the downspouts to at-grade runnels that cross a pedestrian zone surrounding the rain garden, then spill water into the recessed central garden zone; sheet runoff from adjacent asphalt areas is captured in trench drains and also directed to the rain garden.

Rainwater that sheets from the parking and play areas enters a forebay of the rain garden via a trench drain, to ensure initial deposit of hydrocarbons and other sediments. The entire garden, including the forebay, is heavily planted to biofilter the stormwater runoff.

The main purpose of this project is to reduce CSOs by managing up to 25-year storms through infiltration. In Portland, this means capturing the first 15 minutes of the 25-year storm. The rain garden infiltration rate is 2 to 4 inches per hour; monitoring revealed that, in the first year, no runoff entering this rain garden discharged to the city sewer system.

Runnels were specified as 2 feet wide, with a concave cross-section 2 inches deep at the lowest point of the curve. Trench drains were carefully sized to meet capacity needs: 18 inches wide, their runnels (under a grate) 6 inches deep. Additionally, concrete surfaces on both sides of the trench drain slope toward it, ensuring positive drainage so that water will move to the sunken garden even if the runnel overflows. Once in the sunken garden, runoff is slowed by initial detention in the forebay. Additionally, the recessed garden has 4 inches of freeboard to increase its volume capacity. As an additional backup measure, an in-system overflow splitter (overflow inlet) sends excess rainwater directly to the storm sewer (but this hasn't been needed yet).

As an infiltration basin, the rain garden recharges groundwater. This was made possible by a combination of existing conditions and design decisions:

- First, the school has no basement, which means infiltration facilities can be located fairly close to the building's edge.
- Second, the design sets the rain garden 10 feet away from the building face, with a 5-foot walkway along the building, then a 5-foot at-grade perimeter planting zone that surrounds the entire infiltration bed.

Figure 4.8. *(left)* The gravel path does triple duty in this system: It receives rain directly from the runnel, providing an initial infiltration zone; when dry, it serves as a path for maintenance workers, and it extends the rainwater axis to dramatize the water trail (design and photograph: Kevin Perry).

Figure 4.9. *(right)* Convenient location at the school's entrance ensures plenty of educational opportunities focused on rain. Note the simple post and chain entry deterrent (design and photograph: Kevin Perry).

Robust plantings in the rain garden provide microhabitat for local fauna.

Amenity

For such a small and low-cost retrofit, the Mount Tabor Middle School Rain Garden gets high marks in all the amenity categories.

This rain garden suits its context well, providing a clear and rich educational opportunity in a high-traffic entry zone of this school. First, the water trail from rooftop to rain garden is explicitly clear: The disconnected downspouts spill water into runnels covered by cast iron grates with wavy lines (reminiscent of flowing water); then, at the edge of the rain garden's at-grade, planted perimeter, the grates end and water visibly flows in the runnels, then drops into the sunken garden. For the two north–south runnels, the water trails are further emphasized by clear lines of monoculture plantings, and running east–west, a straight pea gravel path links the line of the western runnel with the line of the eastern trench drain. In addition to the perimeter pathway, an entry plaza provides great viewing opportunities for class-related exploration. And, in case the function isn't clear, a bright sign at the main entry provides brief text and visuals explaining the garden's stormwater management.

The rain garden is strategically located to ensure daily encounters in travels to and from school, providing a delightful landscape moment. Seating in the entry plaza also provides the opportunity to linger and enjoy the rain garden scene.

Entrance into the rain garden is visually discouraged by a 5-foot-wide, at-grade perimeter planting and a post-and-chain fence surrounding the sunken rain garden space. Rainwater-carrying runnels and trench drains are covered with cast iron grates whose curving lines mimic moving water, promoting both awareness of and safety from contact with the runoff.

This project hits a lot of great public relations hot buttons. Clearly the school states that "We care, we're environmentally responsible, and we want you to learn about stormwater" through the high visibility and educational opportunities afforded by this design, and the low cost and future infrastructure savings also proclaim that "We're fiscally responsible, mindful of the community's financial well-being," while the mitigation of CSO problems says, "We care about the community's physical well-being." Finally, the project's transformation of an "asphalt oven" into a beautiful, functional landscape says, "We're smart, resourceful, clever, and opportunistic."

The lines of the visible rainwater conveyance make this design an effective ARD: Without the clear, straight water trails (downspout-to-grated-runnel-to-exposed-runnel-to-aligned-plantings-or-gravel-path), this might not read as a stormwater management facility, but the lines are so crisp and clear as to make the function unmistakable. Color and texture are also important: The varied and robust plantings provide a vibrant foil to the surrounding hard surfaces. Finally, this design also offers audible delight: Large rain events offer the special opportunity to listen to the sound of water flowing from the conveyance runnels into the rain garden from four different directions.

Of Note

- This retrofit is an example of the economic advantage of green infrastructure: Portland's BES claims that the total, site-wide, green infrastructure cost of $780,000 represents more than $500,000 in savings compared with retrofitting gray infrastructure to address local CSO issues.
- The Mount Tabor rain garden is intentionally easily replicable, serving as an exemplary model for other projects.
- This project was designed with maintenance in mind. First, the planting plan is so robust (plants were installed 15 to 30 inches on center) that the occasional weed goes almost unnoticed, and the 2-foot-wide pea gravel corridor in the sunken garden not only visually links two rainwater entry points but also serves as an access pathway for maintenance crews, avoiding disturbance to plants or soil structure. And to allow the school to ease into the rain garden maintenance responsibility, the BES and the Portland Public Schools have a shared maintenance agreement until 2017 (in part because the BES is using the project as a design, construction, maintenance, and management case study).
- The success of this project is due in part to an effective community partnership between the school system, the city, and the local community.
- The rain garden at Mount Tabor has become an educational resource for other school groups who take home educational and inspirational ideas.
- A school is an ideal context for an ARD: What better way to enlighten future generations about the value of rain?

Sources

ASLA Professional Awards. 2007. "General Design Honor Award: Mount Tabor Middle School Rain Garden." http://www.asla.org/awards/2007/07winners/517_nna.html. Accessed November 11, 2013.

Liptan, Tom. 2013. Personal correspondence with authors.

Perry, Kevin Robert. 2013. Personal correspondence with authors.

Portland Bureau of Environmental Services. n.d. "BES Design Report: Stormwater Retrofit at Mt. Tabor Middle School." http://www.portlandoregon.gov/bes/article/217429. Accessed November 11, 2013.

CASE STUDY

Swarthmore Science Center, Swarthmore, Pennsylvania

- Reduce pollutant loads in rainwater
- Reduce downstream damage from runoff
- Safely move, control, and contain rainwater
- Capture rain for reuse

- **EDUCATION**
- Recreation
- Safety
- Public relations
- Aesthetic richness

Figure 4.10. A sittable raised runnel carries rain from the "water steps" (in the underpass, upper right) to drop into a pebble-filled basin. The water trail edges this public campus space, and a small sign in the pebble basin explains the rainwater strategy, creating an overall educational system (design: ML Baird & Co., Einhorn Yaffee Prescott; photograph: Stuart Echols).

Date: 2004

Size: Approximately 10 acres

Location: Swarthmore College, Swarthmore, Pennsylvania

Owner: Swarthmore College

Designers: ML Baird & Co.; Einhorn Yaffee Prescott

Background

Swarthmore College is a small liberal arts school, historically renowned for progressive thinking, on Philadelphia's Main Line. The 400-acre campus sits on a hill north of the village of Swarthmore; to the west of the built campus, 200 acres of steep, forested hillside, known as Crum Woods, tumble down to Crum Creek. Crum Woods, a laboratory for many college courses in natural sciences, is part of Swarthmore's Scott Arboretum.

In the late 1990s, Swarthmore acted on a need to significantly update and expand its science facilities, which the college considered a strategic move to attract outstanding science faculty and students. Part of "The Meaning of Swarthmore" campaign, the science facility expansion needed to meet a range of ambitious goals: It was to unite the college's science programs in a facility that would encourage collaboration, serve as a campus gathering place for the entire college community, express the college's historical commitment to progressive thinking, and address Crum Creek and Woods, both by improving watershed quality and by reconnecting Crum Woods to the main campus.

The resulting Science Center has stitched together the northern side of campus in a fabric of buildings and landscape spaces that promotes gathering, learning, and awareness of rain. The Science Center is one component in a campus-wide commitment to water management, sustainable practices, and teaching and learning opportunities that promote environmental stewardship.

Utility

The basic stormwater management concept at the Swarthmore Science Center is capture, convey, cleanse, and either infiltrate, reuse for irrigation, or detain and discharge. Rain is captured in two massive butterfly roof structures and conveyed to basins that collect and filter the rainwater. Some infiltrates to replenish groundwater, some is stored in an underground cistern for reuse in irrigation, and some is directed to another stormwater detention vault and discharged to the Crum Creek watershed in a controlled release. Porous pavement and additional 2-foot-deep infiltration beds (some planted as gardens in an interior courtyard, some as grass on the edge of the college's central quad) ensure that rain hitting the landscape recharges groundwater. The entire design strives for a zero-runoff environment to prevent erosion and degradation of Crum Woods and Crum Creek.

Water going into this system comes from roofs and surrounding landscape. Swarthmore has high standards for sustainable landscape maintenance, so pollution is not extensive. But the infiltration beds do filter sediments.

The major intention in this treatment system is to prevent runoff from eroding the forested hillside of Crum Woods or degrading Crum Creek. According to the final LEED report on the project, the post-development 1.5-year, 24-hour peak rate and quantity do not exceed predevelopment levels (in fact, the runoff has been reduced). Runoff from only 2.66 acres now flows to the preexisting storm vault, where a controlled release via a level spreader–like discharge system reduces point source erosion within Crum Woods; runoff hitting the remaining 3.1 acres is captured for groundwater recharge or reuse.

Because this sustainable stormwater strategy was voluntary rather than mandated by code, it did not address a regulated design storm size. And although multiple infiltration beds welcome large quantities of rainwater, the backup system sends overflow during large storms to the cistern in the central quad; any additional overflow is piped to the preexisting detention vault. This system strives to ensure that runoff primarily recharges the upper water table rather than directly affecting Crum Creek.

Some runoff is captured in a 22,000-gallon cistern below the adjacent grassy quad; that harvested runoff is reused for irrigation. Additional site runoff infiltrates two landscaped beds and an underground seepage bed in the main campus quad.

Figure 4.11. *(left)* At the upper terrace, a simple conveyance system carries roof runoff via tilted roof surface to a gap in the stone wall; rain then drops down a slate wall to a raised runnel and drops again into the pebble-filled basin, headed to an underground cistern and used for irrigation (design: ML Baird & Co., Einhorn Yaffee Prescott; photograph: Stuart Echols).

Figure 4.12. *(right)* The glass walls of Eldridge Commons ensure that both rainwater systems (upper and lower terrace) are visible even from indoors (design: ML Baird & Co., Einhorn Yaffee Prescott; photograph: Stuart Echols).

Amenity

In keeping with Swarthmore's commitment to progressive thinking, the college encouraged the design team to make the center an example of responsible principles and values, using the concept of sustainability as inspiration. Consequently, this is an ARD where stormwater management is visible from different spaces both indoors and out, appropriately piquing interest and offering teaching moments.

Two parts of the stormwater management system offer particularly striking lessons in the hydrologic cycle. One is the "Water Wall," near the main campus quadrangle. Here, runoff drains from one of the huge butterfly roofs and runs down a narrow, black slate wall; the rainwater then flows horizontally in a steel runnel within a 2-foot-high stone wall. The runnel wall reaches away from the building and out into a gathering terrace; a square basin of large river stones forms a pit between runnel and terrace, into which rainwater mysteriously disappears.

The "Stormwater Stairs" form the other visible system. Here, surface flow runoff is directed to the top of a set of water stairs that parallel a wide pedestrian stairway linking the upper Harry Wood Garden with the Glade Garden 13.5 feet below. At the bottom of the stormwater stairs, the rain flows horizontally, again in a steel runnel within a 2-foot-tall sittable concrete and stone wall. This time, the runnel wall, which steps down in three tiers, runs far into the space along a terrace edge of the garden. Here, too, water drops at the end to disappear into a river stone–filled pit.

In the upper space, the "Water Wall" sign explains, "Rainwater falling on the roof of Eldridge Commons flows down the wall at the right and into an underground cistern. It is then pumped through a site irrigation system to nourish plants in adjacent gardens." The "Stormwater Stair" sign explains, "Rainwater falling on the science center roof and into the Harry Wood Garden flows into this channel and empties into a cistern behind Martin Hall. The stored water is slowly released into the Crum Creek watershed." The rainwater trails, in both cases, do a fine job of presenting the main idea of this design: Rain should go into the ground! And both systems clearly read whether wet or dry.

The Science Center design team did an outstanding job of ensuring many different encounters with the stormwater system, indoors and out. Thanks to glass curtain walls on both sides of Eldridge Commons, one can look down on the Stormwater Stair runnel to the north or look out to the Water Wall to the south. Additionally, both systems are found on the edge of outdoor gathering places. And, finally, it's worth noting that in winter the rain ices over, creating fascinating ice displays.

In keeping with the infiltration theme, there is no visible standing water in this design and no runnel at grade. The most interaction one can have with the rain is by trailing a hand in a raised runnel.

The central message is, "We care, we are environmentally responsible, and we want you to learn about stormwater" (achieved both through its visibility and through educational programming). Additionally, "We're smart, we know you'll notice the treatment if it's fun" is a message particularly appropriate in a college context.

The lines of both upper and lower water trails tell the story in this ARD: Their straight, rectilinear clarity stands out in the landscape surroundings. The repetition of runnel wall to river rock basin also clarifies that, in both spots, the system does the same thing.

Of Note

- The project landscape architect cites the client's insistence on "true collaboration across the professional disciplines" as the foundation for this project's success.
- This ARD answers the question, "Yes, but what about in cold climates?" The answer: Because the rain display in ARDs doesn't depend on pipes, they pose an unusual opportunity to let ice happen.

Sources

Baird, Mara. 2013. Personal correspondence with authors.

Einhorn Yaffee Prescott, Architecture & Engineering. n.d.. "Building as an Integrated Teaching Tool: The New Science Center at Swarthmore College." http://www.pkal.org/documents/EYP-Swarthmore1.pdf. Accessed June 11, 2013.

"Green Design: The Scott Arboretum of Swarthmore College." n.d. Brochure. http://www.scottarboretum.org/publications/GreenDesign-2.pdf. Accessed December 2, 2013.

"Rethinking Form and Function: Swarthmore College Unified Science Center by Einhorn Yaffee Prescott and Helfand Architecture." *ArchNewsNow*, July 19, 2005. http://www.archnewsnow.com/features/Feature171.htm. Accessed October 17, 2013.

Swarthmore College Science Center, Swarthmore College. 2005. "LEED Project 122 Final LEED v2 Review." http://www.swarthmore.edu/NatSci/sciproject/ScienceCenterLEED.pdf. Accessed December 2, 2013.

"Ten Years of the Science Center: A Celebration." 2012. http://www.mfairleydesign.com/Science_Center_folding.pdf. Accessed June 23, 2013.

CASE STUDY

"Growing Vine Street" (The Beckoning Cistern and Cistern Steps), Seattle, Washington

Reduce pollutant loads in rainwater

Reduce downstream damage from runoff

Safely move, control, and contain rainwater

Capture rain for reuse

Education

RECREATION

Public relations

Safety

Figure 4.13. This huge "hand" (note human figure in photo), its thick wrist a cistern, playfully suggests its yearning for rain to all passersby (design: GAYNOR, Inc., Carlson Architects, SvR Design Company, Buster Simpson; photograph: Stuart Echols).

Date: 2003

Size: Beckoning Cistern 700 square feet, Cistern Steps 1,200 square feet

Location: Vine Street between 1st and Elliott Avenue, Seattle, Washington

Owner: City of Seattle; managed by Growing Vine Street Committee & Friends of Belltown P-patch

Designers: GAYNOR, Inc.; Carlson Architects; SvR Design Company; Buster Simpson

Background

In the late 1990s, as the Belltown neighborhood of Seattle was becoming a haven for artists, members of the Belltown P-patch community garden were interested in improving pedestrian and residential quality of life on Vine Street and improving the quality of urban water discharged into Elliott Bay. The idea arose to convert eight blocks of Vine Street into an urban watershed through a series of artistic interventions that would both reduce local CSOs and improve water quality of runoff entering Elliott Bay, then Puget Sound. As Peggy Gaynor, landscape architect on the "Growing Vine Street" project, explains, there were four fundamental project intentions:

- Create a prototype Green Street that is pedestrian friendly and ecologically sustainable.
- Bring the qualities of the P-patch community garden onto and up the street.
- Deal with urban runoff and water quality.
- Blur the edges between built and natural environment, cars and people, water and earth.

"Growing Vine Street" implementation faced many challenges, especially resistance from the city because of health and safety concerns (according to Gaynor, at the time city regulators were more comfortable with open swales and rain gardens in more suburban neighborhoods, and they worried about green infrastructure in a densely urban context). Permits and maintenance agreements with city agencies took a long time to obtain, and the city didn't permit street runoff to be managed, as originally desired by proponents.

To date, two blocks of Vine Street are enlivened by two separate artistic systems that manage roof runoff from some adjacent buildings. Beckoning Cistern at 81 Vine and Cistern Steps adjacent to the Belltown P-patch form a two-block rainwater-focused sequence that tumbles down the Vine Street hill toward Elliott Bay.

Utility

The basic stormwater management concept for the Beckoning Cistern is capture, convey, cleanse, and reuse for irrigation; the Cistern Steps' intent is to capture, convey, cleanse, and either infiltrate or detain and discharge.

Beckoning Cistern is a 15-foot-tall, 6-foot-diameter galvanized aluminum cylinder that captures rainwater from the roof of the adjacent 81 Vine building; roof runoff is first filtered in rooftop planters, then falls via downspout to the cistern, where a flow splitter sends some runoff into the container while the rest drops into the first of three round planters, set in a bed of native plants, that cascade down the hill; a concrete scupper extends from each planter to spill rainwater overflow to the next planter. Notably, the rest of the roof runoff is carried to the city storm system via an unusual candelabra-form downspout. This playful, creative infrastructure uses two separate lumiére-like interludes of plant-topped arms to force runoff diversion and oxygenation.

Cistern Steps, designed to capture roof runoff from the Vine Building across the street, is a tiered series of four concrete biofiltration basins that, like the Beckoning Cistern system uphill, each discharge overflow to the next via a concrete scupper. Rainwater that makes it to the end disappears in a final, carved jade basin that connects to the city storm system.

Runoff that flows into the Beckoning Cistern system is first cleansed in the rooftop planters on 81 Vine; the runoff that is subsequently directed through the tiered planters is further biofiltered. In the Cistern Steps, all cleansing is achieved through biofiltration in the sequential planters.

A major impetus of this project was mitigation of CSOs and damage to Elliott Bay and Puget Sound. According to Gaynor, all runoff in the Beckoning Cistern system is retained either in the cistern or in the planters, with none discharged; in the Cistern Steps system, a great deal of the water is retained in the planters, and some discharges to the city system.

Runoff reaches the Beckoning Cistern via a closed downspout; there a flow splitter sends some water to the cistern and some to the bioretention planters. All remaining conveyance and containment in this entire ARD system follows the "always slow it down, spread it out, soak it in" mantra through dispersal of the rainwater in a number of basins and planters. The "safety backup" is that overflow from both systems can discharge to the city system.

Figure 4.14. *(left)* Across the sidewalk from the Belltown P-patch community garden, tiered infiltration basins step down the slope, with any overflow at the bottom directed to the city sewer system (design: GAYNOR, Inc., Carlson Architects, SvR Design Company, Buster Simpson; photograph: Stuart Echols).

Figure 4.15. *(right)* Other roof runoff at 81 Vine is directed to these candelabra downspouts, whose playful forms evapotranspire some rainwater and oxygenate the rest (design: Buster Simpson; photograph: Stuart Echols).

The Beckoning Cistern holds 300 gallons of roof runoff, harvested to irrigate plantings in front of 81 Vine. All the rest of the runoff in these systems, except for the small amount discharged from the Cistern Steps into the city sewer, irrigates the planters of the stormwater management system, one of the effective symbioses possible in green infrastructure.

Amenity

Within a community of artists, this quirky, fun ARD makes a fitting statement about the place. First, 81 Vine discharges its roof runoff into two eye-catching downspout art pieces by artist Buster Simpson, one against the building and one in the right-of-way between sidewalk and street. The downspout closest to Western Avenue was described earlier: Two plant-topped candelabra arms make the downward water flow obvious and fun; one can imagine the falling water caught and pushed up into each arm to water the plants. The other downspout and the Beckoning Cistern present a tongue-in-cheek interpretation of Michelangelo's Sistine Chapel painting of Adam reaching his finger to gain life from God, but this time it's the cistern extending a "finger" to receive water. The downspout providing that life-giving water peels away from the building, angling out to meet the cistern "index finger," a piece of half-round downspout, jointed to bend like a human finger. Three other downspout sections extend from the cistern to form the remaining fingers, and a fifth—the "thumb"—serves as a scupper that sends some of the runoff to the tiered bioretention basins below. A red-and-white dipstick protrudes from the cistern top, showing the volume currently contained.

The rest of the green infrastructure presents a more subdued landscape amenity, with rainwater cascading down the hill in two separate series of planted basins located between street and sidewalk.

This fun system says a lot about rainwater. First, Simpson's two pieces—the candelabra downspout and the Sistine Chapel knock-off—both identify rain as a life-giving resource for the plants in the lumiéres and for people in the Beckoning Cistern. In both, there's a clear narrative and a clear water trail; together they make the message obvious. And location of the stormwater systems also contributes to its educational value: Stormwater is managed in the right-of-way, where it simply cannot be missed, and the Cistern Steps system is adjacent to the P-patch community garden. The lifegiving link between water and plants is clear.

Placement of the system in the street right-of-way ensures that everyone will encounter this ARD: drivers, bikers, pedestrians. Another way the design facilitates lingering interaction is in the Cistern Steps, where pedestrian stairs cascade down the hill next to the tiered basins. Four arced sets of steps with wide treads and low risers each extend their arc around to greet the stormwater system, providing inviting seating right next to each basin's scupper.

The main rainwater harvesting in this system occurs in an abovegrade, enclosed container, separating viewers from the large water volume, but the design of the cistern tells the water story while its containment ensures safety. Throughout the linear, green infrastructure installation, pedestrians walk right next to the basins and, technically, could step over a low curb and into the system. If they do, the low freeboard of each basin ensures that any ponded water they encounter would be very shallow.

This project clearly states, "We care, we are environmentally responsible, and we want you to learn about rainwater," while the artistic eccentricity also proclaims, "We're smart, and we know you'll notice the treatment if it's fun."

Both the Beckoning Cistern and the candelabra downspout serve as eye-catching focal points that make passersby notice the rainwater message. Other visual interest is created by the rhythm and repetition of the tiered basins on both blocks: uphill a theme of circles, downhill a theme of trapezoids next to arcing stairs. This rhythm punctuates the rainwater's movement down the hill. Finally, tactile interest is found in wetness: This design invites pedestrians on the steps to reach out and actually touch rainwater falling from scuppers.

Of Note

- Collaboration with artists can result in memorable "identity imagery" in ARDs.
- Public–private partnerships can help ARD funding. In this project, dollars raised by the community were matched by the city's Department of Neighborhoods.

Sources

Enlow, Claire. 2003. "A Watershed Moment on a Belltown Street." *Seattle Daily Journal of Commerce*, February 19, 2003. http://www.djc.com/news/ae/11142097.html. Accessed September 17, 2013.

Gaynor, Peggy. 2013. Personal contact with the authors.

Growing Vine Street Revisited 2004. 2004. http://www.growingvinestreet.org/book.html. Accessed November 13, 2013.

Whitman, Maryann. 2003. "Growing Vine Street." Reprint from *Wild Ones Journal*, Jan/Feb 2003. http://www.wildones.org/download/GrowingVineSt.pdf. Accessed November 13, 2013.

CASE STUDY

Ridge and Valley at the Penn State Arboretum, University Park, Pennsylvania

Reduce pollutant loads in rainwater

Safely move, control, and contain rainwater

Capture rain for reuse

Education

RECREATION

Safety

Public relations

Aesthetic richness

Figure 4.16. On this small bluestone terrace, it's fun to trace the water system of the local Spring Creek Watershed, whether wet or dry (design: Stacy Levy with MTR Landscape Architects, Overland Partners; photograph: Fred Weber).

Date: 2009

Size: 924 square feet (42 × 22 feet)

Location: Penn State Arboretum Overlook Pavilion, Park Avenue and Bigler Road, University Park, Pennsylvania

Owner: Penn State

Designers: Stacy Levy with MTR Landscape Architects; Overland Partners

Background

One of the reasons for the location of Penn State's arboretum is that the 370-acre site is a major aquifer recharge area and wellhead protection zone for Penn State. In this karst landscape of sinkholes and underground caverns, groundwater is the source of potable water. Consequently, it made sense to use this site for a function that could recharge groundwater and benefit, not harm, the aquifer.

Arboretum development began in 2007, with a gift for the construction of the botanic gardens occupying 30 acres along Park Avenue; the Overlook Pavilion and its environs were part of this initial development. So called because the building offers extensive views both toward campus and toward the larger landscape of rolling fields and ridges, the Overlook Pavilion houses the arboretum's volunteer operations hub and rest rooms, and its terraces provide a scenic venue for many events, from donor appreciation dinners to weddings. A collaboration between an artist, the pavilion architects, and the botanic gardens landscape architects resulted in a small terrace adjacent to the pavilion that offers a lesson in geography and rain: "Ridge and Valley," a bluestone, ground plane, to-scale map of rivers and streams in the local watershed that presents a living, active version of the Spring Creek watershed. Shallow runnels follow the courses of all local surface water bodies, which are named on the terrace "map," and three sittable boulder "ridges" are located to represent the watershed's linear mountains.

Penn State's arboretum, still in phased development, has been funded almost exclusively by private donations. This ARD was funded by a donor who is very active both at Penn State and in the local environmental community, especially in the Clearwater Conservancy, a nongovernment organization that strives to protect water quality in this watershed. Consequently, when the artist developed the idea to harness water from the Overlook Pavilion roof to make a statement of "rooftop to river," the idea was a natural fit with the donor's interests. Additionally, according to the artist, "The client liked that there would be a reason to visit a site in inclement weather. They may have just gone for a map of the watershed, but making the connection of the rain to the streams using live rain seemed to make the watershed map much more visceral."

Utility

The basic stormwater management concept at the Ridge and Valley is capture, convey, cleanse, and infiltrate. Rain falling on the pavilion is collected and channeled through a scupper that protrudes from the roof. During small rain events, rain drips from the scupper onto river pebbles, then flows to the bluestone map; in large events, rain arcs from the scupper to fall directly onto the map, where all rivers and streams in the watershed are incised, each as a ¼-inch-deep runnel, transforming the map during small rain events into the watershed in miniature. The whole terrace is gently sloped to make the rain follow the watershed's configuration. As the rain leaves Bald Eagle Creek, the final tributary on the map, it flows into an adjacent hidden inlet, where the rainwater is piped about 750 feet to a "wet meadow" infiltration basin that connects to Penn State's well fields.

Runoff is biofiltered in the heavily vegetated wet meadow near the major campus entry road, Park Avenue, before it infiltrates into the ground.

This is a very simple system: Small rains find the runnels and are conveyed, whereas large storms sheet flow across the bluestone terrace. Either way, runoff is carried to the inlet and piped to the infiltration basin. If a rain event overwhelms the piped system, the backup is for rain to simply flow into the adjacent planting bed and irrigate the plants.

The management intent of this system is to recharge groundwater, which is accomplished in the wet meadow infiltration. This wet meadow was designed to ensure both biofiltration and infiltration for essential groundwater recharge in a major lowland recharge zone along the Park Avenue edge of the arboretum.

Figure 4.17. *(left)* Roof runoff falls from a scupper onto splash pebbles, then flows across the sloped, incised map to a hidden inlet. The rainwater is then piped to a wet meadow infiltration basin nearby (design: Stacy Levy with MTR Landscape Architects, Overland Partners; photograph: Fred Weber).

Figure 4.18. *(right)* Sittable stone "ridges" complement the playful rivulets, making this terrace a delightful destination that displays local geography in relief, and because the "water system" terrace is surrounded by plantings, the rooftop-to-landscape message is very clear (design: Stacy Levy with MTR Landscape Architects, Overland Partners; photograph: Fred Weber).

Amenity

This beautiful work of environmental art presents a resounding celebration of rain in a public spot that draws visitors from destinations as close as the adjacent neighborhood and as far as across the state. As the artist, Stacy Levy, puts it, “This project gives a role to the rain: to activate the watershed map and make the terrace an interesting place.” She adds, “The artwork is both a placemaking object and an engineering system; and it gives visitors a way to celebrate the hydrologic cycle.” Levy also suggests that a celebration of rain is a natural for an arboretum; in her words, “An arboretum is really as much about its weather as its plants. The rainfall dictates what grows in a particular place, so the presence of rain needs to be featured in a compelling way. This project makes the rain a piece of the landscape, and connects the rain to the watershed. Also, with students coming from many other regions, it seemed an essential moment to introduce people to the watershed that Penn State inhabits.”

Whether wet or dry, this terrace tells the story of water in the Spring Creek Watershed, depicting both surface waters and ground waters (sinks and springs). In any weather, it offers a wonderful teaching moment when visitors, locals, or school kids look for geographic spots they know and tangentially realize how water is at work in those locales. During rain events, the system reveals the hydrologic cycle with crystal clarity, from rooftop to river.

This ARD’s location makes it hard to miss, adjacent to the main event terrace and visible through a “window” between the public rest rooms at the pavilion. As in all outdoor rooms of the arboretum, visitors are enticed in; once they are there, the long limestone benches provide a great spot to pause and peruse the map.

Because the incised runnels are so shallow—only ¼ inch deep—and the runoff is from a roof, this is one ARD where it’s perfectly safe to walk on the rain and reach down to touch it. And the rain’s disappearance into the hidden inlet ensures no standing water.

This clever design carries many useful messages: “We care, we’re environmentally responsible, and we want you to learn about stormwater” is expressed by the ARD’s high-visibility location and the design’s facilitation of programming educational activities. “We’re smart and know you’ll notice the treatment if it’s fun” is another clear message thanks to the easy-to-follow water trail and the design’s invitation to walk and play on the watershed map.

The entire Ridge and Valley functions as a water-related focal point within the arboretum, but its compositional lines are the real draw. From the line of rain falling from the roof to the rainwater-carrying water runnels, this design makes the eye follow the rainwater trail. An added delight is the fact that the design allows visitors to touch the water, whether falling from the scupper or running in a miniature “river.”

Of Note

- This design presents a great example of environmental art that functions as green infrastructure, and it raises the point that ARDs can be enhanced—or completely created—by artists.
- Because plants depend so greatly on rainwater, an arboretum offers an ideal spot for a learning opportunity to ensure that visitors enhance their awareness of the resource value of rain.

Sources

The Arboretum at Penn State. 2008. http://www.arboretum.psu.edu/planning/index.html. Last updated September 18, 2008.

The Arboretum at Penn State. 2013. Promotional brochure created for information and donor relations. University Park, PA: Penn State Publications.

Levy, Stacy. 2013. Personal correspondence with the authors.

CASE STUDY

Southwest Recreation Center, University of Florida, Gainesville, Florida

Reduce pollutant loads in rainwater

Reduce downstream damage from runoff

Safely move, control, and contain rainwater

Capture rain for reuse

Restore or create habitat

Education

RECREATION

Safety

Public relations

Aesthetic richness

Figure 4.19. Whether you're walking to the Recreation Center or simply walking by, this design is fun to encounter and prompts exploration of the water trails from building to bioswale (design: RDG Planning and Design; photograph: Eliza Pennypacker).

Date: 2010

Size: 52,000 square feet

Location: Southwest Recreation Center, 3150 Hull Road, Gainesville, Florida

Owner: University of Florida

Designers: RDG Planning and Design

Background

In 2008, the University of Florida proposed an expansion of the Southwest Recreation Center to alleviate crowding; the building addition and new hardscape added nearly 25,000 square feet of impervious surface and left very little room for a variety of program elements, including stormwater management. This already daunting scenario was heightened by two more realities. First, municipal stormwater regulations require that discharge not exceed preconstruction rates and that rainwater be treated on site for quality and volume. And second, the only land available for stormwater management was in front of the building, along busy Hull Road. The result is a noteworthy ARD that proves you can make lemonade from stormwater lemons if you focus the landscape design on the rain instead of managing it "out of sight, out of mind."

The stormwater challenge became an opportunity to showcase rain and the hydrologic cycle front and center, visible to all pedestrians passing by or entering the facility, as well as to bicyclists and drivers on Hull Road. Runoff from the building roof is conveyed via six runnels away from the front building facade and out into a richly planted bioswale that runs parallel to both the building and Hull Road. The rainwater "roof-to-river" message, already clear, is made more vibrant by sculptures and night lighting that add color and narrative (made possible by a "1 percent for art in state buildings" requirement). In addition, the university chose to make this landscape an educational opportunity for students in a range of majors: science, horticulture, landscape architecture, and art. And as David Bowles, director of the university's Department of Recreational Sports put it, "The use of landscape, rain gardens and the artwork in front of the Southwest Recreation Center demonstrates the ability to use conservation in an aesthetically pleasing way"—just the kind of public statement you want to hear from a proud ARD client.

Utility

The basic stormwater management concept at the Southwest Recreation Center is capture, convey, cleanse, detain, and discharge. Roof runoff falls via downspouts into six pebble-filled cast stone bowls at the base of the building facade; as the bowls overflow, water cascades into pebble-filled runnels that carry the rain across the entry sidewalk to a tiered bioswale filled with native plants and boulders. When it reaches the bioswale, each runnel edges a checkdam that controls water dropping into the adjacent lower basin. The bioswale filters the runoff and detains it in a series of seven tiered basins in all, with some infiltration occurring before the runoff is slowly discharged into the municipal stormwater system.

Stormwater is filtered by traversing the bioswale.

The system of tiered basins in the bioswale slows, spreads, and detains discharge, allowing some to infiltrate and evapotranspire. No monitoring has been conducted to determine the amount of runoff detained.

The system runnels and bioswale were sized to hold and convey a 100-year design storm. Worth noting is that the tiered system of basins, which is so useful in slowing and detaining runoff in the bioswale, was in part a response to a 5-foot drop across the site, existing utilities, and mature live oaks that became part of the design.

Because the bioswale sits on a layer of clay, only a small portion of runoff recharges groundwater (the designer estimates that only about 5 percent of the runoff infiltrates).

Robust native plantings in the wide and long bioswale provide habitat for local fauna.

Figure 4.20. *(left)* Rainwater enters the tiered bioswale via runnels from the building; each runnel then continues and drops via weir in this clever checkdam and weir design (design: RDG Planning and Design; photograph: Eliza Pennypacker).

Figure 4.21. *(right)* Each rainwater runnel extends visually across the bioswale, over a gentle berm, all the way to the public sidewalk via fitted stone paving. This design overtly invites interaction (design: RDG Planning and Design; photograph: Eliza Pennypacker).

Amenity

"Let the rain shine" became a key intention in this artful rainwater solution, and so the rain-focused landscape provides a bold statement of university values and a rich entry experience at the Recreation Center. And with six runnels reaching out from the front facade to six brightly (and differently) colored rain-related sculptures, each runnel extending beyond to the lush bioswale that fronts the entire building, this is a rain amenity that will not be missed.

Befitting its university context, this ARD is loaded with educational content. First, the legibility of the rainwater trail, from roof to runnel to bioswale, clearly tells the hydrologic story. The rain narrative is enhanced by six tall, cylindrical sculptures that stand at the junction of each runnel with a bioswale checkdam. The site-specific art installation, by David Dahlquist of RDG Dahlquist Art Studio, is collectively titled "Thirst." The six metal columns vary only in color (from neon magenta to neon green), their consistent filigree pattern intended to suggest the cell structure of a palmetto drawing nutrients from the water and soil of the bioswale. Each sculpture also contains a cylinder that, at night, glows with cool blue light (just in case the water role is unclear). Native plants, stormwater management, landscape design, and art also provide opportunities for classes across the university to use this ARD as a learning laboratory for a variety of different majors, from the sciences to arts.

This is a particularly inviting ARD that is delightful to encounter. Not only is it at the front door of the Recreation Center and along a busy street, but the design ensures that pedestrians experience the intent. First, those walking between building and bioswale can't miss the six runnels they cross, each linking a building downspout to a sculpture and the bioswale beyond. More unusual is the invitation to enter the stormwater system, extended to pedestrians on the Hull Road sidewalk. There, hand-fitted warm tan sandstone walkways extend from the sidewalk to meet the bioswale, beckoning passersby to enjoy the beautiful garden.

Two deft design moves render the rain highly visible but very safe. First, the runnels crossing the entry walkway are covered in Corten grates, and because black Mexican river pebble runs the entire length of each runnel, from a water-receiving bowl at the facade to the length of a bioswale checkdam, a pedestrian safely crossing the runnel is fully aware of the water conveyance below her feet. Second, both the columnar sculptures and plantings at the bioswale edge serve as vertical barrier to dissuade visitors from entering the management system.

The university succeeded in making its environmental values quite clear in this design. The ARD proclaims, "We care, we're environmentally responsible, and we want you to learn about stormwater" and, "We're smart, resourceful, and clever" in its bold and opportunistic location along the entire front of the new building. The design also states, "We're smart, and we know you'll notice the treatment if it's fun" and "We're sophisticated and distinctive" through the unusual use of art and lighting.

This design is delightfully varied yet unified and truly eye-catching overall. Each splash bowl and each sculpture becomes an intriguing focal point focused on rain, and the bright, varied colors of the six sculptures complement the color and texture of plantings, sandstone, Corten, and black river pebbles. Variety is unified by the lines of the six narrow runnels and checkdams that cross the linear bioswale in a consistent rhythm, tying the whole site together like warp and weft.

Of Note

- Sometimes site constraints become the parameters for outstanding Artful Rainwater Design. Why *not* present stormwater management at the front door?
- The "State Public Art" and "Percent for Art" programs required in many states can provide a means to enrich ARDs.
- Whether required by the state or not, collaboration with artists on ARDs can provide experiential benefits.
- Don't forget to consider the experience of your ARD at night. Lighting can extend the design's message around the clock.

Sources

Martin, Jonathan. 2013. Personal correspondence with the authors.

Martin, Jonathan. n.d.. "Artfully Functional: Form Follows Function at the University of Florida." LandscapeOnline.com. http://www.landscapeonline.com/research/article/17887. Accessed September 27, 2013.

CASE STUDY

Stephen Epler Hall at Portland State University, Portland, Oregon

 Reduce pollutant loads in rainwater

 Reduce downstream damage from runoff

 Safely move, control, and contain rainwater

 Capture rain for reuse

 Education

 **RECREATION**

 Safety

 Public relations

 Aesthetic richness

Figure 4.22. This "bio-alley" forms the public space outside a new dormitory, office, and classroom building. It's an appropriate context to present a fun "stormwater puzzle" that begs to be deciphered (design: Atlas Landscape Architecture, KPFF Consulting Engineers, Mithun; photograph: Stuart Echols).

Date: 2003

Size: 20,000 square feet (courtyard only)

Location: 1136 SW Montgomery Street, Portland, Oregon

Owner: Portland State University

Designers: Atlas Landscape Architecture; KPFF Consulting Engineers; Mithun

Background

Once a 2-year college, Portland State University has grown into a large (and Oregon's only urban) public university of 23,000 students. As it has expanded, and appropriate to the renowned ethos of the city, Portland State has become committed to green environmental strategies and education; in fact, their current tagline is "Learn, live, work, relax, and be green." So when the university decided to construct a new six-story building to house five floors and 130 units of student housing, with offices and classrooms on the first floor, green was a given. Stephen Epler Hall, named for the first leader and champion of the university, was one of Portland State's first LEED projects, intended from the beginning to showcase sustainable strategies.

At the time, the city of Portland faced significant problems with CSO discharge into the Willamette River; so the city advocated reduction of storm flows into their sewer system wherever possible. The city's needs and Portland State's commitment aligned well, and to provide some incentive for sustainable stormwater management, the city gave Portland State a $15,000 grant to develop an innovative system that would reduce offsite stormwater impacts.

Considerable budget constraints meant that everyone involved—owner, developer, regulatory officials, designers—had to work effectively together to ensure that the project's lofty goals were met (and the city's small grant, and resulting expectations, made green features hard to "value engineer" out of the project). Fortunately, all members of the team had something to gain. The result is a groundbreaking project: a LEED Silver building, the first in Oregon to use rainwater to flush toilets, fronting a "bio-alley" where a dispersed, sustainable stormwater management system reduces offsite stormwater impacts and potable water use in a particularly engaging celebration of rain.

Utility

The basic stormwater management concept at Stephen Epler Hall is capture, convey, cleanse, and either reuse for irrigation or toilet flushing or detain and discharge. Roof runoff falls via four downspouts into river pebble-filled splash boxes; scuppers at the base of each box spill water into runnels that safely convey runoff across the space into biopaddies (sunken flow-through filter planters). Biofiltered water is piped from each biopaddy to a belowgrade 10,000-gallon cistern, where bacteria are removed with ultraviolet radiation. The filtered water is used for irrigation and toilet flushing. Large storms send excess runoff from each biopaddy to the next in sequence via runnels; water that exceeds the biopaddy and cistern capacity goes straight to the storm sewer.

Rainwater is first biofiltered in the biopaddies (sunken flow-through filter planters) to remove sediments and other contaminants; secondary treatment by ultraviolet rays in the cistern kills bacteria. This renders the rainwater suitable for toilet flushing as well as irrigation.

The big stormwater management idea here is reduction of offsite impact, especially on the sewer system. Thanks to adsorption, absorption, evapotranspiration, and retention in the biopaddies, plus detention and reuse through the cistern, runoff discharge from the project is significantly reduced. All of this results in a 26 to 52 percent diversion (depending on time of year) of runoff from the city's storm system, according to on-site monitoring.

Safety in both utility and amenity is a project hallmark. On the utility side, safety is ensured largely through redundancy and backup systems. For example, if the scuppers on the splash boxes clog, backed-up rainwater is sent to underground overflow pipes that carry the water to the biopaddies. Another safety measure is the dispersal of runoff in five separate, shallow biopaddies, a strategy to

Figure 4.23. *(left)* Roof runoff falls via downspout to hit a splash block, then spreads out to fill the pebble-lined splash box. A spout, placed low in the box, discharges most of the rain into the runnel, which heads for a biopaddy, safely carrying the water below pedestrian feet by spaces between the granite sets (design: Atlas Landscape Architecture, KPFF Consulting Engineers, Mithun; photograph: Stuart Echols).

Figure 4.24. *(right)* The system of granite set runnels and cuts in the curbs of the sunken biopaddies provokes the curious to figure out how the system works: Water overflowing an upper biopaddy moves to the next one downhill, and so on, as the size of a rain event demands (design: Atlas Landscape Architecture, KPFF Consulting Engineers, Mithun; photograph: Stuart Echols).

hold a lot of water without any one container being dangerously deep. But it's also important that the biopaddies have a 12-inch minimum freeboard to hold some volume before overflowing. If they do overflow, the design ensures that the excess rainwater is carried down the system from one biopaddy to the next via connecting runnels, and if the volume is too great for all five biopaddies, the last biopaddy in sequence sends excess to the storm sewer.

The system sends about 111,000 gallons of water annually to the 10,000-gallon cistern. About 10,000 gallons of retained runoff are used for irrigation, and 100,000 gallons flush first-floor toilets in Stephen Epler Hall.

Amenity

The stormwater management system at Stephen Epler Hall presents a fun and engaging celebration of rainwater. Because it's so dispersed throughout the "bio-alley" site, the stormwater management system surrounds pedestrians—one simply can't miss it. When dry, the system is like a puzzle: Its sequence and function beg to be deciphered (appropriate on a college campus). When wet, the system puts on such a stormwater show that students emerge from dorm rooms to watch.

The intriguing and highly visible water trail ensures that viewers get a clear "rain as resource" message: Rain falls from the roof, is conveyed across the space, and spills into planters that filter, and are nourished by, the rain. If a planter is inundated, the water clearly moves to the next, and so on down the line. Figuring this out takes a bit of effort, but the design's necklace of water trails and biopaddies makes the function both playful and fairly clear. And if by chance a visitor doesn't understand, a small sign with brief text and a diagram explains the system. One additional piece of information is provided in first-floor bathrooms, where signage proclaims that toilets are flushed with rain.

This project is just plain fun: It immerses visitors in a landscape of plaza-crossing runnels and sunken planters like a stormwater jigsaw puzzle. Just passing by on the way to a friend's dorm room, a student can't miss the stormwater system. And when it rains, strategically located covered seating across from the downspouts and splash boxes offers a perch to watch the stormwater show.

As mentioned in the "Utility" section, safety is a hallmark of this ARD; on the amenity side, this means that viewers are fully aware of the rainwater but are never in danger. The first noteworthy safety move is found in the plaza-crossing runnels: These channels are "paved" with granite blocks mortared only at the bottom. This means the water is visible and audible, while pedestrians can pass right over without hazarding a wet or twisted foot. Another safety move is found in the biopaddies: A raised concrete "curb" surrounds each (except at the runnel entry and exit points), providing both impromptu seating and a safety edge to dissuade people from stepping into the sunken planter.

If Portland State seeks a reputation for being green, this project proclaims the message loud and clear. First, it says, "We care, we're environmentally responsible, and we want you to learn about stormwater," but it also conveys a cleverness on the university's part, a message that "We're smart because we know you'll notice the stormwater system if it's fun" and "We're smart to opportunistically use a small space and disperse the system throughout so you can't miss it." The overall message is that Portland State is both environmentally responsible and light-hearted, even hip—a particularly appropriate set of messages outside a college dorm.

The strictly rectilinear site composition provides an appropriately urbane theme in this "bio-alley." A system of orthogonal runnels crisscrosses the site, intersecting the rectangular volumes of the biopaddies. Thanks to the consistent compositional strategy and the dispersal of the system across the site, the whole design is unified by the repetition and rhythm of the rectilinear runnel and biopaddy pattern. Additionally, color and texture add richness through contrast of soft sedges and spiky rushes in the biopaddies with black river pebble (at the base of each runnel inlet to control erosion) and gray granite.

Of Note

- This project embodies the benefits of being opportunistic with space: Dispersal of the stormwater system throughout a tight site can ensure that the ARD becomes a focus and theme.
- CSO reduction earned the project a $79,000 rebate on system development fees levied on new construction by the city.
- The sunken biopaddies are the only planted zones in this green infrastructure system, which makes maintenance clear and simple.

Sources

McDonald, Steve. 2006. Interview with authors (architect from Mithun).

Miller, Terrence. 2002. "From Pollution Source to Resource via Value-Added Design." A report for the Hixon Center for Urban Ecology and in fulfillment of F&ES 546a, Yale School of Forestry and Environmental Studies.

"Stephen Epler Hall." 2012. *Landscape Voice*. http://landscapevoice.com/stephen-epler-hall/. Accessed November 7, 2103.

Turner, Cathy. 2005. "A First Year Evaluation of the Energy and Water Conservation of Epler Hall: Direct and Societal Savings." Masters of environmental management project, Department of Environmental Science and Resources, Portland State University. http://www.lafoundation.org/research/landscape-performance-series/scholarly-works/?benefit=benefit_id_7. Accessed November 8, 2013.

Wilson, Nick. 2013. Personal correspondence with authors (principal of Atlas Landscape Architecture).

Historic Fourth Ward Park, Atlanta, Georgia

Reduce pollutant loads in rainwater

Reduce downstream damage from runoff

Safely move, control, and contain rainwater

Capture rain for reuse

Restore or create habitat

Education

Recreation

Public relations

SAFETY

Aesthetic richness

Figure 4.25. It's hard to believe that this inviting park is a detention basin that can manage well beyond a 500-year storm. Everywhere within its very different two blocks of recreation space, this design presents simple safety features that prevent contact with the rainwater (design: HDR; photograph: Eliza Pennypacker).

Date: 2009–2011

Size: 17 acres over 2 city block phases (Phase 1, 5 acres; Phase 2, 12 acres)

Location: Angier Avenue NE, Atlanta, Georgia

Owner: City of Atlanta

Designers: Phase 1, HDR (detention basin park); Phase 2, Wood+Partners (multipurpose recreation park)

Background

Historic Fourth Ward is the only remaining "ward" of six in Atlanta's original subdivision. By the early 2000s, this neighborhood, which contains Martin Luther King Jr.'s birthplace, had become what *The Atlanta Journal-Constitution* called "a barren expanse of cracked concrete, weeds and towering trees surviving against a background of neglect." Change was both necessary and imminent, thanks in part to the Atlanta BeltLine, a 22-mile network of parks, trails, and transit proposed to connect forty-five neighborhoods, planned to run along the east side of the ward. In 2008, the city consequently undertook the Old Fourth Ward Master Plan, the guiding principle of which was sustainability: environmental, social, and economic.

One site in the ward needed particular attention: a barren, contaminated, lowland area in the Clear Creek watershed, just west of the proposed BeltLine, that was subject to flooding in large rain events. If the city could alleviate flooding of this site, land in the area would become more attractive for development lured by the BeltLine. But the existing 9- × 13-foot combined sewer pipe was inadequate, and in the city's effort to mitigate flooding, they discovered that a detention basin designed for a 500-year storm would actually be cheaper than a standard gray infrastructure solution. The city also realized that if the basin were conceived as the centerpiece of a park, that amenity could jumpstart redevelopment of the area. And so this brownfield site became a stormwater-managing park, a jewel on the BeltLine necklace that has spurred more than $400 million in private investments abutting the new Historic Fourth Ward Park.

The park comprises four city parcels: The middle parcel focuses on the sunken detention pond and includes overlooks, plazas, trails, fountains, and an amphitheater. The hillside south parcel of the basin offers an upper lawn, Atlanta's first skate park, a splash pad and playground, and a stream of recirculating rainwater that tumbles along trails and wildflower meadows.

Utility

The basic stormwater management concept at Historic Fourth Ward Park is capture, convey, cleanse, and either reuse in water features or detain and discharge. A deep, 2-acre wet detention pond was dug to the water table; Clear Creek, piped in this area, feeds the pond with 425 gallons of water per minute. Additionally, runoff from the surrounding 800-acre drainage area is piped to the detention pond. Some water from the pond is recirculated to form the south parcel's naturalized stream; some goes to a 20,000-gallon cistern for irrigation. Any stormwater overflow slowly discharges to the Highland Avenue combined sewer through a controlled release.

Rainwater is cleansed in a variety of ways: The recirculating stream aerates and biofilters, and three different fountains in the pond aerate water while sediments deposit at the pond bottom.

The detention and reuse system has significantly reduced peak flow into the combined sewer, but no data are available on the amount.

Sizing for management of runoff from 800 acres meant thinking big: The 35-foot deep, 2-acre wet detention basin has capacity to hold a 500-year design storm. Gray infrastructure for piping is enormous and includes a 24-inch tap into an existing 9- × 13-foot trunk sewer and nearly 1,000 linear feet of 6- × 3-foot box culvert.

The cistern holds 20,000 gallons of combined creek and rainwater used to irrigate the park landscape, and recirculation of creek and rainwater to flow in the stream and fountains presents a creative amenity reuse.

Native wildflower meadows and streamside urban forest plantings characterize the south parcel, and riparian plants in the wet pond create wetland habitat.

Figure 4.26. *(left)* The wet detention basin, at 35 feet deep and 2 acres in size, has significantly mitigated a serious local flooding problem. Some detained rain is diverted to the south parcel's recirculating naturalized stream, and some goes to a cistern for irrigation. Overflow discharges via controlled release into the city sewer system (design: HDR; photograph: Eliza Pennypacker).

Figure 4.27. *(right)* This spiraling water trail carries rain from the upper terrace to the detention basin; water disappears into the nautilus shell–shaped drain cover at the spiral's inner end, to reappear tumbling down a water stair to the detention basin below (design: HDR; photograph: Eliza Pennypacker).

Amenity

Historic Fourth Ward Park celebrates water everywhere: In the south parcel, water appears in a stream and splash pad; in the detention basin parcel, runnels, terraced channels, fountains, plazas, and of course the huge pond present the delight of water in many forms. But a visitor has to really look at these features to realize that much of this is, in fact, *rain*. Three features in the design make clear rainwater statements:

- A spiraling conveyance channel on the upper terrace of the detention pond

- A stepped channel along which rain tumbles from the upper terrace down to the wet pond
- Two horizontal lines of river rock inlaid into the otherwise granite detention basin walls that mark water levels achieved by different size rain events

In the south parcel of the park, curious visitors decipher a captivating rainwater trail that tells the story of rain. First, at the southern terrace above the sunken pond, a curious stone runnel meanders down the gently sloping length of a brick entry plaza. Its source near the street is invisible, but the channel almost seems to be an urbanized extension of the naturalized stream in the adjacent parcel (a nod to Clear Creek). At its lower end, near the pond overlook, the runnel spirals inward, and a beautiful nautilus-shaped drain receives the water. Visitors naturally move from that overlook terrace down a wide, long stairway toward the pond below, and once on those stairs they see a huge discharge pipe in the terrace wall that shunts water from the upper level down a conveyance channel that steps, alongside the pedestrian stairs, all the way down to the pond. So that's where the water on the terrace went! And judging by the size of that pipe orifice, the pond is clearly the destination for the spiraling runnel water and a whole lot more. Once down in the pond zone, surrounded (but amazingly not cramped) by soaring 35-foot-tall granite walls, curious pedestrians notice two perfectly horizontal river rock lines mortared into those walls, one about 4 feet above the path, one about 6 feet. There are only two spots in the entire design where their significance is revealed: At about the pond middle, on opposite sides, letters chiseled in the granite read "100-year storm" on the lower line and "500-year storm" on the upper. Suddenly the rainwater story is clear.

Of course the detention pond itself is a recreation destination where paths and plazas invite visitors to stroll and sit, but the design also ensures encounters with the rainwater system. We're enticed to jump across the shallow, spiraling runnel, to descend the stairs next to the tiered rainwater channel, and to meander the paths along the design storm lines marked in the basin wall.

Safe water viewing is a hallmark of this design, especially from the inviting walkways that meander along the recirculating rainwater stream and the wet pond. In both instances, visitors are kept from straying into the stormwater management systems by stainless steel railings reinforced with thin cables that edge gracefully curving paths; their thin, silvery meanders allow full water visibility while establishing a safe vertical barrier. Down at the detention pond, these lilting paths fly over the water in elegant curves; here, the number of cables is maximized (twelve from top to bottom) to make a water entry unlikely, and a littoral shelf (a planted shelf just below the water level) ensures that anyone taking a plunge won't go deep.

This design makes two statements found in so many effective ARDs: "We care, we're environmentally responsible, and we want you to learn about stormwater" and "We're smart, and we know you'll notice the treatment if it's fun." Befitting its recreational use, everything about the rainwater messages here is fun, encouraging both mental and physical sleuthing to figure them out.

Within this complex, multifaceted design, two aesthetic aspects stand out. First are the lines of water trails that vary throughout, from a tumbling "stream" that zigzags down a hillside to a spiraling runnel, from an arcing stair of water to curving pedestrian paths that feel nearly liquid as they soar over the pond. Also noteworthy is the vast volume of the sunken pond: This is a massive basin obviously capable of managing huge storms, but it is cleverly designed so that, while on paths 35 feet below grade, we never feel claustrophobic.

Of Note

- This ARD proves that green infrastructure can be less expensive than gray: The city estimates that this stormwater management system saved approximately $10 to $15 million.
- This project also proves that a rainwater-focused park can effectively manage rain and promote redevelopment, enhancing both the community and the tax base.
- This project was chosen as one of seven ASLA SITES pilot projects in Georgia.

Sources

Astra Group. n.d. "Clear Creek Combined Sewer Basin Relief." main.astragroupinc.com/wp-content/uploads/2012/01/Clear-Creek.pdf. Accessed December 1, 2013.

Burke, Kevin. 2013. Personal communication with the authors.

HDR, Inc., and Wood + Partners. n.d. "Atlanta's Historic Fourth Ward Park." LandscapeOnline.com. http://landscapeonline.com/research/article/17483. Accessed September 23, 2013.

Tunnell-Spangler-Walsh and Associates. 2008. *Old Fourth Ward Master Plan*. Prepared for the City of Atlanta Department of Planning and Community Development. http://georgiaplanning.org/pdfs/2009_awards/old_fourth_ward__plan_document3.pdf. Accessed March 3, 2015.

The Outwash Basin, Stata Center at MIT, Cambridge, Massachusetts

- Reduce pollutant loads in rainwater
- Reduce downstream damage from runoff
- Safely move, control, and contain rainwater
- Capture rain for reuse

- Education
- Recreation
- **SAFETY**
- Public relations
- Aesthetic richness

Figure 4.28. The Outwash Basin provides an aesthetic foil to Frank Gehry's iconoclastic Stata Center and serves as a nearly inaccessible, sunken rain management system for a large area of impervious surfaces (design: OLIN, Nitsch Engineering; photograph: Stuart Echols).

Date: 2003

Size: 300- × 75-foot basin

Location: Building 32, Vassar Street, Cambridge, Massachusetts

Owner: Massachusetts Institute of Technology

Designers: OLIN; Nitsch Engineering

Background

The city of Cambridge had a major problem with combined sewer overflows (CSOs), including the combined sewers at Vassar and Main Streets, near the project site, which were prone to flooding. Although stormwater was routed from those pipes to a treatment plant, large storm overflows went, untreated, straight to the Charles River. Because discharge from MIT contributed to the problem, in 1998 the university faced stiff fines from the Environmental Protection Agency (EPA). But rather than simply paying for their past environmental sins, MIT worked with the EPA to develop some environmentally responsible solutions for the future. As MIT's director for environmental programs, Jamie Lewis Keith, put it, "MIT's approach is to integrate legal compliance with initiatives to make our campus more environmentally sustainable. This not only reaps greater benefits for the environment, but also reduces regulatory burdens and serves as a potent educational message to our students about environmental responsibility."

When MIT proposed the new Stata Center to house facilities for sciences and humanities, the university committed to addressing Cambridge's stormwater management requirements in sustainable ways for this project. The Outwash Basin at Stata Center was designed to combine form and function in a landscape that would fulfill city requirements by managing all rainwater volumes and flows from half-inch rains to 100-year storms.

According to Steve Benz, lead civil engineer on the project, the design team committed to an integrated process to meet the project's lofty goals. They were determined to usefully marry landscape form and performance, creating a landscape that would be a stormwater management workhorse while offering a unique visual amenity for people walking across the site. As Benz puts it, "This was the first time anything like this had been done, so there was a great deal of trust needed—in the process, product, and team." The team faced many challenges, from budget to regulations; and the functional intentions evolved, with early ideas leading to new ones. The result is a most unusual ARD: a landscape "non sequitur" on the MIT campus and one of the most technologically complex ARDs we've encountered to date.

Utility

The basic stormwater management concept at the Outwash Basin is capture, cleanse, and either reuse for toilets and irrigation or detain and discharge. Rain captured from the Stata Center plaza and roofs, as well as the roofs of three adjacent buildings, is piped to the site; some goes directly to an underground detention vault, and some is piped to the landscaped detention basin, where it is biofiltered, along with sheet runoff from surrounding paved surfaces. Solar-powered pumps recirculate rainwater through the landscaped basin, maintaining wetland moisture needed for the plants while continuing the water cleansing. Because the landscaped basin is lined, it stays moist, but holes in the liner release water to the detention vault below. The vault maintains a 5-day supply of water for flushing toilets and for irrigation; excess flows out to a pump station that sends it on to the sewer system at Vassar Street.

Runoff that goes directly to the detention vault is first cleansed of large particles by a vortex separator (a device that separates suspended solids from stormwater), and runoff that goes directly to the landscaped basin is biofiltered there. Recirculation of rainwater in the basin further cleanses it, and ultraviolet radiation in the detention vault destroys bacteria. Pollutants are reduced by 80 percent.

A major goal of this project was to reduce CSOs and environmental damage to the Charles River. The landscaped basin itself is large enough to detain water from 100-year storms, but it is designed for 24 hour maximum ponding, while the major detention is accomplished in the 50,000-gallon detention vault below grade. Thanks to both this detention and aggressive rainwater reuse, the system reduces peak rate of flow by 90 percent.

This ARD is the most complex of all our case studies, including a lot of gray infrastructure; here, conveyance to the system occurs via pipes rather than a visible water trail. Most of the rainwater is held underground in the detention vault, while water in the landscaped basin—which can reach 100-year volumes without flooding—is released into the detention vault within 24 hours.

Because the site was formerly a brownfield, infiltration was precluded, but more than a million gallons of rainwater per year are reused for irrigation and toilet flushing.

Figure 4.29. *(left)* The curb-like gabion edge not only dissuades entry into the basin (its wire grid is coarse and sharp) but also serves as a trash rack, intercepting debris while accepting water from runoff sheet flow across the plaza and into the basin (design: OLIN, Nitsch Engineering; photograph: Stuart Echols).

Figure 4.30. *(right)* The basin landscape, designed to evoke a New England riverbank and/or drumlin or moraine outwash, was intended as a landscape to view while passing by (or over, via the bridge) (design: OLIN, Nitsch Engineering; photograph: Stuart Echols).

Amenity

Immediately before this project, the site was a sea of asphalt with a two-story World War II building—a zone of service parking and pedestrian scurrying, not a campus attraction. OLIN's concept for the landscaped basin design—the visible, green infrastructure component of this complex system—was to present an abstracted New England riverbank landscape through a sculpted, planted, sunken basin, a subtle expression of water and its ephemerality. The name *Outwash Basin* is a nod to regional glacial geomorphology, where rock and gravel outwash forms linear glacial deposits (drumlins or moraines). The sunken basin, edging Whitaker Building to the south and an asphalt-paved area to the north, was designed as a landscape to view while passing by, not as a place to enter.

OLIN designs are typically aesthetically rich but intentionally not overtly didactic. The Outwash Basin is subtle in its river and geomorphology reference and challenging to understand as a stormwater management system unless a major rain has just filled the sunken basin. When we first visited in 2006, we were disappointed that such an ambitiously engineered system functioned invisibly—and at MIT, where the design would be both understood and appreciated. Since that time, MIT has added a sign that explains the system's function.

This ARD is to be viewed while one passes by, offering a change of scenery in a nod to regional natural landscapes. Two sides of the sunken rectangular basin comprise tiered gabions, which are sittable but pretty uninviting.

The Outwash Basin invites viewing but discourages entry into the system in a variety of ways. First, a bridge crosses the basin, permitting direct access to Whitaker Building; the bridge suggests that the basin is a water container, and its metal mesh-faced railings prevent access. Two sides of the basin that edge the adjacent paved area are lined by terraced gabions; the combination of rock pieces and coarse metal grid provides an uninviting surface for walking or sitting. The south side edges a walkway along Whitaker; although the landform meets grade here, thick planting and boulders in the ARD dissuade access.

Until explanatory signage was added, the message conveyed by the Outwash Basin was, "We want to provide a beautiful landscape to view." But as stated earlier, it was a "landscape non sequitur": a vaguely riverine, inaccessible basin on the edge of a chaotic multiuse asphalt zone. It's amazing what a bit of signage can accomplish: Now the project proclaims, "We care, we are environmentally responsible, and we want you to learn about stormwater," and "We are thorough in our stormwater management, willing to use extensive, complex methods to accomplish sustainable goals." Both messages seem particularly appropriate for the context of this particular university.

Aesthetically, this design first presents a sinuous, green, naturalistic landscape within a hard-edged campus context. The line of its lilting landform curves elegantly, emphasized by its meandering, boulder-strewn edge (suggesting glacial deposit); it contrasts dramatically with the rectilinear form of the basin, suggesting this piece of nature is found by peeling back the local campus grid. Also noteworthy is the contrast in texture and color of plantings and rocks in the basin with surrounding buildings and paved surfaces.

Of Note

- Engineer Steve Benz uses a "landscape performance" strategy in all of his ARDs: Make the landscape function so that it becomes essential to the project.
- The Outwash Basin presents an innovative and effective combination of green and gray infrastructure.
- Plants in the landscaped basin were arranged in grid or other clearly intentional patterns to make weeds obvious for the maintenance crew.
- Postcompletion addition of explanatory signage serves as a reminder: Don't miss the opportunity to educate viewers about the functioning landscape, especially in learning environments!

Sources

Baird, C. Timothy. 2004. "Stata Center Constructed Wetland System." Unpublished document prepared for Landworks Studios, as data relevant to another MIT project.

Benz, Steve. 2013. Personal communication with authors.

Sales, Robert J. 2001. "MIT to Create Three New Environmental Projects as Part of Agreement with EPA." *MIT News*, April 25, 2001. http://web.mit.edu/newsoffice/2001/epa-0425.html. Accessed September 27, 2013.

The Rain Garden at the Oregon Convention Center, Portland, Oregon

Reduce pollutant loads in rainwater

Reduce downstream damage from runoff

Safely move, control, and contain rainwater

Capture rain for reuse

Restore or create habitat

Education

Recreation

SAFETY

Public relations

Aesthetic richness

Figure 4.31. This rain garden presents an abstracted river landscape against a huge blank wall of the Convention Center. Its location on the center's back side, its separation from pedestrians, and its tiered basin system render it safe in spite of managing rain from 5.5 acres of Convention Center roof (design: Mayer/Reed; photograph: Stuart Echols).

Date: 2003

Size: 0.5-acre rain garden for 544,000-square-foot building expansion

Location: NE Martin Luther King Jr. Boulevard, Portland, Oregon

Owner: Metropolitan Exposition Recreation District

Designer: Mayer/Reed

Background

Because of combined sewer overflow problems that became dire in the 1990s—in part due to discharge impacts on endangered species of native fish—the City of Portland has very strict stormwater management requirements for all new projects. In this case, a major expansion of the Oregon Convention Center necessitated thoughtful rainwater quality treatment, retention, and detention, particularly because the center is located near a combined sewer outfall directly into the Willamette River. The nature of the project was challenging: 5.5 acres of convention center roof were divided into five different roof watersheds. The logical site area for stormwater management, along Martin Luther King Jr. Boulevard, was disrupted in two spots—by a fire and life safety pathway and by a parking garage access drive—and the rest of that side of the building presented a massive blank wall.

The solution was to create an abstraction of a native river landscape, fed by five huge and highly visible scuppers along its length. The two required access points were addressed by bridges over the "river," and the windowless building wall became a useful neutral backdrop for the dramatic display of stormwater, with scuppers spewing rain into the exuberantly planted river-like landscape. Also important is the designers' exploitation of the center's use by out-of-towners to showcase in this "river" the plants and geologic formations characteristic of the Pacific Northwest and to convey the importance of improving water quality in local rivers and streams.

The Rain Garden's compelling narrative and public relations value were instrumental in winning project approval in both the design and environmental regulatory review processes.

Utility

The basic stormwater management concept of the Rain Garden at the Oregon Convention Center is capture, convey, cleanse, and either infiltrate or detain and discharge. Five scuppers each drain a different "watershed" of the 5.5-acre roof, dramatically dropping runoff into a river rock–lined series of tiered biofiltration basins that form the "river." The sequential basins step down a gentle slope to ensure gravity flow, separated by dressed stone checkdams. Much of the runoff infiltrates into the subgrade, and any that reaches the end of the biofiltering system is discharged to the Willamette River.

Two treatment strategies reduce runoff pollutants: The basins are planted to ensure biofiltration, and the checkdams slow rainwater flow and promote sediment deposition.

The intent of this rain garden is to significantly reduce combined sewer overflows and rainwater discharge to the Willamette by infiltrating much, and detaining the rest, of runoff from the roof. Although impacts have not been monitored, anecdotal information suggests that little runoff reaches the river.

The Rain Garden "river" is sized to contain up to a 25-year design storm. The basins are generously sized and tiered to promote a slow gravity flow. In an overwhelming rain event, water would overflow the lowest basin to the adjacent street. As designer Carol Mayer Reed quipped, "At that point we should all head for the hills!"

Runoff infiltration promotes groundwater recharge. Carol Mayer Reed reports anecdotally that nearly all runoff infiltrates.

Robust native and ornamental plantings in the Rain Garden provide habitat for local fauna.

Figure 4.32. *(left)* Within the system, a tiered series of basins is generously sized to slow the rain and promote filtration and infiltration (design: Mayer/Reed; photograph: Stuart Echols).

Figure 4.33. *(right)* Materials characteristic of the region (including basalt columns and native plantings) help this garden achieve its intention to showcase the Pacific Northwest. Note the size of the scupper above, relative to the human figure below; this system manages a huge amount of water (design: Mayer/Reed; photograph: Stuart Echols).

Amenity

The Rain Garden at the Oregon Convention Center is a delightful surprise, tucked along a quiet side of the facility. It is beautiful and eye-catching, transforming the center's blank wall into a verdant showcase of the Pacific Northwest. The rainwater celebration is clear whether wet or dry, if one simply looks up the wall to the bold, huge scuppers: "Rain from rooftop to river" is the obvious message.

This ARD educates in two ways. First, the narrative is made very obvious in the design: We clearly see the water trail as it flows through an elegantly designed version of a regional river. Second, an overlook terrace that provides conventioneers a moment of fresh air holds a helpful informational sign on its railing. Graphics and text permit the curious to learn how this design manages rain. Other ideas can be learned as well, about native riparian plant types, wildlife, and regional geology (thanks to beautiful basalt columns that punctuate the design in the horizontal and vertical).

The Rain Garden runs along a sidewalk and street, permitting easy viewing by passersby; it's also the logical focal point for those who step outside the convention center onto the overlook terrace. But the design additionally beckons the adventuresome to actually enter the system. Flat-laid slabs of long basalt extend out from the rain garden checkdams toward the sidewalk; these breaks in the otherwise thickly planted river edge invite entry and permit easy exploration on the flat, smooth rocks. The dressed stone checkdams offer delightful sitting spots, and a bit of clamoring over rocks in other places rewards the interloper with great spots to sit and beautiful views of the system.

The Rain Garden is set back from the sidewalk across a wide strip of mown grass, its edge lushly planted in most spots to dissuade entry; consequently, most viewers never actually enter the system. But for those who find the beckoning entry points mentioned earlier, the system's distribution of rainwater into a sequence of tiered, shallow basins safely controls water depth and velocity.

The Rain Garden at the Oregon Convention Center was conceived as an important public relations statement about the city and the region. It succeeds in proclaiming, "We care, we're environmentally responsible, and we want you to learn about our natural landscape, from rain to river and from vegetation to geology." The design also conveys, "We're smart, resourceful, and clever" in its opportunistic transformation of the center's blank wall into a message-bearing landscape amenity. Finally, its location along the road and sidewalk, and below a terrace with signage, ensures that both passersby and convention attendees get these messages loud and clear.

The massive metal scuppers puncturing the center's upper wall serve as important focal points in this narrative; the "rain from roof to river" message begins there. Then the line of the falling runoff and its transformation into a "river" gently flowing through a regional landscape clarifies the importance of rain. Thoughtful use of materials results in eye-catching color and texture contrasts: the verdant native and ornamental plants against smooth basalt and river rock, the exuberant plantings within the abstracted river "tamed" by a weathering steel edge against the smooth mown lawn.

Of Note

- Public facilities—especially those focused on tourism and frequented by out-of-towners—present a noteworthy opportunity to make a statement about the importance of rain in the local landscape.
- Blank walls can be used to advantage in ARD design.

- One small way that the designers clarified maintenance needs was to use low, weathered steel edging to separate the landscape that demands weekly maintenance (mown lawn) from that which demands maintenance only once a month (the rain garden).

Sources

Mayer Reed, Carol. 2013. Personal correspondence with the authors.

Thompson, William. 2004. "Remembered Rain: In Portland, a Stormwater Garden Celebrates Rain Falling on an Urban Setting." *Landscape Architecture* 94 (9): 60, 62–64, 66.

Queens Botanical Garden, Flushing, New York

- Reduce pollutant loads in rainwater
- Reduce downstream damage from runoff
- Capture rain for reuse
- Restore or create habitat
- Education
- Recreation
- **SAFETY**
- Public relations
- Aesthetic richness

Figure 4.34. Rainwater in this design is often accessible but never dangerous, thanks to its shallow depth and low flow (design: Atelier Dreiseitl with Conservation Design Forum; photograph: Stuart Echols).

Date: 2004

Size: 39-acre botanical garden, 4-acre visitor center site

Location: 43–50 Main Street, Flushing, New York

Owner: Queens Botanical Garden

Designers: Atelier Dreiseitl with Conservation Design Forum; BKSK Architects

Background

In *The Great Gatsby* (1925), F. Scott Fitzgerald characterized this now-reclaimed site as a "valley of ashes." In 1939, the site was repurposed as part of the New York World's Fair, and in 1964, in preparation for another World's Fair, the Queens Botanical Garden was moved to this spot. Located in the most ethnically diverse county in the United States, the Queens Botanical Garden continues to evolve to meet diverse local needs, most recently through a masterplan adopted in 2001 and a new visitor center and administration building completed in 2008.

Two factors in particular drove the direction of the 2001 masterplan. First, the site's former spine, Mill Creek, was long ago piped and the land was subsequently flood-prone; in keeping with the times, the client was eager to adopt a sustainable solution to stormwater management. Second, the Botanical Garden was already extensively used by the diverse community for a wide range of functions, from beekeeping to tai chi, and the community-driven planning process resulted in recognition of the importance of water to all cultures. In their effort to accomplish even more for the community to foster cultural connections and provide opportunities for learning and recreation, the designers decided to highlight rainwater. By cleansing and recycling rain in a variety of site amenities and rainwater celebrations, the design accomplishes a high level of environmental stewardship and responds to the community's cultural values.

Utility

The basic stormwater management concept at the Queens Botanical Garden is capture; cleanse; reuse in water features, cleaning, and toilet flushing; or infiltrate. Rainwater is managed in a variety of ways in different parts of the site. A new "parking garden" infiltrates rain in pervious paving plus "parking fingers" (islands) that biofilter and infiltrate; runoff from large rain events flows to a large rain garden. Surface runoff from the maintenance courtyard and other dirty areas needs more management: It is treated with a mechanical filter, runs through a biotope (an artificial shallow pond with vegetation and gravel substrate), is stored in a cistern, and is then reused for irrigation and cleaning machinery. Roof runoff from the visitor center is addressed in two ways. Rain falling on the auditorium roof is filtered and retained by a green roof. Rain hitting the rest of the visitor center feeds a complex harvesting system: Runoff falls from a scupper into a cleansing biotope, then is stored in a cistern where ultraviolet radiation destroys bacteria. The processed rainwater is then pumped to a fountain at the edge of the Main Street entry plaza, which feeds a "stream" that flows back to the biotope at the visitor center, bringing the rain full circle. Finally, the entire site drains toward a depressed central spine, recalling Mill Creek, that can hold up to a 100-year storm rainwater volume.

Rainwater is cleansed in many ways on this site: in infiltration basins; in biotopes, bioswales, and rain gardens; and in cisterns where bacteria are destroyed by ultraviolet rays. This extensive filtration prepares the rain for reuse in human and natural systems.

One of the goals of this design was to manage all rainwater on site to prevent any downstream discharge. According to the designers, all rain is retained on site.

"Reduce, reuse, recycle" could be the slogan for water use in the new Queens Botanical Garden. Every effort was made to reduce use of potable water site-wide and to reuse rainwater in a variety of ways. Some rain is reused in natural systems, including recharging groundwater through infiltration and irrigating the green roof and plants on site; the rest is harvested for reuse in water features, cleaning machinery and tools, and toilet flushing. In the new visitor center, potable water use is 80 percent lower than in a traditional building of the same size.

To restore depleted soils and showcase regional plant associations, all areas not planned for intensive use were replanted with native species. In other words, all new plants in the rain garden, biotope, bioswales, and green roof are native. This, in combination with extensive areas of surface water, provides habitat for a variety of small fauna in this densely developed area of the city.

Figure 4.35. *(left)* Rain is cleansed and controlled as it traverses a circuit. Here, recirculated rainwater drops from the "fountain stream" via level spreader (lower left) into a channel that gently carries it back to the visitor center, thanks to shallow tiers that brake the water's speed (design: Atelier Dreiseitl with Conservation Design Forum, BKSK Architects; photograph: Stuart Echols).

Figure 4.36. *(right)* This sparkling, touchable fountain at the main entry plaza recirculates rainwater (design: Atelier Dreiseitl with Conservation Design Forum, BKSK Architects; photograph: Stuart Echols).

Amenity

Because this is a botanical garden in a neighborhood of extraordinary diversity, the stormwater management strategy was intended to showcase rainwater and graywater recycling and cleansing technologies in ways that would especially inform children and older adults. And so it is easy to follow rainwater trails from parking lot to rain garden and from roof to biotope, but only thanks to signage do we learn one of the outstanding features of this ARD: Water that flows from a fountain to a stream and back to the biotope at the visitor center—water that is not only visible but also touchable, splashable—is *all* rain. Within this beautiful, well-used community garden, rainwater is the unifying feature.

The rainwater trail here is visible, but in many spots it's not clearly rain; the only overtly visible rainwater is the roof runoff that falls via scupper into the visitor center biotope. It's a surprise, in fact, to learn that the fountain and "stream" are fed by rain, a feature visitors learn through signage. Indeed, throughout the garden information systems tell the story, from signs to pamphlets to a multilingual touchscreen explanation of water conservation and reuse strategies in the visitor center lobby. The site design also provides places, especially in the entry plaza and at the visitor center building, for group gathering to facilitate educational activities.

Throughout the garden, visitors find many opportunities to walk along or sit beside rainwater features. Adding to the delight, water cascading from the gently tiered fountain is touchable, and the rain that flows from that fountain into a stream invites visitors to touch and splash, thanks to pavers that step down to the stream edge. Likewise, outside the visitor center, steps cascade down to the biotope water, inviting interaction.

Surface rainwater everywhere in this ARD is spread out to control its depth. The fountain feature doesn't pool at all; the stream it feeds is a few inches deep, and the biotope near the visitor center slopes in depth from merely splashable nearest walking surfaces to 18 inches deep at the far end (furthest from the building). At the visitor center, low edging on one side and a metal railing on the other prevent missteps into the biotope pool from two boardwalks that cross it; in high-traffic events, planters are added near the low edging to prevent an inadvertent stumble. Rainwater velocity is also controlled by vertical drops: In the fountain, rainwater cascades down 18 inches in a series of twenty semicircular tiers, the result a gentle bubble, and a level spreader dissipates rainwater energy where the stream drops into a channel that returns water down a tiered system to the visitor center biotope.

The public relations messages at Queens Botanical Garden are many and clear. First, "We care, we're environmentally responsible, and we want you to learn about stormwater" is nearly a mantra, thanks to extensive signage explaining the equally extensive environmentally responsible stormwater management. One message found less often in our case study ARDs is, "We care, and we want you to know you can do this yourself," which is particularly apparent in the parking garden. Here, the homeowner might note the porous paving strategy (regular pavers set in pea gravel) and think, "I could do this at home!" Visitor access to the rainwater at the fountain, stream, and biotope is delightful and most unusual in the United States, where liability concerns typically preclude touching rain (sounds a bit silly, doesn't it?). The message conveyed by touchable rainwater is, "We are progressive and innovative," because we care about and know how to make it safe for human access. Finally, that physical access combined with the variety of water movement—cascading, sheeting, flowing, splashing—says, "We're smart; we know you'll notice the stormwater treatment if it's fun."

Between the visitor center and the entry plaza, the line of the water trail leads visitors throughout this complex site, and the entry plaza fountain is a fitting focal point that marks the spot where stored rainwater reemerges to traverse the system. Color and texture are important as well: First we find different textures of water, from the frothy fountain to the burbling stream to the still, clear pools around the visitor center; additionally, the stream presents a "human" texture on the plaza side (stepped rectangular white pavers) and a "natural" texture of plantings and shallow stream bank on the other.

Of Note

- This ARD proves that, with some regulation-required cleansing, roof runoff can flow in accessible water features, to the delight of users.
- Characteristic of Atelier Dreiseitl's approach, the process for this design was highly participatory. As Herbert Dreiseitl explains, "Our first workshop was an art event to find the idea . . . [with local citizens and stakeholders]. We made water experiments, had an evening of water stories from each of the participants, and were drawing already a first outline of the final design."
- The water trail can serve as a spine to lead visitors through a complex site.

Sources

AIA/COTE. 2009. "Queens Botanical Garden Visitor Center." AIA/COTE Top Ten Green Projects. http://www2.aiatopten.org/hpb/site.cfm?ProjectID=1018. Accessed September 20, 2013.

American Society of Landscape Architects, Ladybird Johnson Wildflower Center, United States Botanic Garden. 2008. "Queens Botanical Garden: Treating Rainwater as a Resource, Not 'Waste.'" In *Draft Guidelines and Performance Benchmarks: The Sustainable Sites Initiative*, p. 87. http://www.cpd.wsu.edu/Documents/SSI_Guidelines_Draft_2008.pdf. Accessed September 17, 2013.

Conservation Design Forum and Atelier Dreiseitl. 2002. "Queens Botanical Garden Master Plan." http://www.queensbotanical.org/media/file/masterplan_complete_web.pdf. Accessed March 3, 2015.

Dreiseitl, Herbert. 2013. Personal correspondence with the authors.

Queens Botanical Garden. n.d. "Sustaining the Future." Brochure obtained at the Queens Botanical Garden Visitor Center on June 19, 2013.

High Point, Seattle, Washington

Reduce pollutant loads in rainwater

Reduce downstream damage from runoff

Safely move, control, and contain rainwater

Capture rain for reuse

Restore or create habitat

Education

Recreation

Safety

PUBLIC RELATIONS

Aesthetic richness

Figure 4.37. At this residential community, sustainable stormwater management is a selling point (design: SvR Design Company, Mithun, Bruce Meyers; photograph: Stuart Echols).

Date: 2000–2010

Size: 120 acres

Location: 6550 32nd Avenue Southwest, Seattle, Washington

Owner: Seattle Housing Authority and others

Designers: SvR Design Company; Mithun; Bruce Meyers; see Seattle Housing Authority website for many additional consultants

Background

The original High Point Garden Community, consisting of 1,300 residential units in 404 buildings, was built in 1941 to house defense workers and their families during World War II. The community sat on the West Seattle plateau above Longfellow Creek, which flows into the Duwamish River, then to Puget Sound, and the majority of High Point's stormwater discharged to Longfellow Creek.

In the 1990s, Seattle adopted a commitment to restore local natural system health, especially in the Puget Sound watershed, and particularly focused on salmon habitat. As one of four urban salmon-bearing streams in Seattle, Longfellow Creek was targeted for environmental mitigation. At the same time, the 60-year-old High Point Garden Community was in need of significant revitalization, by that time consisting of 716 units of public housing in one- and two-story buildings.

In 2000 the Seattle Housing Authority (SHA) obtained a Housing Opportunities for People Everywhere (HOPE) VI grant from the Department of Housing and Urban Development, which required redevelopment rather than rehabilitation of existing housing. SHA committed to creating a unique, mixed-income neighborhood grounded in the goal of building community. That mission expanded when the Seattle Public Utilities (SPU) proposed also to make High Point a model for sustainable urban neighborhood development. To do that, the SPU approached the SHA about a partnership to address the city's Integrated Drainage Plan project requirements through a natural drainage system. SHA agreed to fund traditional drainage systems required by code, and SPU agreed to fund the cost difference to create the natural drainage system.

High Point became Seattle's first large-scale green neighborhood, integrating New Urbanist principles of walkability and community building with environmental responsibility in building and landscape design, including stormwater management to mitigate environmental damage to Longfellow Creek. The result is a thirty-four-block, mixed-use community planned for up to 1,600 units (both owned and rented, affordable and market rate, from apartments to single family homes), including a branch library, medical center, and planned neighborhood shopping. All existing infrastructure was replaced (water, separated sanitary and storm sewer, electricity, phone, cable), including roadways changed from curving to grid for easy wayfinding, their widths reduced for traffic calming. Each of the thirty-four "superblocks" has a pocket park, and the community is enriched by about 23 acres of additional open space (12.5 acres on site and 11 acres nearby).

The process was not easy: Interagency and interdepartmental agreements were made, codes had to be changed, and High Point–specific requirements and standards were created (because, in 2001, no examples of neighborhood-wide natural drainage system or green infrastructure applications existed). Additionally, the project's success required a highly collaborative and integrated approach to design and construction. The result is a design that most unusually uses its stormwater system as a means to build community.

Utility

The basic stormwater management concept at High Point is capture, convey, cleanse, and either infiltrate or detain and discharge as much as possible, through a site-specific, sequential combination of management techniques on each block. Roof runoff travels via downspout to a flow-through filter planter, rain barrel, conveyance furrow, or pipe/pop-up emitter, then to a rain garden. Additional runoff infiltrates through porous paving or flows via turf-lined swales to dispersal trenches along sidewalks. If that doesn't address all rain volume, excess runoff then moves to natural drainage system bioswales that run along street rights-of-way, and any remaining runoff from huge storms goes to a large, central wet detention basin. Overall, High Point strives to achieve a 40 percent pervious to 60 percent impervious ratio (compared with the city's typical 25 to 75 percent ratio) and successfully reverts 8 percent of the Longfellow Creek basin to emulate predevelopment pasture conditions.

Stormwater filtration occurs throughout High Point, with parcel-specific techniques including flow-through filter planters, rain gardens, turfed or vegetated swales and furrows, and gravel trenches. Most notably, 3 miles of rights-of-way throughout the community are richly planted bioswales that cleanse runoff not captured by the sequential systems within each block.

At High Point, every effort is made to prevent damage to Longfellow Creek and its salmon population. To that end, a site-specific sequence of techniques on each block ensures maximum reasonable infiltration, including the vegetated swales that edge many roads and capture runoff not managed by systems within the blocks. In the case of larger storms, city storm drains carry overflow from the bioswales to the wet detention pond near the northeast site corner; water from the pond is slowly released into Longfellow Creek.

Figure 4.38. *(left)* If runoff exceeds the capacity of community-wide infiltration strategies, overflow is sent to this 5.2-million-gallon wet detention pond, with controlled release to Longfellow Creek (design: SvR Design Company, Mithun, Bruce Meyers; photograph: Stuart Echols).

Figure 4.39. *(right)* Focus on rain is even evident in sidewalks, incised with concentric circles to look like raindrops on water. Note porous sidewalk in background, adjacent to robust bioswale plantings on left (design: SvR Design Company, Mithun, Bruce Meyers; photograph: Stuart Echols).

Thanks to project-wide emphasis on infiltration and layered management techniques in each block, large volumes of stormwater are rarely contained or conveyed on site; rather, carefully sized pipes, furrows, and swales quietly contain and convey generally small amounts of excess runoff. Design criteria for conveyance and containment include the following:

- Pipe conveyance for peak flow of the 25-year storm
- Detention of 100-year storm in a 5.2-million-gallon wet detention pond
- Safe discharge of the 5,000-year storm from the detention pond

In addition to extensive neighborhood-wide infiltration for groundwater recharge, the High Point *Site Drainage Technical Standards* document (for design and construction of future phases) recommends rain barrels for water harvesting in appropriate contexts.

Native plants mix with ornamental plants throughout High Point to create habitat.

Amenity

Rarely have we encountered an ARD that so joyfully celebrates rain—and in a 120-acre community, no less! The developers' commitment to use the natural drainage system as a means to promote community is insightful, commendable, and evident throughout the property. High Point's branding message focuses on environmental stewardship, and especially rain. The prevalence of this unified message undoubtedly contributes to a sense of place and community: Residents of High Point know what this place is about, and ideally they value this ethic. Let's hope that High Point's "rain brand" becomes a national model.

At High Point, reminders of the hydrologic cycle are found everywhere: in residential splash blocks sculpted to represent salmon swimming "upstream" toward downspouts, in densely planted bioswales along rights-of-way and porous sidewalks where signage clarifies their stormwater management roles, in brass dragonfly decorations on drain inlets, and in sidewalks incised with concentric circles to look like raindrops splashing on a pond. In the many different treatment techniques, often supplemented by colorful, brief signage, designers at High Point have tried to make people aware of the presence, movement, and significance of rain and the ways that the designed landscape ensures its resource value. The community has put additional effort into neighborhood and external outreach through multilingual brochures and hosting hundreds of tours for interested people from all over the United States and beyond.

The rain-focused imagery at High Point is not only educational, it's delightful. And it's both strategically located and impossible to miss: One can't walk far without encountering "raindrop sidewalks" or colorfully planted swales. The wet detention pond presents a particularly strong recreational amenity: Platforms overlook both the pond and water cascades, while sloping lawn and pond-circling pathways provide opportunities to pass by, exercise, or sit and observe.

Emphasis on stormwater dispersal and infiltration, often in heavily planted swales and rain gardens, ensures a high level of safety; water volume and speed are never problematic. In spots where water flows or ponds, the designs allow people to safely observe the rain. Raised walkways cross bioswales, stairs and overlooks at the wet detention pond are safely railed, and the pond's edge has a low fence to allow views but restrict access.

Here lies the amenity brilliance of High Point: As mentioned earlier, the rainwater stewardship message is everywhere, saying, "We care, and we want you to learn about rain so you'll care, too"; "We are smart, resourceful, and clever in our multifaceted approach and our ability to make it beautiful and fun; we hope you share our environmental commitment (how could you not?) and value our community"; and, most important for marketing, "We hope you want to be part of this unique, environment-focused community." In sum, the messages at High Point are clear, ubiquitous, and effective.

It's challenging to briefly characterize all the aesthetic qualities of a 120-acre community; instead, we present one key overall compositional strategy: Hundreds of highly visible, often richly planted stormwater management techniques throughout the community establish an aesthetic theme of rhythm, repetition, and unity focused on rain, as well as rich colors and textures that, cumulatively, create visual interest unusual in a mixed-income housing project—once again proclaiming, "High Point is special."

Of Note

- ARD can foster a sense of community and serve as a branding or marketing strategy. At High Point, artist Bruce Meyers's rain-focused works, from splash blocks to "raindrop sidewalks," contribute significantly to the message.
- The *High Point Community Site Drainage Technical Standards* and the *High Point Community Natural Drainage and Landscape Maintenance Guidelines* have been key to presenting requirements for maintenance and for future development in this complex, phased project.
- Contractors at High Point were held to unusually high standards of environmental performance. Two strategies to avoid failure have been:
  - Using traditional construction materials and language to minimize bidders' fear of the unknown
  - Explaining environmental intentions to construction crews, who then became part of the solution by offering helpful suggestions

Sources

Cornwall, Warren. 2005. "Neighborhood Tries to Honor Mother Nature's Runoff Rules." *The Seattle Times*, June 10, 2005. http://community.seattletimes.nwsource.com/archive/?date=20050610&slug=storm10m. Accessed October 22, 2013.

"The High Point Neighborhood Wins 'Show You're Green' Award." In *Welcome to the High Point Neighborhood*. http://www.thehighpoint.com/show_youre_green.php. Accessed October 14, 2013.

Mithun/SvR. 2008. "High Point: Restoring Habitat in an Urban Neighborhood." In *Sustainable Sites Initiative Guidelines and Performance Benchmarks, draft 2008*. Sustainable Sites Initiative: 35.

Seattle Housing Authority. 2002. *Final Environmental Impact Statement, High Point Revitalization Plan*.

Staeheli, Peg. 2013. Personal contact with the authors.

SvR Design Company. 2006. *High Point Community Site Drainage Technical Standards*. https://static1.squarespace.com/static/528fd58de4b07735ce1807b2/t/541a1cf3e4b0f8281ce77756/1410997491349/High-Point-Technical-Drainage-Standards_LID_GSI_green-stormwater-infrastructure_web.pdf. Accessed March 3, 2015.

Pacific Cannery Lofts, Oakland, California

- Reduce pollutant loads in rainwater
- Reduce downstream damage from runoff
- Safely move, control, and contain rainwater
- Capture rain for reuse
- Education
- Recreation
- Safety
- **PUBLIC RELATIONS**
- Aesthetic richness

Figure 4.40. In the Entry/Dining Room Court, the design proclaims rain stewardship through a clever design element: Downspouts discharge into runnels within sittable concrete walls at townhouse entry doors (design: Miller Company Landscape Architects, David Baker Architects; photograph: Miller Company Landscape Architects).

Date: 2009

Size: 2.7 acres

Location: 12th and Pine Street, Oakland, California

Owner: Holliday Development Company

Designers: Miller Company Landscape Architects, David Baker Architects

Background

One hundred years ago, this westernmost neighborhood of Oakland teemed with activity in industrial warehouses and provided their workers convenient housing in Victorian bungalows, but with the demise of the industries, the area became a brownfield zone of abandonment criss-crossed by raised highways and rail lines. But the location—close to downtown Oakland, a transit station, and the Bay Bridge—made this area ideal for transit-oriented housing. And so the Central Station neighborhood was conceived: 30 acres of largely forgotten opportunity would become 1,000 housing units with parks, commercial services, and an urban farm.

Pacific Cannery Lofts is part of that vision: 163 units (lofts and townhouses) repurpose the old cannery with housing and gardens grounded to place by artfully used industrial artifacts. The old cannery roof was partially peeled away to reduce impervious surface and create two rain-receiving interior courtyards; two others were created by the addition of new buildings flanking the old. These gardens not only serve for gathering, but also offer some very interesting statements about, and management of, rain. Each courtyard has a name and a distinct identity that provides a unique sense of home for each different resident group. There's the Entry/Dining Room Court, offering a generous table for residents to gather around; the Living Room Court, where banquette seating surrounds the central walkway, both providing gathering space and ensuring interaction with passersby; the Grove, where edible plants create a virtual forest of color and texture; and the Lew Hing Court, an Asian-inspired garden named for the cannery's original owner. In all four, the access walk forms a central spine, allowing the rest of each space to be a themed garden that houses unit terraces and entries as well as gathering areas. The client was open to the designers' commitment to these garden courts as important social spaces that provide both identity and clear public–private transitions for the residents, and to creative stormwater management approaches.

Utility

The basic stormwater management concept at Pacific Cannery Lofts is capture, convey, cleanse, and either infiltrate or detain and discharge. The core structure of all four courts—central walkway spine with extensive plantings on the sides—provides plenty of garden landscape for cleansing and infiltration. Additionally, porous paving used for the path in the Grove and a raised boardwalk in the Lews Hing Court both increase cleansing and infiltration; and the rainwater in the Entry/Dining Room Court falls from roofs via downspouts at unit entry doors into river pebble–filled runnels in bench structures, then into infiltration trenches filled with tumbled, recycled glass that line both sides of the central walk.

Rainwater cleansing is achieved in the biofiltering landscapes of each courtyard, including the gravel infiltration trenches of the Entry/Dining Room Court and the porous paving of the Grove.

Much of the rainwater that falls on this site is retained from the storm system. Although the system has not been monitored, designer Jeffrey Miller estimates that 180,000 gallons per year are retained in the Entry/Dining Room Court; because the old warehouse roof was peeled off to create the Lew Hing and Living Room courts, Miller estimates an additional 35,000 gallons of retention per year thanks to those rain-absorbing courtyard landscapes.

The stormwater system in the Entry/Dining Room Court is sized to manage a 2-year storm. Rain moves from four downspouts to four raised runnels, each 16 inches wide; that water then drops into infiltration trenches filled with recycled glass. In large rain events, if these infiltration trenches overflow, the designers placed backup drain inlets just below the recycled glass to carry the excess to the storm drain system. Because these inlets aren't visible, small wheels from the old machinery were pressed into the concrete adjacent to those inlets to let maintenance personnel know where they are.

Runoff from roofs surrounding the other courts goes directly to the city sewer. If downpours flood the Lew Hing or Living Room landscapes, underdrains and surface drains carry the excess to the city storm system.

Infiltration is the goal in this stormwater management system, with a hearty amount of runoff captured for groundwater recharge. Additionally it's worth noting that rain entering the courtyards supplements the automatic irrigation system, which is "dialed back" during the winter rainy period.

Figure 4.41. *(left)* In each distinct courtyard, walking is confined to a central spine, and landscape functions as an infiltration sponge. This idea is most apparent in the Lew Hing Court, named for the cannery owner (design: Miller Company Landscape Architects, David Baker Architects; photograph: Miller Company Landscape Architects).

Figure 4.42. *(right)* In the Entry/Dining Room Court of this cannery-turned-housing, focus on rain is proclaimed through infiltration trenches filled with recycled tumbled glass, lit with LED wavy lines along the central sidewalk (design: Miller Company Landscape Architects, David Baker Architects; photograph: Miller Company Landscape Architects).

Amenity

The design of Pacific Cannery Lofts isn't focused on stormwater; it's really focused on community. It provides social spaces that promote interaction, linking with the surrounding community and creating different place identities for different groups of residents. But in the designers' effort to address the latter, part of the placemaking strategy was to create four separate courts, each of which says something about rain.

The most overt rain statement occurs in the Entry/Dining Room Court. Here, roof runoff is gathered at four townhouse doorways in clever multipurpose structures. At each, a raised concrete bench extends 8 to 11 feet from the building into the space and offers a spot for the resident to perch next to his or her entrance, whether to read mail or chat with neighbors; that bench contains a 16-inch-wide, river pebble–filled runnel that carries roof runoff from the downspout to the end of the runnel bench, where it drops into an infiltration bed that runs along the central courtyard walkway. These linear infiltration beds bracket the central walkway and very clearly suggest "rain" thanks to the fact that they are filled with 4 inches of tumbled, clear, recycled glass. But there's more: LED lights trace wavy lines under the glass pebbles; at night, these sinuous ribbons come to life, unmistakably marking this as a water-receiving place.

One could argue that the other three courtyards don't speak of rain; but their consistent structure—narrow, central walkway up the middle with lush landscape on each side—subtly suggests that we're invited to partake, but the space is as much about rain and plants as it is about people. The Lew Hing Court is particularly rain sensitive. The walkway spine through it is a raised boardwalk, subtly enforcing the idea that we should stay off this rain-receiving landscape. The rain awareness in all these spaces is enhanced by the courtyard enclosure: rain falling into a courtyard seems so much more intense and noticeable than rain in the larger landscape, thanks to the small, focused "rain column" created by surrounding buildings.

Rain in the Entry/Dining Room Court is just plain fun, whether by day or night. We can sit next to the bench runnel or walk right next to the glass-filled infiltration trench. In the Grove, we can watch the rain disappear into the porous decomposed granite central walkway as we traverse its length. In the Lew Hing Court, we tread lightly on the narrow, linear boardwalk above the rain-slurping landscape. In each, when rain happens, it is visible and close.

Within this design, stormwater is managed with neither ponding nor runnels that we walk across; at the same time, we are made aware of rain, especially in the Entry/Dining Room Court, where the water trail reads whether wet or dry. One of the key contributors to our perceived safety is the fact that our movement through these landscapes is restricted to the designed paths: Stepping off the hard surfaces means stepping into the water-receiving landscape.

The main message here is, "We value and promote community," and a secondary message is, "We're environmentally responsible and want you to notice the importance of rain here." Particularly in the Entry/Dining Court, the clever multipurpose runnel benches, and the grays and whites of concrete, stone, and glass pebbles all say, "We're smart, innovative, and sophisticated," and the glass-filled and LED-lit infiltration trenches say, "We're hip" and "We know you'll notice the rain if it's fun!"

In the Entry/Dining Room Court, line is key: The visible line of the rainwater trail takes it from roof to ground in an elegant set of vertical-to-horizontal runs, then the LED-lit infiltration trenches transform the central walkway into a symbolic stream of water and people. In each space, the contrast in texture and color and the presence of a thin, central walkway axis with lush plantings on both sides strongly suggest that the landscape and rain own the courtyard, while we move through or pause in the "human zones" only.

Of Note

- Overflow drains in the glass-pebble-filled infiltration trench are invisible (under the glass pebbles); to help maintenance workers find them, gear handles from the old cannery are embedded in the concrete in spots next to the drains.
- Recycled glass is such a great material for ARDs! It should be used much more often.
- The landscape architect on this project had worked with the same client on a number of successful projects, resulting in a level of trust by the client in the designer. A strategic way to embark on your own ARD approach to stormwater management is to suggest it to a client with whom you already enjoy a track record of success.

Sources

ASLA. 2010. "Honor Award: Pacific Cannery Lofts, Oakland, CA USA." Residential Design 2010 ASLA Professional Awards. http://www.asla.org/2010awards/161.html. Accessed December 8, 2013.

ASLA. 2013. "Case Study: Pacific Cannery Lofts, Oakland, California, USA." *Designing Our Future: Sustainable Landscapes.* http://www.asla.org/sustainablelandscapes/cannerylofts.html. Accessed December 13, 2013.

Calkins, Meg. 2012. "Pacific Cannery Lofts." *The Sustainable Sites Handbook.* Hoboken, NJ: Wiley.

Miller Company Landscape Architects. n.d. "Pacific Cannery Lofts." http://millercomp.com/projects/pacific-cannery-lofts. Accessed December 7, 2013.

Schnitker, Jeremy. 2010. "Bringing the Indoors Outdoors." *San Francisco Chronicle* January 31, 2010, p. H-6. http://www.sfgate.com/realestate/article/Bringing-the-indoors-outdoors-3201516.php#ixzz0eOqn3hzX. Accessed December 14, 2013.

Venhaus, Heather L., and Dreiseitl, Herbert. 2012. "Case Study: Pacific Cannery Lofts." *Designing the Sustainable Site: Integrated Design Strategies for Small Scale Sites and Residential Landscapes.* Hoboken, NJ: Wiley.

CASE STUDY

Pierce County Environmental Services, University Place, Washington

- Reduce pollutant loads in rainwater
- Reduce downstream damage from runoff
- Safely move, control, and contain rainwater
- Capture rain for reuse
- Restore or create habitat
- Education
- Recreation
- **PUBLIC RELATIONS**
- Safety
- Aesthetic richness

Figure 4.43. Rainwater stewardship messages abound at this combined recreation–public works facility. Here, visitors are reminded that roof runoff falling from the scupper relates to Puget Sound in the background (design: Bruce Dees & Associates, SvR Design Company, The Miller|Hull Partnership; photograph Stuart Echols).

Date: 2002

Size: 22 acres

Location: 950 64th Street West, University Place, Washington

Owner: Pierce County Public Works and Utilities

Designers: Bruce Dees & Associates; SvR Design Company; The Miller|Hull Partnership; Arai/Jackson Architects and Planners

Background

Steilacoom gravel was extracted from this site and an additional 900 contiguous acres for 100 years. By the 1990s, environmental degradation of the whole "Chambers Creek Property" was so bad—especially to its 3 miles of river estuary and 2 miles of saltwater shoreline along Puget Sound—that in 1997 Pierce County created a 50-year masterplan to heal the 930-acre site. Called "Reclaiming Our Resources," the masterplan proposed to transform the huge site into a sustainable and community-beneficial resource with a particularly unusual pairing of program elements. This site would house both environmental services (wastewater, solid waste, and surface water management) and extensive public recreation facilities, from golf course to dog park to play fields. This seemingly odd marriage is actually quite cunning in an environmentally responsible way: By using cutting-edge sustainable strategies in all of the environmental facilities and then encouraging citizens to visit, learn from, and play near these facilities, Pierce County achieves a high level of public environmental education and awareness, both of the county's stewardship efforts and of residents' individual responsibilities.

The Pierce County Environmental Services Building (PCESB) was the first significant project grounded in the "Reclaiming Our Resources" masterplan, and in keeping with that plan, it combines environmental management with public education and recreation. The main building houses offices for county Environmental Services (public works and utilities) on one side and public meeting rooms and didactic exhibits on the other (popular for retreats and even weddings). The site includes a well-screened service garage and yard on the southwest corner (linked to the wastewater treatment plant offsite, where biosolids are converted to fertilizer pellets) and a major community pedestrian and bike trail linking to onsite playing fields and a concession stand. Other public trails throughout the site afford pleasant walks to, for example, the onsite Chambers Creek Labyrinth. And in keeping with the overall "stealth environmental education" strategy, stormwater management at this site is extensive, multifaceted, and highly visible.

Utility

The basic stormwater management concept at PCESB is capture, convey, cleanse, convey and cleanse more, then infiltrate, accomplished in a linear sequence of multiple treatment techniques. Roof run-off from the main building falls from a scupper into a concrete basin (made with Steilacoom gravel aggregate, a nod to the site's history); the basin is incised with a spiral, so runoff spirals through it and on to a created wetland. Any overflow from the wetland continues via pipe across the building entry plaza to bioretention gardens; excess runoff continues down a bioswale that also accepts runoff from adjacent parking lots and the main pedestrian path. Bioswale overflow is carried via pipe across a road to a backup in-system flow splitter that's pretty unique: Two valves divert half of the runoff into a grass-lined swale and half into a wetland plant–lined swale, and a third valve, currently unused, will divert some runoff into a yet-to-be-developed type of system based on future advances in technology. All remaining runoff, including from the playing fields, infiltrates.

Because of Pierce County's commitment to clean groundwater recharge, filtration is emphasized throughout the sequential system: first in the wetland that receives roof runoff, then in the bioswale that filters runoff from roads and parking lots, next in the grass-lined and wetland plant–lined swales (which are monitored to collect data about which lining filters more effectively), and finally in the grass-covered infiltration basin.

One of the most important stormwater goals in this project—characteristic of nearly every project in the greater Seattle area since the 1990s—is mitigation of damage to surface water bodies, especially those where salmon live and spawn. Here, degradation of Puget Sound was extensive, at the same time that the underlying soil conditions readily permit infiltration. The result was the logical decision to prevent all discharge to surface waters by infiltrating all runoff.

Conveyance and containment techniques on this site are carefully sized to avoid flooding or high-velocity water movement: Pipes and swales are sized for the 25-year storm, and catch basins are set to prevent the overflow of a 100-year storm. And the sequential system allows excess runoff to move on to the next treatment phase, with some infiltration occurring at most steps.

Again, all rain infiltrates on this site, recharging groundwater. This occurs via bioswale, infiltration basin, and porous paving (including, in different places, grasscrete pavers, porous asphalt, and natural resin paving).

Figure 4.44. *(left)* At the end of the 270-foot long infiltrating bioswale overflow is directed to one of two different swales: on the left, a pebble-and-riparian plant-lined swale, on the right a grass-lined swale, both of which function, as the sign states, as "Micro Water Filters" (design: Bruce Dees & Associates, SvR Design Company, The Miller|Hull Partnership; photograph Stuart Echols).

Figure 4.45. *(right)* The axial bioswale is strategically located adjacent to a major pedestrian and bicycle path that leads to community play fields in the background. Note interpretive sign at the flow splitter plaza beyond (design: Bruce Dees & Associates, SvR Design Company, The Miller|Hull Partnership; photograph Stuart Echols).

One of the tenets of the Chambers Creek Master Plan is reintroduction of native species to help restore site health. In the PCESB site, native wildflower meadows and wetland species help to fulfill the masterplan intentions.

Amenity

The PCESB site design successfully combines public recreation and site reclamation in a multifaceted landscape that not only celebrates rain but visually links the resource of rain to the larger natural landscape and educates visitors at every turn.

From the building scupper at one corner of the site all the way to the infiltration basin at the far end, every facet of the sequential rainwater system is adjacent to public amenities (trails and recreational fields). And for 270 feet of that sequence, the bioswale runs straight as an arrow along parking and the major community trail, on axis with Mount Rainier and Mount Olympus to link rain on this site to the larger natural context. And at the end of this axis, we find an interesting learning opportunity in the flow splitter plaza: Here, signage clarifies that three valves on the axis divert runoff through different swales on its way to the infiltration basin (one grass-lined, one wetland plant–lined, one "awaiting future technologies"). This design not only manages rain sustainably in many ways, it also ensures that visitors notice, thanks to the very visible water trail. Throughout, clever and effective signage provides detail. Along all paths, yellow signs each provide just a snippet of information; because every sign is both brief and intriguing, visitors soon find themselves looking for the next yellow marker to learn another environmental tidbit. By the time they've reached their destination, visitors have learned a great deal about the environmental intentions of this design. In sum, it's the best example of "stealth education" we've seen.

A key characteristic of this design is strategic location of stormwater management adjacent to public paths and destinations. Local residents can't go from home to play field, or from car to building, without enjoying a view of some part of this ARD. And the overall Chambers Creek strategy—wedding recreation with water management of all kinds—is a great idea for any ARD.

Two very different safety strategies are found here: First, visitors are encouraged to view the wetland via a boardwalk, but it's edged with cabled railings that promote visibility but preclude access. Elsewhere the various bioretention gardens and long bioswale disperse runoff to minimize ponding depth.

The PCESB design is a public relations masterpiece, happily chirping environmental "do good/feel good" messages of all kinds: "We're smart, and we want you to learn about stormwater," "We're progressive and experimental" (evident in signage that highlights such features as resin paving), and "We know you'll notice the treatment if it's visible and fun." The entire site proclaims the county's environmental stewardship and commitment to community.

As we've found in so many great ARDs, the line of the water trail is the key to the rainwater story. At PCESB, the water line from the building scupper all the way down the axial bioswale to the flow splitter plaza is the spine of the entire design.

Of Note

- Site design that puts visitors next to the stormwater management wherever possible is a great strategy for ARD.
- Combining public utility with public recreation can create unexpected synergy.
- At the design team's suggestion, Pierce County Public Works decided not to pursue LEED certification, using those funds instead to create interpretive displays and signage throughout the site.
- This design achieves amazing success in "stealth education" through its signage strategy: Keep the text brief, focus on one point on each sign, locate signs along pedestrian trails, and use eye-catching color to alert pedestrians in advance to the next tidbit of info.

Sources

AIA/COTE. 2004. Pierce County, Washington Environmental Services Building (Pierce County Environmental Services). In "AIA/COTE Top Ten Awards." http://www2.aiatopten.org/hpb/ratings.cfm?ProjectID=162. Accessed November 8, 2013.

Dees, Bruce. 2013. Personal contact with the authors.

Pierce County. 2003. *Chambers Creek Properties Standards and Guidelines.* http://www.co.pierce.wa.us/?nid=3032. Accessed February 5, 2014.

Pierce County Public Works and Utilities Department. 2007. *Chambers Creek Properties Master Site Plan.* http://www.co.pierce.wa.us/?nid=3032. Accessed February 5, 2014.

Washougal Town Square, Washougal, Washington

- Reduce pollutant loads in rainwater
- Reduce downstream damage from runoff
- Safely move, control, and contain rainwater
- Education
- Recreation
- Safety
- PUBLIC RELATIONS
- Aesthetic richness

Figure 4.46. Washougal Town Square was built as a downtown anchor and catalyst for development. Its central courtyard proclaims the town's commitment to clean water through numerous installations, including this splash sculpture that receives roof runoff via the long aqueduct visible on the right (design: GreenWorks, Sienna Architecture Company, Ivan McLean; photograph: Stuart Echols).

Date: 2005–2007

Size: 100- × 80-foot courtyard

Location: 1700 Main Street, Washougal, Washington

Owner: Lone Wolf Investments

Designers: GreenWorks; Sienna Architecture Company; Ivan McLean

Background

Washougal, Washington is a tiny but growing city (currently around 15,000 population) about 20 miles east of the bustling vibrancy of Portland, Oregon, and Vancouver, Washington. The city, whose name means "Rushing Waters," sits at the confluence of the Washougal and Columbia Rivers, at the gateway to the Columbia River Gorge and within eyeshot of the Cascades. It's a place of natural beauty and resources, including excellent water quality and quantity in both surface and groundwater sources. And, of course, both rivers are home to abundant salmon and steelhead trout.

By the early 1990s, when Washougal's population was below 5,000, the tiny city lacked a vital downtown core but was sprawling with residential development on its periphery, and so Washougal responded to the Washington Growth Management Act by developing the "City of Washougal Comprehensive Plan for Growth Management Act Compliance" to accommodate future needs without sacrificing the city's character and resources. Within the expansive plan were a vision for the downtown to become "a dense, unified area with a common design theme and streetscape elements" and a commitment to effective groundwater protection and stormwater management. By 1998, ultraviolet ray treatment was added to the city's sewer treatment plant to protect the Columbia River fish population from effluent discharge (so serious was their commitment to natural resources); by 2002, the city approved its Downtown Revitalization Plan; and by 2007, Phase 1 of the Washougal Downtown Revitalization Project was complete.

Redevelopment of Washougal's downtown has been grounded in New Urbanist principles of density, walkability, and legible fabric. In keeping with the city's values, one of the clear design themes of the new downtown is stormwater management. Christopher Freshley Landscape Architects designed stormwater swales along downtown streets, robustly planted and punctuated by horizontal basalt columns intended to evoke the log rafts of Washougal's logging history. And the major Washougal booster, Lone Wolf Development, built Washougal Town Square, a two-story, mixed-use building, as an anchor and catalyst for development. The building, chosen for the LEED Neighborhood Development pilot program, features underground parking and an interior courtyard that enthusiastically celebrates rain.

Utility

The basic stormwater management concept at the Washougal Town Square courtyard is capture, convey, cleanse, detain, and discharge through effective separation and dispersal of roof runoff into management systems throughout the space. Roof runoff is carried by downspouts and drain pipes to five separate flow-through detention planters around the edges of the space, and three additional flow-through planters are fed by a long, sculptural scupper. The planters cleanse rainwater and hold it before it is discharged into the city's stormwater system.

All roof runoff is biofiltered by plants and soil in the flow-through filter planters.

This is an effective detention system in which the flow-through detention planters hold rainwater from 23,000 square feet of roof, which slows and delays peak discharge.

Five downspouts plus a scupper carry runoff from the surrounding roof. Six flow-through filter planters were designed to contain rainwater and offer a controlled release into the sewer system (two additional planters in the space do not collect runoff).

Figure 4.47. *(left)* Multiple green downspouts discharge roof runoff into splash boxes that in turn discharge it, via level spreader, into flow-through filter planters. The mesh-covered column in the planter is the supporting structure for a "vine tree" (design: GreenWorks, Sienna Architecture Company, photograph: Stuart Echols).

Figure 4.48. *(right)* The entire courtyard space is activated by flow-through filter planters on a grid, ensuring that visitors grasp the rainwater stewardship message (design: GreenWorks, Sienna Architecture Company, Ivan McLean; photograph: Stuart Echols).

Amenity

The Washougal Town Square interior courtyard ARD truly symbolizes the spirit of the city's revitalization: It's fun, it's lively and colorful, and it clearly says, "Rainwater is a resource to celebrate."

This ARD needs no signage, because the rainwater narrative here is crystal clear. A visitor in the space is surrounded by water trails that very clearly trace the hydrologic cycle from roof to landscape in different ways. On one side, green downspouts stand out against burnt sienna–colored metal building walls, with each downspout "kick" just visible above the top of a rectangular, two-tiered stone basin. It's obvious that rainwater falls from the downspout into the upper basin, then flows out small-but-very-visible box level spreaders into a thickly planted lower basin. Some of these basins have an added feature: a green metal "tree" in the plantings, whose "trunk" is a hollow drain pipe and whose "canopy" an inverted pyramid of metal screening. Vines are training up the "trees," with the eventual result a "living" (albeit vine-covered) tree. In other spots, the vine-clad drain pipes, some in tiered and some in single-level flow-through planters, receive water directly, acting as lower downspouts for the building. All of these clever features make it obvious that rain from the roof is nourishing the courtyard plants. And yes, there's more: The central feature of the courtyard is an exuberant 15-foot-tall metal sculpture by artist Ivan McLean that looks like a joyous splash of raindrops flying upward after hitting the ground. A long, thin scupper reaches from one of the courtyard walls out to this central sculpture, bolstered by two vine-covered green metal drain pipes along the way (each in its own flow-through planter). The sculpture stands in the upper, stone-filled level of a two-tiered square basin, with rainwater clearly flowing out of four box level spreaders, one on each side, to water plants in the lower basin. You just can't miss the message here!

The strategic location of this ARD, filling an interior courtyard of the new Town Square, is highly visible from courtyard entries and windows in the two-story building. The coping of the planters isn't quite sittable, a bit too narrow, but plenty of paving makes this courtyard inviting for events and movable chairs, and the delight of the ARD can't be missed.

Water is conveyed to the splash sculpture high above the reach of visitors, and the thickly vegetated flow-through planters preclude access to standing water.

In this ARD, a civic-minded developer chose to overtly present the town's commitment to its abundant natural resources and their preservation. The design makes a range of statements: "We care, we're environmentally responsible, and we want you to learn about stormwater"; "We're progressive and innovative, sophisticated and distinctive," all thanks to the unusual rainwater-themed forms; and "We're smart, and we know you'll notice the stormwater if it's fun." In sum, the ARD courtyard is a microcosm image of the city's energetic and environmentally conscious vibe.

There's a host of focal points here, each rainwater focused, from "rain trees" to the rain sculpture. Their repetition establishes a rhythm and theme that makes the entire courtyard a rain celebration. And, of course, the lines of the rainwater trails, whether in downspouts, scuppers, or "tree trunks," cumulatively let us grasp the rainwater story, while color and texture of the green plantings and vine-covered "rain trees" contrast with the bright building colors to make the rain-and-plant theme stand out.

Of Note

- A courtyard conceived as ARD can effectively surround a visitor with the rainwater experience.
- Washougal Town Square's courtyard-wide dispersal of flow-through filter planters epitomizes the basic stormwater management adage of separation and dispersal.
- Collaboration with an artist can produce a memorable ARD focal point.

Sources

Benkendorf Associates Corporation. 1994. "City of Washougal Comprehensive Plan for Growth Management Act Compliance." http://www.cityofwashougal.us/city-services/community-development2/planning-division2/resources/the-comprehensive-plan.html. Accessed November 30, 2013.

Christopher Freshley Landscape Architects website. "Downtown Washougal Renewal." http://freshleylandscapearchitect.com/community-one. Accessed November 30, 2013.

Downtown Washougal website. http://www.downtownwashougal.com/. Accessed November 30, 2013.

Faha, Mike. 2013. Correspondence with authors.

Hastings, Patty. 2012. "Washougal's Downtown Growing Up." *The Columbian*, September 17, 2012. http://www.downtownwashougal.com/2013/04/23/washougals-downtown-growing-up/. Accessed November 30, 2013.

"Lone Wolf Washougal Project Picked for Pilot." *Vancouver Business Journal*. November 29, 2007. http://www.vbjusa.com/news/news-briefs/5888-lone-wolf-washougal-project-picked-for-pilot. Accessed November 30, 2013.

Perove, Alex. 2013. Personal correspondence with the authors.

Topal, Margarita. 2013. "Washougal—a Growing Destination." *Vancouver Business Journal*, January 25, 2013. http://www.downtownwashougal.com/2013/04/23/downtown-washougal-a-growing-destination/. Accessed November 30, 2013.

CASE STUDY

10th@Hoyt, Portland, Oregon

- Reduce pollutant loads in rainwater
- Reduce downstream damage from runoff
- Safely move, control, and contain rainwater
- Capture rain for reuse
- Education
- Recreation
- Safety
- Public relations
- **AESTHETIC RICHNESS**

Figure 4.49. Roof runoff falls via a five-story downspout (upper right) to tumble down the central stepped runnel into the river rock–filled, raised detention vault. Recirculated rain washes over the Corten "weir boxes" for up to 48 hours, reminding residents of rain's beauty and ephemerality (design: Koch Landscape Architecture; photograph: Stuart Echols).

Date: 2004–2005

Size: 6,900-square-foot courtyard, 40,000-square-foot watershed

Location: 925 NW Hoyt Street, Portland, Oregon

Owner: Prometheus Real Estate Group

Designers: Koch Landscape Architecture; Ankrom Moisan Associated Architects

Background

Two challenges confronted the landscape architect for this project. The first was pressure from the city of Portland to achieve required stormwater mitigation (especially impact on combined sewer overflows); the second was a zero lot-line apartment building with below grade parking in the city's Pearl District. In other words, while the city demanded that stormwater impacts on the metro sewer system be mitigated, there was little space for green infrastructure. Now add a building envelope with an interior entry courtyard and a developer who recognized how important the courtyard would be in creating an image and inviting entry for the five-story apartment building. Landscape architect Steven Koch responded to all these issues by adapting historical water garden traditions that activate and accentuate the sensual qualities of water. Koch respects ways that many cultures have historically used and revered water as a precious resource, and the enclosure of the courtyard afforded him a context appropriate to emulate some of these historical strategies. As Koch puts it, "My intent was to creatively adapt methods used in ancient Persian and Mughal gardens for a modern urban context and public enjoyment."

This ambitious design idea succeeded because of the support of the prime architect and the developer's vision of a focal point courtyard. The design needed to fulfill that vision while demonstrating that environmentally responsible design could both address the city's stormwater mitigation requirements and prove financially responsible. The result is 10th@Hoyt, an elegant oasis of a courtyard where residents and visitors are invited to enjoy rain that lingers awhile, helpfully detained from the city storm system. Here, rainwater is seen, heard, and touched in a variety of runnel conveyances and rainwater-recycling fountains, and at night the drama is enhanced through lighting and luminous colored glass.

Utility

The basic stormwater management concept at 10th@Hoyt is capture, convey, detain, reuse in water features, and discharge. The city of Portland requires all developed and redeveloped sites with 500 square feet or more of impervious surface to mitigate stormwater on site, using a 10-year storm as the design storm event. The 10th@Hoyt site posed a challenge to this requirement, because the entire landscape of this project is located on a concrete slab over a belowgrade parking garage; consequently, there was no opportunity for infiltration and aquifer recharge. In other words, 10th@Hoyt is essentially a green roof over a belowgrade parking garage.

Three copper downspouts carry all roof runoff down into the courtyard. One, on axis with the entry gate, carries half of the runoff into a 33-foot-long, 2,500-gallon raised concrete detention vault. Two other downspouts in the courtyard corners convey the other half of the runoff, each into a shallow, abovegrade concrete container. Water recirculates to the surface of the large central vault, flowing over sculptural Corten weir boxes and recirculating in a closed system not only during a rain event but for a slow, extended drainage period up to 48 hours.

Because this ARD treats only roof runoff, the need for filtration is minimal. Rainwater from the roof is oxygenated by flowing down a contemporary chaddar (a textured, sloping runnel) and recirculating over Corten weir boxes. Additionally, the extended detention of rainwater in this central cistern allows suspended sediments to settle out.

The most important rainwater management here is detention from discharge into the city's storm system. The 3,000-gallon cistern in the 3-foot-high raised concrete box manages runoff to meet Portland's strict requirements. The two other raised concrete rainwater containers on either side of the space are only 12 inches deep; water in these containers mostly evaporates, whereas runoff from huge rain events overflows into the city system.

Safety in conveyance and containment is an important characteristic of this management system. First, Koch worked carefully to size the runnels, creating full-scale concrete mockups. In spots, including one right-angled turn, modifications had to be made to the final runnel design. Second, the main cistern has the capacity to detain 15 percent of a 10-year storm and up to 100 percent of lesser storms. When a rain event exceeds the cistern capacity, excess flows immediately to the city storm system.

Figure 4.50. *(left)* A second rain-receiving system to one side of the space sends roof runoff down a stepped runnel to enter a raised basin via level spreader; most rain held in this 12-inch-deep basin simply evaporates (design: Koch Landscape Architecture; photograph: Stuart Echols).

Figure 4.51. *(right)* The courtyard's bilateral symmetry, with the axial rainwater system as a central focal point, is elegant and serene, and the water movement adds a playful element (design: Koch Landscape Architecture; photograph: Stuart Echols).

Rainwater is reused through a system that recirculates it to run fountains. This reuse provides both visual and auditory interest, some rainwater cleansing through oxygenation, and some evaporation to decrease water eventually going to the sewer system.

Amenity

The rainwater celebration at 10th@Hoyt is both elegant and fun. It presents a serene symmetry from the main street entrance, but upon entry, what seemed peaceful and understated reveals a playful dimension in different Rube Goldberg-esque conveyance systems on each side. Ephemeral qualities are also important here: A rain event activates the recirculating rainwater system, transforming the quiet, elegant space into a noisy, bubbly, water-focused place, and night reveals a colorful, dramatic side thanks to lighting strategically placed behind colored glass "buttons" in the Corten water-spreading surfaces (a move inspired by Mughal gardens). The combined drama and ephemeral enrichment of place by rain poses a great way to make us treasure rain's value.

10th@Hoyt achieves education only partially, but it's worth noting its strengths. First, the visible and engaging water trail is amazing: In three different locations and ways, the design merrily cajoles viewers into noticing that roof runoff flows into three large raised concrete boxes. The rest, though, is a mystery: The rainwater simply disappears into large river rocks in each box, and one might not realize that recirculating rainwater activates the fountains. But residents or other frequent visitors probably notice that water activity occurs only after a rain event and may be able to decipher the system's detention function.

This design makes up in recreational value what it may lack in education. The rainwater celebration here provides a delightful experience, whether wet or dry. When dry, the space is elegant yet engaging; when wet, it is lively, noisy, and fun. And the fact that this is the apartment building's main entry courtyard means that comings and goings include immersion in the design, and seating encourages lingering. The space also invites visitors from the street: Grand gates decorated with rushes usually stand open during the day, and the elegant symmetry of the central downspout axis definitely entices.

An important facet of this design is providing experience of rainwater without physical contact in accessible pools. To meet this challenge, all water-receiving basins appear to be filled to the brim with large river rocks. Rainwater tumbles down from the roof, then disappears into the rock-filled basins, magically reappearing in ephemeral fountain recirculation, then disappearing once more. Rain's destination is puzzling, mysterious—in a way, this means of addressing safety increases our appreciation for the fickle nature of rain.

Many messages cumulatively state that this apartment complex is sustainable, sophisticated, and fun—just right for their urban professional demographic. "We're environmentally responsible" is obvious in the clear water trail, the system's main courtyard location proclaims, "We want you to notice," and the variety of conveyance systems and appearances plus ever-changing experience say, “We’re making it fun.” At the same time, “We’re sophisticated” is conveyed by the elegantly simple composition, refined materials, restraint in diversity of materials and forms, and manicured appearance. And all of this public relations transfers to residents, who subtly proclaim through their housing choice, “I live in a place that is environmentally responsible and makes it look cool!”

Aesthetically, 10th@Hoyt is a stunner. The overall courtyard appropriately focuses on the central, downspout axis with elegant seating, planters, and Corten weir boxes all serenely and symmetrically arranged. Additional visual interest comes from the varied lines of two other conveyance systems. Color and texture are huge here, from the colorful glass buttons contrasting with their Corten surfaces to a thoughtful planting plan of various textures that all contrast luxuriously with concrete, river rock, Corten, and glass. And, of course, water sound adds interest when the rain is active. This design is simultaneously simple and complex, a multifaceted aesthetic experience.

Of Note

- 10th@Hoyt teaches that the most urban context can still provide an ARD opportunity.
- The fact that the water runs only after a rain event heightens awareness of rain’s ephemerality.
- State codes that strictly limit storage and access to collected rainwater don’t preclude ARD.
- An ARD can be a cost-effective marketing device: 10th@Hoyt’s developer believes the building leased exceptionally quickly because of the courtyard design, and the capital investment premium for the ARD approach (approximately $75,000) had a very positive return on investment.

Sources

Koch Landscape Architecture. 2005. “Narrative Summary” written as general public relations information on the project.

Koch, Steve. 2013. Personal communication with authors.

Rodes, Benjamin J. 2007. *10th@Hoyt Courtyard*. Unpublished study completed in partial fulfillment of BLA at University of Idaho.

The Dell at the University of Virginia, Charlottesville, Virginia

- Reduce pollutant loads in rainwater
- Reduce downstream damage from runoff
- Safely move, control, and contain rainwater
- Capture rain for reuse
- Restore or create habitat
- Education
- Recreation
- Safety
- Public relations
- AESTHETIC RICHNESS

Figure 4.52. The Dell presents an elegant two-celled pond, fed by water from a daylighted stream, routed via the raised stone channel in the background. Whether wet or dry, it's a beautiful view and recreational amenity for all (design: Nelson Byrd Woltz Landscape Architects with Biohabitats, Inc., PHR&A with Nitsch Engineering; photograph: NBW).

Date: 2005

Size: 12 acres

Location: Emmett Street, Charlottesville, Virginia

Owner: University of Virginia

Designers: Nelson Byrd Woltz Landscape Architects with Biohabitats, Inc.; PHR&A with Nitsch Engineering

Background

This site, bordering a residential neighborhood to the north and west and a main road through campus on the east, has been a place of campus respite since the time of Thomas Jefferson; it has also been a water source thanks to Meadow Creek, which historically meandered through the site but was piped in the 1950s. In 1999, the landscape architecture and civil engineering team of Andropogon and Cahill created the University of Virginia (UVa) Stormwater Masterplan, which included recommendations for restoring and daylighting streams throughout campus. A few years later, The Dell project was funded to mitigate the stormwater impact of the John Paul Jones Arena, built a mile downstream. As is often the case, initial project funding was adequate only to create basic stormwater facilities and to daylight 1,200 feet of Meadow Creek, but faculty, students, and residents from the adjacent neighborhood encouraged the university administration to strive for more. University administrators were won over by the resulting park-with-stream-fed-pond proposal, which succeeded in referencing past histories of the site, retaining tennis and basketball courts and a sixty-car parking lot, and providing some recreational lawn space.

Today, The Dell is a bucolic 12-acre park that mediates between campus and neighborhood, with the daylighted Meadow Creek meandering downhill, straightening along the tennis courts, then coursing on to drop into a peaceful, three-quarter-acre pond that offers a pastoral view from Emmet Street and Route 29.

Utility

The basic stormwater management concept at The Dell is capture, cleanse, convey, reuse in water feature, detain, and discharge. Runoff sheeting into the daylighted Meadow Creek is first cleansed and partially infiltrated to ensure that the creek is as clean as possible; the meandering creek is subsequently channeled and drops into a two-cell wet detention pond. Water drops sediment in the forebay, then overflows into the second detention cell. The detained water later slowly discharges to the storm sewer at a controlled rate that doesn't overtax the gray infrastructure. According to UVA and state monitoring, the project meets or exceeds all water quality and quantity goals, significantly reducing and delaying peak stormwater discharge and reducing sediments and nutrient loading downstream.

A variety of techniques filter the water. First, rain gardens edge Meadow Creek around the tennis courts, biofiltering first flush stream bank runoff; in other spots, vegetated swales provide further purification; next, water pausing in the forebay of the wet pond deposits sediments; and, finally, the main pond's edge is planted along one side with wetland species for further biofiltration.

The project manages runoff from a maximum 2-year storm for 170 surrounding acres. As a backup to prevent flooding, water in excess of 2-year storm volume is diverted by an in-system overflow splitter (a raised drop inlet located in the restored stream) into the creek's old pipe, which carries the excess to the storm sewer. Water that reaches the pond is detained, then slowly released into the storm sewer system.

Meadow Creek courses to the main pond via 1,200 feet of daylighted, naturalized stream and then a straight, constructed runnel; it then drops into the pond forebay. Note that the upstream pipe flow-splitter protects the project from damaging flood flows. A stepped weir also controls flow rate, releasing water from the forebay into the main pond. Pond banks are sloped to provide capacity for additional water volume beyond normal pool.

Daylighting of Meadow Creek was intended, in part, to mitigate groundwater recharge lost by its piping. Additional recharge is accomplished through the design of infiltrating vegetated swales and rain gardens along the daylighted creek.

Lush native plantings edge the northern side of Meadow Creek and the detention pond, providing habitat for local fauna.

Figure 4.53. *(left)* Water in the pond forebay is visibly cloudier than water in the main pond, indicating that water is dropping sediment there and moving to the second cell much cleaner (design: Nelson Byrd Woltz Landscape Architects with Biohabitats, Inc., PHR&A with Nitsch Engineering; photograph: NBW).

Figure 4.54. *(right)* The checkdam between the two pond cells invites crossing when dry (design: Nelson Byrd Woltz Landscape Architects with Biohabitats, Inc., PHR&A with Nitsch Engineering; photograph: Stuart Echols).

Amenity

The Dell is a complex stormwater management system that presents as a pastoral, 12-acre park whose centerpiece is a beautiful pond. The only shortcoming of The Dell as an ARD is that its stormwater management function isn't obvious, but a number of visible characteristics suggest that water is doing something special here.

Perhaps because designer Warren Byrd taught plant identification at UVa, this project was conceived as an opportunity to educate students in local flora and fauna. To that end, the planting plan didactically presents vegetation characteristic of the three main physiographic provinces of Virginia—mountain, piedmont, and tidewater—arranged in three descending zones along the course of the creek. Other educational facets of the design require keener observation: After a large rainfall, for example, the cloudy water in the forebay contrasts with the clearer water of the wet pond beyond; a thoughtful viewer would surmise the cleansing function of the forebay. Similarly, the character of water movement in the system changes dramatically after a major storm: As the volume increases, water sheeting off the elevated runnel into the forebay angles out, away from a quiet, vertical drop, and water overflowing the forebay noisily roils over the entire checkdam rather than gently and compliantly flowing within the confines of the central weir opening. A thoughtful observer would note that this project surely has something to do with rain, and in case she misses the lessons, informational signage fills in the gaps.

Water, in the form of natural stream or pond, had been absent from the UVa campus for generations; this design returns the amenity of water to campus. And it's both accessible and very visible, bordered by a neighborhood on one side and a well-traveled state route through campus on the other, with plenty of paths and grassy areas that invite wandering. The fact that tennis and basketball courts and a parking lot had to be retained is in some ways a plus: People traveling to and from these recreation destinations can't miss The Dell. In sum, the design offers many opportunities for recreational interaction, from enjoying the scene while passing by, to walking through en route to play tennis or go home, to sitting on the pond bank or carefully walking across the pond checkdam.

The design team gave careful consideration to safety along the pond. A continuous shallow-water safety bench around the perimeter of the pond (a planted bench on one side, and open water gravel-lined benches on the other) ensures that visitors can't fall into deep water.

The location and design of this graceful detention pond proclaim some important messages about UVa. The prominent, highly visible location suggests, "We care about the environment, and we want you to notice," while the elegant design carries on the UVa tradition begun by Mr. Jefferson that "We are sophisticated and aesthetically refined." And the project name, "The Dell," is also a fitting statement: The fact that it is named makes it an instantly identifiable destination, and the name itself suggests a place of quiet repose.

This design makes a compositional statement about the meeting of piedmont stream hydrology and campus grid. The lilting curve of the meandering daylighted stream contrasts with, yet flows gracefully into, the rectilinear grid of campus; nature (water) meets culture and is elegantly tamed. So the line of Meadow Creek intentionally shifts from casual curve to straight runnel in its meander from upland to campus, while the outline of the detention pond embraces both: rectilinear on the campus side, curving on the other. Meanwhile, the multilevel, rectilinear planes of the raised stream runnel and tiered check-dam align with the campus grid vocabulary, appropriate because their function is to control the water. Finally, the rich colors and textures of the plantings along the creek and on the curving side of the pond contrast effectively with the smooth, rectilinear stonework, and grassy plane on the campus side.

Of Note

- The Dell design shows that a highly visible, beautiful, recreation-focused design can effectively manage stormwater.
- The designers report that nuisance Canada geese are kept away by border collies. A contractor provides them in unpredictable visits, so the geese can't detect any routine.
- To ensure effective maintenance, the designers conducted site walk-throughs with maintenance supervisors and staff focused on selective removal of invasives and concepts of managed succession. To facilitate maintenance, plants were massed so weeds have little room to grow and are easily recognized by the maintenance crew.

Sources

American Society of Landscape Architects. 2009. "Honor Award: The Dell at the University of Virginia." 2009 Professional Awards. http://asla.org/2009awards/567.html. Accessed September 29, 2013.

Byrd, Warren. 2013. "Lessons from a Dell." Video of presentation at Artful Rainwater Design Symposium. Stuckeman School, Penn State, April 10, 2013. https://www.youtube.com/watch?v=P3PZIsn0LxM.

Byrd, Warren. 2013. Personal communication with the authors.

UVA Dell. 2013. Nelson Byrd Woltz Landscape Architects. http://www.nbwla.com/featured/dell.htm. Accessed November 4, 2013.

CASE STUDY

Shoemaker Green at the University of Pennsylvania, Philadelphia, Pennsylvania

- Reduce pollutant loads in rainwater
- Reduce downstream damage from runoff
- Safely move, control, and contain rainwater
- Capture rain for reuse
- Restore or create habitat
- Education
- Recreation
- Safety
- Public relations
- **AESTHETIC RICHNESS**

Figure 4.55. This design transformed a grayfield in front of Penn's iconic Palestra and Franklin Field athletic buildings into an inviting grassy quadrangle edged along 33rd Street by this lush rain garden (design: Andropogon Associates Ltd., Meliora Design LLC; photograph: Barrett Doherty).

Date: 2012

Size: 2.85 acres

Location: 33rd Street between Walnut and Spruce Streets, University of Pennsylvania, Philadelphia, Pennsylvania

Owner: University of Pennsylvania

Designers: Andropogon Associates Ltd; Meliora Design LLC

Background

Before its development as Shoemaker Green, this site had both problem and potential: On one hand, it was an underused grayfield with aging tennis courts, a few trees, and stormwater runoff problems; on the other, it sat at the front doors of the Palestra and Franklin Field, two of the University of Pennsylvania's iconic athletic facilities, and on the edge of 33rd Street, with the potential to link Penn's Locust Walk with Penn Park along the Schuylkill River. The impetus to transform this site came when the university, led by president Amy Gutmann, committed to becoming a leader in sustainable design and planning. They undertook a new campus master plan, linked to the university's 2009 Climate Action Plan and to the city of Philadelphia's aggressive 2009 Green City, Clean Water program. Bottom line: When the decision was made to transform the shabby-but-significant site into Shoemaker Green, there was no question that sustainability would guide the change.

Shoemaker Green was conceived as a traditional college green with a variety of added intentions: In addition to a large grassy area, the sloping site provides barrier-free access to the surrounding buildings and is adaptable for a wide range of uses at many scales. And, not surprisingly, the client agreed to make this a pilot project for SITES, the voluntary rating system that measures landscape sustainability, which entailed both creation of a high-performance landscape and a long-term site monitoring program developed in conjunction with Penn's Department of Earth and Environmental Science. Rainwater management here is elegantly addressed both as utility and amenity, most obviously in a site-draining rain garden that defines the 33rd Street edge of the Green.

Utility

The basic stormwater management concept at Shoemaker Green is convey, cleanse, and infiltrate or reuse for irrigation. The stormwater concept reduced existing impervious surfaces by 49 percent and was designed so that 86 percent of rainwater flows from surrounding buildings down walkways, where it is intercepted by perpendicular trench drains and conveyed either to the lawn or to the rain garden. The lawn is actually an infiltration basin that accepts runoff from trench drains (and, in summer, air conditioning condensate), then a network of drain pipes conveys it to a 20,000-gallon cistern under the lawn. Although this stormwater management component doesn't clearly read on the site, the rain garden's role is very clear: Trench drains cross sidewalks to feed the rain garden through visible curb cuts and a visible water trail, and the rain garden then biofilters and infiltrates in a two-cell basin system. Rain that is not adsorbed or absorbed by plants and soil is harvested in the cistern for reuse in site irrigation.

Biofiltration is key in this ARD, both in the rain garden and in the turf-covered infiltration basin. In both spots, plants and soil cleanse runoff. Additionally, the rain garden basin is divided into a forebay and main basin by a stone checkdam with a central weir; this two-basin system allows sediments to settle in the forebay before reaching the infiltration basin beyond.

The Shoemaker Green design significantly reduces discharge into the city's stormwater system through its infiltration and harvesting strategy. According to the designers, "We believe no stormwater has left the site from May 24, 2013 to October 11, 2013 [a time period that included 2013's Hurricane Andrea], indicating that the site can manage a 3.14" storm at a minimum, which is well above the design requirement of the site to manage a 1" storm."

Sheet flowing runoff is intercepted in multiple spots by perpendicular trench drains sized for a 1-inch design storm at a minimum; two of these feed the grassy infiltration basin, which is sized to hold up to 13,000 gallons; and three trench drains feed the rain garden, which is sized to contain up to to 8,500 gallons.

In the 180-day spring and summer of 2013, the 20,000-gallon cistern below the rain garden harvested an equivalent of 123,469 gallons of water per year, used for site irrigation.

One project goal was to increase biodiversity. The densely planted rain garden provides native habitat for small fauna, including yellow warblers, an important indicator species for migratory bird habitat.

Figure 4.56. *(left)* Trench drains cross many of the sloping walks, catching and redirecting rain—in this case, to the main rain garden runoff entry point (design: Andropogon Associates Ltd., Meliora Design LLC; photograph: Stuart Echols).

Figure 4.57. *(right)* From the rainwater entry point in figure 4.56, a meandering white river pebble line clearly presents the water trail when wet or dry. Rainwater follows this path through robust plantings to drop into the main infiltration basin via the weir in center of photograph. Note the bench in the background: Visitors are invited to stop and enjoy (design: Andropogon Associates Ltd., Meliora Design LLC; photograph: Stuart Echols).

Amenity

Shoemaker Green succeeds in presenting the traditional feel of a college quad while adding a low-key celebration of rain: Visible water trails clearly lead into the rain garden, where a "stream" and "tributaries" of white river stones highlight the rain's meander as it flows into the rain garden basins, with the main stream tumbling merrily over a stone weir. The design takes advantage of the site's slope down to 33rd Street and places the rain garden at the low point, an eye-catching focal point for all who pass by.

This ARD isn't overtly educational: No signage explains the management system, although there is a recording accessible by phone that describes the project components for those curious enough to learn about the green. But in this intriguing design, the visible water trail provides just enough information for the curious to decipher what's happening. First, long steel grates extend perpendicularly across walkways all over the site to capture runoff from impervious surfaces; some lead straight to curb cuts at the edge of the rain garden, where white river stones then meander into the plantings. It's obvious that these spots receive sidewalk runoff intercepted by the steel-grated trench drains. Less obvious is the role of the grates that seem to butt into the curbing of the turfed quad, although a semi-sleuth can guess that rain must be gathered under the lawn. And for those who need a bit more clarity, the rainwater entry point at the northern corner of the rain garden is a complete giveaway: Here the trench drain edges granite pavers that step down to meet broad, flat granite slabs that clearly define a water channel, made visible even when dry by a "streambed" of white river stone that meanders into robust native plantings toward a broad stone checkdam.

Placement of the colorful, intriguing rain garden along the 33rd Street sidewalk edge of this site ensures that it receives maximum visibility and invites all passersby to notice and decipher its function. Two long, arcing granite benches along that sidewalk edge further invite lingering enjoyment of the garden's beauty. And one more feature doesn't exactly invite but beckons adventuresome folks to actually enter the rain garden: The wide, flat granite slabs that separate the forebay from the main basin extend almost all the way from edge to edge of the rain garden, stopping about 2 feet short of the curb. A gentle jump allows the nimble to walk across the checkdam, perhaps pausing to sit a bit at the weir, offering yet another way to enjoy this delightful garden.

Many design features ensure visitor safety. First, trench drains across walkways are covered by grates that permit awareness of water without danger. Additionally, entry into the rain garden is dissuaded by very thick edge plantings in combination with seemingly unwalkable dry stream beds of white river stone (they look like ankle-turners). And anyone who dares to walk across the stone checkdam is likely to stay on that granite slab path simply because the plantings around it are too lush—there's really nowhere else to go. Finally, the broad two-basin system of the rain garden spreads rainwater, preventing any dangerous depth, and the weir waterfall and ponding in both basins ensure slow water velocity.

Shoemaker Green clearly shows Penn's commitment to sustainable principles and the richness of the college green tradition and elegant sophistication through high-end materials. Cumulatively, the design says, "We care, we are environmentally responsible, and we want you to learn about stormwater" as well as "We are sophisticated, aesthetically refined, and traditional." Of additional note is the design's status as a certified SITES pilot project. Though not visible on site, this recognition is of significant value to the university.

At Shoemaker Green, rain is celebrated especially through line. The bold lines of trench drains clearly lead to meandering lines of white river stone in the rain garden; the water trail is easy to see and follow, and it's essential to the narrative of this design. Color and texture are also key, along with contrast: The rich rain garden plantings contrast with the smooth grassy quad and granite paving, white river stone, and metal grates boldly marking the water trails.

Of Note

- If your client seeks major recognition for sustainable efforts, consider pursuing SITES certification for your ARD.
- In order to meet SITES postconstruction monitoring requirements, a partnership was created with Penn to make monitoring part of the science curriculum, a strategy that could be replicated at other educational institutions.
- A rain garden can be an elegant addition to a campus quadrangle, which is typically conceived as a simple turf field.
- Robust plantings in rain gardens can have major impact, both on visitors' appreciation and on dissuading them from entering the garden. Such thick plantings can also help reduce the maintenance weeding regimen.

Sources

Alminaña, José. 2013. Personal correspondence with authors.

McWilliams, Julie. n.d. "Shoemaker Green: Penn's Newest Public Common." University of Pennsylvania website. http://www.upenn.edu/spotlights/shoemaker-green-penn-s-newest-public-common. Accessed September 23, 2013.

Meliora Design website. http://melioradesign.net/Project-UPennShoemaker.html. Accessed September 23, 2013.

"Shoemaker Green: The Red and Blue Turn Grey into a Green Sustainable Site." *University of Pennsylvania Almanac* 57, no. 01 (2010). http://www.upenn.edu/almanac/volumes/v57/n01/shoemaker.html. Accessed September 23, 2013.

"SITES™ Certifies Three More Projects." Land: E-News from ASLA. https://www.asla.org/land/LandAr. "Shoemaker Green." In "Certified Projects" of the Sustainable Sites Initiative. http://www.sustainablesites.org/cert_projects/show.php?id=56. Accessed November 27, 2013.

CASE STUDY

NE Siskiyou Green Street, Portland, Oregon

- Reduce pollutant loads in rainwater
- Reduce downstream damage from runoff
- Safely move, control, and contain rainwater
- Capture rain for reuse
- Education
- Recreation
- Safety
- Public relations
- **AESTHETIC RICHNESS**

Figure 4.58. Two parallel curb extensions near the intersection of Siskiyou and 35th Street provide color, texture, and beauty to this quiet residential street (design: Portland Bureau of Environmental Services; photograph: Stuart Echols).

Date: 2003

Size: 590 square feet

Location: NE Siskiyou Street between 35th St. and 36th St., Portland, Oregon

Owner: City of Portland

Designers: Portland Bureau of Environmental Services; Kevin Perry, ASLA

Background

This is a humble project that shows the multiple benefits that can be accomplished with small but creative ARDs. Because of city-wide combined sewer overflow (CSO) problems impacting the Willamette River, Portland's Bureau of Environmental Services (BES) proposed a small, first-of-its-kind retrofit demonstration on NE Siskiyou Street, in a leafy residential neighborhood that they considered representative of conditions in other areas. Kevin Perry, then designer with BES, chose this one-block section of NE Siskiyou Street because it was a low-volume residential street that would be low-risk in terms of small traffic flow modifications. In addition, Perry felt that the street had an inherently beautiful quality, and he just happened to be a resident of the neighborhood, so his personal investment as both BES designer and resident was seen as a way to overcome possible neighborhood concerns.

According to Tom Liptan, recently retired environmental specialist for the BES, the idea was to cleanse, detain, and infiltrate street runoff in symmetrical stormwater curb extension biofiltration basins on each side of the street. The BES team reasoned that this retrofit would not only manage rainwater but also provide traffic calming and pedestrian safety by narrowing the street, and beautify the area through plantings.

Some local residents had reservations about altering the street, including fears about reducing on-street parking. But the BES design team had multiple street-side chats with the local homeowners to discuss the actual footprint of the curb extensions and the minimal amount of parking loss. In addition, BES made the extensions literally reversible by attaching them to the existing curb, which remained in place; if residents don't like it, the BES team reasoned, the basins will be removed with nary a trace.

Two parallel basins, each 50 feet long and 7 feet wide, were installed immediately uphill from a combined storm sewer inlet near the intersection of Siskiyou and 35th Street. Construction took 2 weeks and cost $20,000 (which included $3,000 in ancillary street and sidewalk repair). The completed project made good on BES's claims, providing all the expected benefits; and, importantly, local residents came to thoroughly embrace the new "street gardens," even helping to weed them. In fact, shortly after the project was installed, hundreds of residents within the immediate and surrounding neighborhoods expressed interest in having similar treatments placed on their streets. By 2005, enough residents on other streets wanted their own stormwater curb extensions that the *Green Street News* published criteria for building new ones:

- Neighborhood support
- Unique opportunity to test for specific types of conditions
- Need to relieve overburdened sewer system
- Site that doesn't conflict with underground utilities

BES monitoring has additionally shown that these humble little landscape areas are a real stormwater management success.

Utility

The basic stormwater management concept of the NE Siskiyou Green Street is capture, convey, cleanse, and either infiltrate or detain and discharge. The two stormwater curb extensions capture runoff from 9,300 square feet of paved surface (note that this is just shy of the 10,000 square feet we recommended in part 3.1); stormwater is admitted on the uphill side through 18-inch curb cuts. Each biofiltration basin has four compartments separated by three checkdams (soil covered in gravel) to slow flow and promote infiltration, including an initial forebay that holds a 2-inch layer of pea gravel. Stormwater is cleansed by plants and soil, then infiltrates. Any overflow that passes through or around the stormwater curb extensions is allowed to enter the city's storm drain system.

Street runoff enters the forebay, where most sediments are dropped; the checkdams delay runoff in each of the three remaining compartments, promoting further sediment drop. Plants and soil then biofilter the rainwater before it infiltrates.

The main purpose of this project was to mitigate stormwater discharge impacts on the city's sewer system. In August 2004, the BES conducted flow tests simulating the peak half hour of a 25-year design storm (1.89 inches in 6 hours, an intense storm with heaviest rainfall in the first 15 minutes) and a

Figure 4.59. *(left)* Street runoff enters the bioretention basin via the large curb cut and entry flow splitter on the uphill side of the system; the smaller, downhill curb cut functions as an overflow splitter for excess runoff in large rain events (design: Portland Bureau of Environmental Services; photograph: Stuart Echols).

Figure 4.60. *(right)* The parallel curb extensions calm traffic, beautify the street, and provide a subtle gateway to Siskiyou Street from 35th (design: Portland Bureau of Environmental Services; photograph: Stuart Echols).

3-year CSO design storm (1.41 inches in a 24-hour summer storm). The tests revealed that runoff discharge was reduced by 88 percent and 85 percent, respectively.

The stormwater curb extensions can manage significant amounts of stormwater runoff. However, during large storm events, the design has a built-in backup plan: Any runoff that cannot be managed within the landscape system is simply allowed to flow through or around and run to the storm sewer inlet, thanks to curb cut flow splitters. The basins are 6 inches deep at the curb, sloping to 12 inches deep at the center, with the checkdams allowing a maximum ponding depth of 7 inches and storage volume of 120 cubic feet per basin.

Water removed from the sewer system by the basins infiltrates for groundwater recharge. Both storm simulations showed a recharge infiltration rate of 2 inches per hour when fully saturated.

Amenity

The NE Siskiyou Green Street provides a multifaceted amenity, not only celebrating rain but also adding garden landscape to the street and slowing traffic by briefly narrowing the street from 28 to 14 feet over the 50-foot length of the curb extension biofiltration basins.

During a rain event, it's easy to see water entering, ponding, and slowly percolating into the basins; the water trail and the basic function of the system are very clear. But in case a passerby doesn't grasp the stormwater management, an interpretive sign in the southern curb extension clarifies with brief text and graphics. The sign's website link offers an impressive amount of information on the project.

Location of the stormwater system along the road, between pedestrians and cars, ensures high visibility and provides a delightful view for passersby.

Because the curb extensions are densely planted and separated from the sidewalk by a traditional turf right-of-way, the basins are visible but not readily accessible by passersby. Additionally, their shallow depth and large horizontal area control rainwater volume at safe levels while checkdams slow the runoff speed. In sum, even in significant storms the basins hold shallow, very temporary amounts of water.

This simple little project says a great deal about the city: "We care, we're environmentally responsible, and we want you to learn about rainwater" as well as "We're smart, resourceful, and clever, opportunistically using a small and unexpected area not only to sustainably manage stormwater but also to slow traffic and beautify the neighborhood."

Plant material was selected to present a rich combination of color and texture in the gray, blue, and green family, with bulbs gaily offering spring color. In addition, nearly all of the plant material is evergreen in order to provide year-round structure to the landscape (and to help slow the flow of water as it moves through the system). And the symmetrical arrangement of the two basins creates a serene gateway near the intersection of NE Siskiyou and 35th Street.

Of Note

- Grounded partly in his experience with this project, Tom Liptan's mantra for convincing wary clients to go with green infrastructure and ARDs is, "Make it small, non-threatening, and reversible."
- This project meets three important goals (stormwater management, traffic calming, and beautification) in a small space and on a tiny budget.
- All plants chosen for the stormwater curb extensions are 3 feet tall or lower, to make the landscape garden-like and somewhat diminutive, not threatening; and they were installed more densely than usually specified to reduce maintenance (less space for weeds) and provide quick aesthetic appeal.
- If at all possible, conduct postconstruction testing and monitoring to ensure system functionality, identify improvements, and—ideally—gain convincing data for your next ARD client.
- BES has concluded that the forebays could be improved by design for easier cleaning (in the first year they were cleaned twice) and that the checkdams deserve more substantial construction, to prevent erosion in large storms.

Sources

City of Portland. 2005. *Green Street News.* Summer 2005.

City of Portland Bureau of Environmental Services. 2004. *Flow Test Report: Siskiyou Curb Extension, August 4, 2004.* http://www.portlandonline.com/shared/cfm/image.cfm?id=63097. Accessed November 12, 2013.

City of Portland Bureau of Environmental Services. 2005. *NE Siskiyou Green Street Project Report.*

Liptan, Tom. 2006, 2013. Personal correspondence with authors.

Perry, Kevin Robert. 2013. Personal correspondence with authors.

Conclusion: Some Parting Thoughts

The XYZ Elementary School principal faced a quandary: The town stormwater official wanted the school to eliminate half their parking, because dirty runoff was flowing right through the school's grass-lined detention basin into a creek, degrading the water quality. Impossible! They needed every parking space as it was. She called a landscape architect she knew, and it happened he'd just read a book on Artful Rainwater Design. He knew that this could be a great test of ideas in the book, and he offered to share some thoughts.

First, he reassured the principal, you don't need to touch your parking. Instead, he proposed a green infrastructure retrofit: Create a bioswale filled with native perennials to carry rain from the roof and parking lot to the detention basin; this would cleanse the water and diminish some volume through infiltration. Deepen the basin by about a foot to retain first flush rainwater volume. Plant ribbons of native perennials in the basin, their deep roots helping to filter and infiltrate some of the rain and their linear massings providing the appearance of water flow. Create a dry stream of river rocks marking the path of small to medium flows in the basin, which would slow the water to let it drop sediments while showing that this is a "water place." Add bird houses and stepping stones for access into the new rain garden. Problem solved: The rain is diminished in volume and cleansed before it leaves the basin, but the result is so much more. It's a new outdoor classroom, where kids learn about groundwater recharge, native plants, habitat for birds, bees, and butterflies, and how it all can work together in a beautiful landscape.

The purpose of this book is to help you rethink stormwater management. Regulatory mandates now require that we proactively address both water quantity and quality, but this book shows that by taking an ARD approach, we can accomplish much more. We hope that the preceding pages have given you plenty of ideas and inspirations so that you, like our fictitious designer in the preceding paragraphs, can create landscapes that manage rain *and* create habitat, experience, and learning—landscapes that make a difference.

But perhaps the most important ideas you can take away from this book are these three:

Idea 1: Put That Landscape to Work!

This is such a simple idea, but it wasn't until we heard it articulated by civil engineer Steve Benz that we experienced the critical "aha!" moment. Steve's point is simple: In every site design project, landscape is needed for project approval and is valuable (especially in the eyes of you, the designer), but as we know, the components of landscape that the designer considers critical are far too often "value engineered" out of the project to ensure adequate funds for other project priorities. The rationale is often that "we can come back later and beef up the landscape" or "the plants will grow; we can install small ones to save money." The result, too often, is the loss of opportunity to implement the significant spaces you've designed to promote social interaction, environmental awareness, improved alternative mobility systems, and so on. Instead of performing a meaningful function, that landscape is relegated to providing skimpy parsley around the turkey, "greening up" (but not too much!) the building.

But here's the thing: All that can change *if the landscape performs as a stormwater management system needed for the site development.* As Benz puts it, "Focus on *performative* landscapes: make them work! Then they're essential to the project, and can't be value engineered out." Wow, what a simple but powerful concept.

So, in your quest to create an ARD—a truly sustainable stormwater management system that also provides an amenity experience—keep the following in mind:

- Take to heart the dictum, "Always slow it down, spread it out, soak it in." Use the entire site as your sustainable stormwater management system. Disperse that water as much as you can, striving to mimic the kind of site-wide rain capture that occurs in natural landscapes. This strategy accomplishes two important goals: It effectively manages rainwater quantity and quality, and it ensures that every inch of your designed landscape is *necessary* to the project.
- Make sure the stormwater management system really works. Size conveyance and containment carefully (then add some extra capacity), and ensure redundancies so that when that bioretention basin overflows, there's a backup system that sends that water where you want it to go, not into someone's basement. Plan backups for your backups, because the last thing you want is for the system to fail and your client to say, "Well, it looks nice but it doesn't really work."
- Don't make the system too technically complicated, because complication means more potential spots for the system to fail. Keep the basic system concept simple, with not too many mechanical parts to stop pumping, or clog, or leak, and so on.
- Use green wherever possible for three fundamental reasons. First, you're required by regulations to return stormwater management on this site to some modicum of predevelopment condition;

what better way to do that than to make a *landscape* do the work? If your goal is to emulate a natural landscape's management of rain, isn't it incredibly sensible to create a landscape to do that? This idea is so simple it's almost embarrassing that it's not our typical stormwater management method—yet. Second, by using green infrastructure, the owner and maintenance crews can avoid a lot of headaches caused by underground problems such as clogged pipes and silted catch basins. Green infrastructure keeps the big maintenance tasks on the land's surface—much more accessible to repair and also much easier to spot the problems before they escalate into maintenance nightmares. Finally, there are now plenty of green infrastructure users who report that it's less expensive than gray, whether in construction or life-cycle costs, and the value added can result in significant economic benefit, too. For corroboration, consider the city of Atlanta and Historic Fourth Ward Park. The city claims they saved $20 million by creating a rain-managing park rather than expanding their sewer tunnels; they also claim that the park has prompted more than $400 million in private development of land abutting the park (for more information, see the Historic Fourth Ward case study in part 4). Or listen to Tom Liptan, retired environmental specialist at Portland, Oregon's Bureau of Environmental Services. On the basis of his work more than 20 years on green infrastructure in that city, he reports that comparative cost analyses make green infrastructure a clear winner over gray.

Idea 2: Make the Landscape Overtly Celebrate *Rain*

We are gratified that people frequently contact us, recommending that we look at a particular stormwater management system for possible inclusion in our case studies. Far too often, though, what we find when we investigate is a design that's an attractive bioswale or a lovely rain garden, not an Artful Rainwater Design. "Wait a minute," you're thinking, "what's wrong with that?" Well, nothing, except that a stormwater management system simply designed to be a visually appealing landscape misses an incredibly important and timely opportunity: At this point in our environmental efforts, we need to educate people about the value of rain. We need stormwater management systems that clearly and entrancingly celebrate rain to make visitors say, "Look what the rain is doing!" or, "Look! That's *rain*." We need especially to make people aware of rain's essential role in the hydrologic cycle: "From rooftop to river" and "from parking lot to pond" are the types of messages we need to convey (messages found in so many of our case studies).

Why is this so important? Landscape architect Leo Alvarez put it beautifully in the May 2013 issue of *Landscape Architecture*. In describing a small but elegant ARD he created for his firm's home office, Perkins + Will in Atlanta, he explained, "One of our goals was to make it visible. A lot of these things are great for the environment, but if no one's seeing it, it's not moving the needle."[1]

Our goal at this point needs to be to move the needle, to help the public realize that rain is our essential ally, not an enemy.

So a true ARD unquestionably must be a beautiful landscape: thoughtfully composed, rich in color and texture. It must be valued for more than treating rain; it must be loved as an environment of value, a place of beauty, because a landscape can be sustained—and thus sustainable—only if people *love* it so that they care enough to retain and maintain that place. So to all the folks who have created sustainable stormwater management systems that are also visually appealing landscapes, we say, "Good work!" The owners of and visitors to those stormwater-managing landscapes have a valuable amenity that we hope will be sustained. But, we respectfully add, next time why not go one step further and really celebrate the rain in that landscape: Surprise, delight, or educate people about rain's significance. That's how we'll move the needle!

Idea 3: It Can't Be Just a Working Dog or Just a Show Dog

Okay, the analogy's not great, but we think you'll get the idea. There are lots and lots of working dogs who perform valiantly and successfully at their jobs of herding sheep or retrieving ducks or leading the blind. It doesn't matter what these dogs look like; their value is in their ability to perform a useful function, and their frequent mutt-ness allegedly makes for a better-tempered animal than one with exclusive bloodlines. Then there are the purebred show dogs, some of whom are so painstakingly bred exclusively for their appearance that their behavior is, well, not great, and their working ability is questionable. Get it?

So let's swiftly abandon the analogy and cut to the point: An effective ARD is neither exclusively a working dog nor a show dog. It must have the strengths of each; it must function very well in its sustainable stormwater management, and it must be attractive to give people the desire to experience and learn from its celebration of rain.

Unfortunately we've seen many well-intentioned examples of ARD working dogs and show dogs. We've seen municipal engineers thrilled by their implementation of green infrastructure systems that look like weed patches in the urban landscape, and we've seen visually stunning rain celebrations that don't treat rain at all effectively. If we want to move the needle, we can't afford to create either of these types. Simply put, we must create ARDs that sustainably manage stormwater *and* are clear celebrations of rain. We must create ARDs that people respect for their rainwater management success *and* enjoy for their beautifully presented message that rain is a resource. Anything less is a woefully missed opportunity.

With those three big ideas in mind, let's now tackle the most common doubts we've heard from designers who want to create ARDs but think they can't.

Doubt 1: "Well, That's Portland. We Can't Do That Here!"

Earlier in this book—more than once—we've pointed out that Portland, Oregon is not some magical Oz where all the restrictions you face in your geographic locale are somehow moot. Put aside your *Portlandia* imagery and realize that the ARD movement in Portland began because the city faced a CSO crisis: An urgent necessity was the mother of invention there. So Portland was simply one of the first of more and more municipalities nationwide facing increasingly demanding stormwater management restrictions, and, in Portland crisis led to creativity. Rather than disregarding ARDs in Portland, or any city outside your geographic region, we should learn from them, because we can significantly improve our own ARD success if we take the time to understand both the why and the how of any successful ARD.

Doubt 2: "Yes, But How Do We Know It Will Work?"

This doubt is very real: Many designers have told us that they want to use green infrastructure, but their clients can't be convinced that this approach will manage rain effectively. But a growing number of projects include postconstruction monitoring (see our case studies in part 4 for many examples). There's also a growing number of projects certified in the SITES program, a voluntary set of guidelines and performance benchmarks for sustainable land design. To obtain SITES certification, projects must be monitored for performance, so SITES-certified projects or case studies provide another useful mine of information. And, as of this writing, the American Society of Landscape Architects also provides very useful data on stormwater case studies nationwide (http://www.asla.org/stormwatercasestudies.aspx). In other words, you can explore the performance and stormwater management methods of plenty of existing projects to find the data you need to make a successful case for ARD green infrastructure.

Doubt 3: "It's Too Expensive!"

Increasing amounts of data show that green infrastructure can be less expensive than gray. Peruse our case studies for some examples, then explore any of the helpful publications on the subject, including the American Society of Landscape Architects' "Banking on Green: How Green Infrastructure Saves Municipalities Money and Provides Economic Benefits Community-wide" (http://www.asla.org/ContentDetail.aspx?id=31301) and the EPA's "Reducing Stormwater Costs Through LID Strategies and Practices" (EPA 841-F-07-006, December 2007, at http://www.epa.gov/nps/lid). By the time you read this, many more such resources will be available, so do your homework to help make your financial case for green.

Once you've passed the green infrastructure hurdle, the next one is spending the money to make that green infrastructure a rain-celebrating amenity. Here, consider your client: Schools and even municipalities increasingly seek the public relations benefits of leadership in sustainable initiatives, and private developers can be convinced of the amenity approach by the prospect of good public relations and return on investment. Consider High Point, our case study that uses stormwater management celebration as a branding tool, or 10th@Hoyt, another case study where the apartment building developer is convinced that the courtyard ARD is a signature that made the rental units there fill quickly. If you can convince your client that ARD is a worthy investment in economics, good will, or product branding, you can overcome this doubt.

Doubt 4: "Yes, but It Freezes Here."

This is a common fallback for those in frosty climes, and it is wholly bogus both from a utility and an amenity perspective. Consider the following:

- If you create a green infrastructure ARD, it will function the same way a natural landscape does: Precipitation will freeze and remain in or on the ground until a thaw, and then it will move through the system. It's that simple.
- ARDs are among the *only* water landscapes where ice can become part of the rainwater celebration. Why? If the rain is conveyed on the surface rather than in pipes, there's no need to worry about pipes freezing and bursting. Consider the Swarthmore Science Center, one of our part 4 case studies, as an effective example. Here, the designer reports that "freezing was never raised as an issue," and the resulting "frozen rain" suspended from runnels provides recognition of rain even in winter (figure 5.1).

Figure 5.1. Frozen rain suspended from runnels at the Swarthmore Science Center makes people recognize the significance of rain even in winter (design: ML Baird & Co., Einhorn Yaffee Prescott; photograph: Mara Lee Baird).

Doubt 5: "Maintenance Is Too Much Trouble."

Getting the maintenance crew onboard with your ARD function and intentions can be challenging, but it's often a matter of education and creative teamwork. Taking the time and energy to do this really makes the difference between a long-term success or a failure in your ARD. The case studies in part 4 offer some simple and some creative approaches:

- The designers of the Dell made the maintenance crew part of the team by meeting with them to clarify the project's maintenance requirements.
- At High Point, a different approach was taken to team-building: Contractors were informed of the sustainable intentions of the place at the outset and invited to make suggestions, which they did, resulting in some very useful refinements and additions to the planned strategies. In some contexts, this could be a great strategy for the maintenance crew. There's nothing like getting people invested in something with noble intentions and encouraging their creative input as part of the team.
- To minimize confusion about intentional plants and invaders, designers of a number of the case study projects planted on a grid or other obvious pattern to make weeds easy to spot, or they planted especially lushly (increasing size or number) to crowd out weeds.
- All stormwater management systems need maintenance, some more extensive than others. To keep an ARD looking the way visitors and neighbors typically prefer landscapes to look (we Americans tend to expect tidy landscapes!),[2] ensure that the maintenance regimen is frequent enough to keep it looking well tended. You don't want local homeowners to see your ARD as a feral eyesore of unkempt, overgrown, tangled plants.
- Be particularly careful of the planting palette. ARDs that we predict will stand the test of time—and plant growth—share some important characteristics: The plants at mature size fit comfortably within the green infrastructure system, and the plants won't acquire a very leggy or floppy character (which the average American sees as undesirably "unkempt").

In sum: Yes, at this point in our sustainable design history, ARDs pose many challenges, but don't let those challenges prevent you from pursuing this extremely functional, educational, and exciting approach to stormwater management. Anticipate the challenges and creatively prepare to address them.

And so with all the preceding pages—the examples, ideas, questions, rebuttals, and resources—we encourage you to make ARD the future strategy of your stormwater management systems. Recognize today's increasingly stringent stormwater treatment regulations as an exciting opportunity rather than a burden. The fact is that we have to manage rain; doing nothing is not an option. Let's be smart and opportunistic by managing rain in ways that accomplish other goals, from education to beautification to stimulating surrounding development to creating green jobs. Let's be smart and let soil and plants do the stormwater management work for which they're so perfectly suited. Let's provide a huge public service by "moving the needle," teaching people to revere rain as the life-giving resource that it is.

As a final thank you to the designers who have created the design innovations that inspired this book, we offer this narrative from a 1997 Apple ad (https://www.youtube.com/watch?v=8rwsuXHA7RA), used in their "Think Different" campaign:

> "Here's to the crazy ones: the misfits, the rebels, the troublemakers, the round pegs in the square holes—the ones who see things differently. They're not fond of rules. You can quote them, disagree with them, glorify or vilify them, but the only thing you can't do is ignore them because they change things—they push the human race forward."

Notes

1. Jonathan Lerner, "The Last Drops," *Landscape Architecture* 2013 (5): 60.
2. For an exploration of this topic, see Eliza Pennypacker, "What Is Taste, and Why Should I Care?," *Proceedings of the 1992 International Conference of the Council of Educators in Landscape Architecture* (Washington, DC: Landscape Architecture Foundation, 1992): 63–74.

Artful Rainwater Design Project List

Name	Location	Designer
Arizona State University Polytech Campus	Mesa, AZ	Ten Eyck Landscape Architects, Inc.
Underwood Sonoran Landscape	University of Arizona, Tempe, AZ	Ten Eyck Landscape Architects, Inc.
Pacific Cannery Lofts	Oakland, CA	Miller Company Landscape Architects, David Baker Architects
Rodgers School	Stamford, CT	Mikyoung Kim Design
Washington Canal Park	Washington, DC	OLIN
Southwest Recreation Center Expansion	University of Florida, Gainesville, FL	RDG Planning and Design
1315 Peachtree	Atlanta, GA	Perkins+Will
Historic Fourth Ward Park	Atlanta, GA	Phase I: HDR; Phase II: Wood+Partners
Lamar Dodd School of Art	University of Georgia, Athens, GA	Ecos Environmental Design
International Student Center Rain Garden	Kansas State University, Manhattan, KS	Department of Landscape Architecture/Regional & Community Planning, KSU
Outwash Basin at Stata Center	Massachusetts Institute of Technology, Cambridge, MA	OLIN; Nitsch Engineering
Maplewood Rain Gardens	Maplewood, MN	Joan Nassauer et al.
Queens Botanical Garden	Queens, NY	Atelier Dreiseitl with Conservation Design Forum; BKSK Architects
10th@Hoyt	Portland, OR	Koch Landscape Architecture
The Ardea	Portland, OR	Mayer/Reed
Atwater Place	Portland, OR	Mayer/Reed
Buckman Heights	Portland, OR	Murase Associates
Gibbs Street Bridge	Portland, OR	Mayer/Reed
Glencoe Elementary School	Portland, OR	Portland Bureau of Environmental Services
Headwaters at Tryon Creek	Portland, OR	Greenworks
Howard Hall, Lewis and Clark College	Portland, OR	Walker Macy

Name	Location	Designer
Mount Tabor Elementary School	Portland, OR	Portland Bureau of Environmental Services
New Seasons Market Arbor Lodge	Portland, OR	Lango Hansen Landscape Architects PC; Ivan McLean
New Seasons Market Seven Corners	Portland, OR	Portland Bureau of Environmental Services
Oregon Museum of Science and Industry	Portland, OR	Murase Associates
Rain Garden at the Oregon Convention Center	Portland, OR	Mayer/Reed
Rigler Community Garden Gazebo	Portland, OR	Liz Hedrick
RiverEast Center	Portland, OR	Greenworks; Group MacKenzie
Siskiyou Green Street Project	Portland, OR	Portland Bureau of Environmental Services
Stephen Epler Hall	Portland, OR	Atlas Landscape Architecture; KPFF Consulting Engineers; Mithun
Southwest 12th Avenue Green Street	Portland, OR	Portland Bureau of Environmental Services
Southwest Montgomery Street	Portland, OR	Nevue Nguyan
Tanner Springs Park	Portland, OR	Atelier Dreiseitl with Greenworks
Water Pollution Control Laboratory	Portland, OR	Murase Associates
Taylor Residence	Kennett Square, PA	Margot Taylor
Liberty Lands Park	Philadelphia, PA	Pennsylvania Horticultural Society and CH2MHill
Salvation Army Kroc Center of Philadelphia	Philadelphia, PA	Andropogon Associates Ltd.
Shoemaker Green	Philadelphia, PA	Andropogon Associates Ltd.; Meliora Design LLC
Springside School Rain Wall and Gardens	Philadelphia, PA	Stacy Levy
Center for Sustainable Landscapes	Phipps Conservatory, Pittsburgh, PA	Andropogon Associates, Ltd.

Name	Location	Designer
Swarthmore Science Center	Swarthmore, PA	ML Baird & Co.; Einhorn Yaffee Prescott
Ridge and Valley	The Arboretum at Penn State, University Park, PA	Stacy Levy with MTR Landscape Architects; Overland Partners
Automated Trading Desk	Mount Pleasant, SC	Nelson Byrd Woltz Landscape Architects; Tinmouth Chang Architects
Ladybird Johnson Wildflower Center	Austin, TX	J. Robert Anderson Landscape Architects; Overland Partners
The Green at College Park	University of Texas, Arlington TX	Schrickel, Rollins, and Associates
Belo Center for New Media	University of Texas, Austin, TX	Ten Eyck Landscape Architects, Inc.
Manassas Park Elementary School	Manassas Park, VA	Siteworks LLC
Campbell Hall Renovations	University of Virginia, Charlottesville, VA	Nelson Byrd Woltz Landscape Architects
The Dell	University of Virginia, Charlottesville, VA	Nelson Byrd Woltz Landscape Architects
South Lawn Commons "water circuit"	University of Virginia, Charlottesville, VA	Office of Cheryl Barton
Cedar River Watershed Education Center	North Bend, WA	Jones and Jones
Waterworks Garden	Renton, WA	Lorna Jordan
2nd Ave Edge Street (SEA Street)	Seattle, WA	Seattle Public Utilities
110 Cascade	Seattle, WA	Seattle Public Utilities
Growing Vine	Seattle, WA	GAYNOR, Inc.; Carlson Architects; SvR Design Company; Buster Simpson
High Point	Seattle, WA	SvR Design Company; Mithun; Bruce Meyers
Pierce County Environmental Services	University Place, WA	Bruce Dees & Associates; SvR Design Company; The Miller|Hull Partnership
Washougal Town Square	Washougal, WA	GreenWorks; Sienna Architecture Company, Inc.; Ivan McLean

References

Part 1

Bay Area Stormwater Management Agencies Association. 1997. *Residential Site Planning & Design Guidance Manual for Stormwater Quality Protection.*

Biswas, A. K. 1970. *History of Hydrology*. Amsterdam: North Holland Publishing.

Carson, R. 1962. *Silent Spring*. New York: Houghton Mifflin.

CIRIA. 2007. *The SUDS Manual C697*. Construction Industry Research and Information Association. http://www.ciria.org/service/AM/ContentManagerNet/Search/SearchDisplay.aspx?Section=Search1&FormName=SearchForm1.

Clean Water Services. 2009. *Low Impact Development Approaches Handbook*. http://www.cleanwaterservices.org/content/.../Permit/LIDA%20Handbook.pdf. Accessed September 24, 2013.

Coffman, L. 2000. *Low-Impact Development Manual*. Prince George's County, MD: Department of Environmental Resources.

Dreiseitl, H., and Grau, D. (eds.). 2005. *New Waterscapes: Planning, Building and Designing with Water*. Berlin: Birkhäuser.

Dreiseitl, H., Grau, D., and Ludwig, K. H. C. (eds.). 2001. *Waterscapes: Planning, Building and Designing with Water*. Berlin: Birkhäuser.

Dunnett, N., and Clayden, A. 2007. *Rain Gardens: Managing Water Sustainably in the Garden and Designed Landscape*. Portland, OR: Timber Press.

Dzurik, A. A. 1990. *Water Resources Planning*. New York: Rowman and Littlefield.

Ferguson, B. 1990. "Role of the Long-Term Water Balance in Management of Stormwater Infiltration." *Journal of Environmental Management* 30: 221–233.

Ferguson, B. 1994. *Stormwater Infiltration*. Boca Raton, FL: CRC Press.

Ferguson, B. 1995. "Storm-Water Infiltration for Peak-Flow Control." *Journal of Irrigation and Drainage Engineering* 121 (6): 463–466.

Ferguson, B. 2005. *Porous Pavements*. Boca Raton, FL: CRC Press.

Göransson, C. 1998. "Aesthetic Aspects of Stormwater Management in an Urban Environment." In *Proceedings of Sustaining Urban Water Resources in the 21st Century*. Rowney, A. C., Stahre, P., and Roesner, L. A., eds., 406–419. New York: ASCE/Engineering Foundation.

Hager, M. C. 2001. "Evaluating First Flush." *Stormwater, the Journal for Surface Water Quality Professionals* 2(6). http://www.stormh2o.com/SW/Articles/219.aspx.

Kent, K. M. 1973. *A Method for Estimating Volume and Rate of Runoff in Small Watersheds*. SCS-TP-149. Washington, DC: U.S. Department of Agriculture Soil Conservation Service.

Law, S. 2011. "River City's Pipe Dream." *Portland Tribune*, November 9, 2011. http://cni.pmgnews.com/component/content/article?id=15327. Accessed January 5, 2014.

Liptan, T. 2013. Telephone interview with the authors. September 2013.

Maplewood, Minnesota. 2013. "Rainwater Gardens." Accessed August 29, 2013. http://www.ci.maplewood.mn.us/index.aspx?NID=456.

McHarg, I. 1969. *Design with Nature*. New York: Natural History Press.

National SUDS Working Group. (2003). *Framework for Sustainable Urban Drainage Systems (SUDS) in England and Wales*. London: CIRIA.

Niemczynowicz, J. 1999. "Urban Hydrology and Water Management: Present and Future Challenges." *Urban Water* 1: 1–14.

Owens Viani, L. 2007. "Seattle's Green Pipes." *Landscape Architecture* 97 (10): 100–111.

Prince George's County Government Environmental Services Division. 1993. *Design Manual for Use of Bioretention in Stormwater Management*. Prince George's County, MD: Department of Environmental Resources.

Roesner, L., and Matthews, R. 1990. "Stormwater Management for the 1990s." *American City and Country* 105 (3): 33.

Schueler, T. 1987. *Controlling Urban Runoff: A Practical Manual for Planning and Designing Urban BMPs*. Washington, DC: Metropolitan Washington Council of Governments.

Schueler, T. R. 1995. *Site Planning for Urban Stream Protection*. Washington, DC: Metropolitan Washington Council of Governments.

SCS. 1975. *Urban Hydrology for Small Watersheds*. Technical Release 55. Washington, DC: U.S. Department of Agriculture Soil Conservation Service.

SCS. 1982. *Computer Program for Project Formulation Hydrology*. Technical Release 20. Washington, DC: U.S. Department of Agriculture Soil Conservation Service.

Stahre, P. 2006. *Sustainability in Urban Storm Drainage: Planning and Examples*. Stockholm, Sweden: Svenskt Vatten.

Strom, S., and Nathan, K. 1993. *Site Engineering for Landscape Architects*. New York: Van Nostrand Reinhold.

Thompson, J. W., and Sorvig, K. (2000). *Sustainable Landscape Construction: A Guide to Green Building Outdoors*. Washington, DC: Island Press.

Tourbier, J. T. 1994. "Open Space through Stormwater Management: Helping to Structure Growth on the Urban Fringe." *Journal of Soil and Water Conservation* 49 (1): 14–21.

Urbonas, B., Roesner, L., and Sonnen, M. 1989. *Design of Urban Runoff Quality Controls*. New York: American Society of Civil Engineers.

Wenk, W. E. 1998. "Stormwater as Civic and Ecological Urban Framework." In *Proceedings of Sustaining*

Urban Water Resources in the 21st Century. Rowney, A. C., Stahre, P., and Roesner, L. A., eds., 434–453. New York: ASCE/Engineering Foundation.

PART 2

Beyard, M. D. 1989. *Business and Industrial Park Development Handbook*. Washington, DC: Urban Land Institute.

Bookout, L. 1994a. *Residential Development Handbook*. 2nd ed. Washington, DC: Urban Land Institute.

Bookout, L. 1994b. *Value by Design: Landscaping, Site Planning, and Amenities*. Washington, DC: Urban Land Institute.

Corbin, J., and Strauss, A. L. 2008. *Basics of Qualitative Research: Grounded Theory Procedures and Techniques*. 3rd ed. Newbury Park, CA: Sage.

Deming, E., and Swaffield, S. 2011. *Landscape Architecture Research: Inquiry, Strategy, Design*. Hoboken, NJ: Wiley.

Echols, S., and Pennypacker, E. 2008. From Stormwater Management to Artful Rainwater Design. *Landscape Journal* 27 (2): 268–290.

Kaplan, R., Kaplan, S., and Ryan, R. L. 1998. *With People in Mind*. Washington, DC: Island Press.

Koch, S. 2006. Interview with the authors, Portland, OR.

Kone, D. L. 2006. *Land Development*. 10th ed. Washington, DC: National Association of Home Builders.

McDonald, S. 2006. Mithun Partners. Interview with the authors, Seattle, WA, March 8.

O'Mara, W. P. 1988. *Office Development Handbook*. Washington, DC: The Urban Land Institute.

Owens Viani, L. 2007. "The Feel of a Watershed." *Landscape Architecture* 97 (8): 24–39.

Whyte, W. H. 1980. *The Social Life of Small Urban Spaces*. New York: Project for Public Spaces.

PART 3

Byrd, Waren. 2006. Interview with the authors. Charlottesville, VA. March 10.

Richman, T. 1999. *Start at the Source: Design Guidance Manual for Stormwater Quality Protection*. San Francisco, CA: Bay Area Stormwater Management Agencies Association.

US Environmental Protection Agency. "Green Infrastructure." http://water.epa.gov/infrastructure/green infrastructure/index.cfm.

PART 5

Lerner, J. 2013. "The Last Drops." *Landscape Architecture Magazine* 103 (5): 52, 54, 56, 58, 60.

Pennypacker, Eliza. 1992. "What Is Taste, and Why Should I Care?" Proceedings of the 1992 International Conference of the Council of Educators in Landscape Architecture. Washington, DC: Landscape Architecture Foundation: 63–74.

Index

Figures/photos/illustrations are indicated by an "f" and tables by a "t."

Island Press | Board of Directors